Factor
Investing

Factor Investing

by James Maendel and
Paul Mladjenovic

A Wiley Brand

Factor Investing For Dummies®

Published by: **John Wiley & Sons, Inc.,** 111 River Street, Hoboken, NJ 07030-5774, www.wiley.com

Copyright © 2023 by John Wiley & Sons, Inc., Hoboken, New Jersey

Published simultaneously in Canada

For general information on our other products and services, please contact our Customer Care Department within the U.S. at 877-762-2974, outside the U.S. at 317-572-3993, or fax 317-572-4002. For technical support, please visit https://hub.wiley.com/community/support/dummies.

Wiley publishes in a variety of print and electronic formats and by print-on-demand. Some material included with standard print versions of this book may not be included in e-books or in print-on-demand. If this book refers to media such as a CD or DVD that is not included in the version you purchased, you may download this material at http://booksupport.wiley.com. For more information about Wiley products, visit www.wiley.com.

Library of Congress Control Number: 2022946843

ISBN 978-1-119-90674-2 (pbk); ISBN 978-1-119-90675-9 (ebk); ISBN 978-1-119-90676-6 (ebk)

Printed and bound by CPI Group (UK) Ltd, Croydon, CR0 4YY

C004380_211022

Contents at a Glance

Table of Contents

Introduction

F actor investing has been flying under the radar for decades as professional money managers have successfully used them for better investment portfolio management and performance. But now anyone can find out about what they are and how they can successfully improve your investment success. Many financial planners, advisors, and portfolio managers have turned to factors so they're not flying blind in volatile and uncertain markets. A factor-based approach has the power to level the playing field.

Factor Investing For Dummies helps you make sense of what has been a tested and proven approach that professional money managers have kept secret for nearly a half century and still popular and proven in today's turbulent markets.

About This Book

Factor investing is generally new to the public and it can be so valuable to anyone managing an investment portfolio, especially stocks and stock-related funds. This book is laid out so you can go from learning what factors are to how to use them and which ones work best in varying economic conditions.

The early part of the book goes in the basics of factors and the different kinds there are. There are factors designed to do well in periods of economic growth and those that hold up well in bad times. Style (or microeconomic) factors are tied to the strength of the individual stocks (and their underling companies), while macro factors are tied to the general economic environment. Stocks and funds with macro factors have a a better chance of succeeding versus the general stock market.

The book doesn't stop at just factors; it rounds out a more complete picture so you don't miss a beat with your overall factor-based investing approach. You will find out that factor-based ETFs and mutual funds can be an easy way to incorporate factors in your investment picture. Need income? See how factors can help you generate dividend income or use call and put options for added income from your portfolio. We don't want you to just generate good gains and income from your factor-based approach; we also want you to keep the fruits of your investment labor by showing you how to use brokerage orders and tax strategies.

Lastly, the book offers a wealth of resources and sites so you can keep learning about the new innovations, strategies, and tactics for successful factor-based investing long after you read your last chapter.

Foolish Assumptions

In writing this book, we wondered what a potential reader would need to know to find this book interesting. Here are some of the assumptions we came up with about you:

>> You have an interest in getting better at investing.

>> You are a novice or intermediate portfolio manager seeking reliable ways to enhance portfolio performance.

>> You have experience with the stock market but want to do better.

>> You are a financial planner or financial consultant seeking better ways to manage stocks and ETFs for yourself or a client.

Icons Used in This Book

In the margins of the book, you'll find these icons helping you out:

TIP

Whenever we provide a hint that makes an aspect of factor investing easier or potentially more successful, we mark it with a Tip icon.

REMEMBER

The Remember icon marks paragraphs that contain a friendly reminder.

WARNING

Heed the paragraphs marked with the Warning icon to avoid potential disaster.

Where to Go from Here

This book is designed so that you can quickly jump to a specific chapter or section that most interests you. You don't have to start with the first chapter — although if you're new to factor-based investing, we recommend that you do so. Understanding the foundation of factor-based investing (which we explain in the early chapters) helps you better apply the techniques that you learn in the later ones to the specifics of your investment activity. The great thing with this book is that even if you are still not sure how best to incorporate factors in your investing approach, we include coverage of factor-based exchange-traded funds (ETFs) that could do the heavy lifting for you.

You can also find the cheat sheet, complete with additional nuggets of information, for this book by going to www.dummies.com and searching for "Factor Investing For Dummies cheat sheet."

1

Starting with Factor Investing Basics

IN THIS PART . . .

Getting the lowdown on what factors are.

Get insights on why you should consider factors.

Learn which factors can work best for you.

Using factors without needing to time the market.

» How factor investing can benefit you

» Identifying the various factors used

Chapter **1**

Counting on Factor Investing

n recent years, the strategy approach of factor investing has been catching on and it may be something that could boost your personal approach in the financial markets. Factor investing takes into account decades of portfolio experience and market research regarding effective approaches to portfolio management that can remove the guesswork about which types of securities are best able to meet a particular investor's needs.

Perhaps the simplest explanation for factors is that they can act like guard rails in your portfolio management choices. The growth in factor investing's popularity is evident in the world of portfolio management. Financial assets managed under the mantle of factor investing grew from under $400 billion in 2013 to exceeding US $1.2 trillion in 2021. In this chapter, you see what the appeal is.

The Essentials of Factor Investing

Factor investing is an investment portfolio general strategy that favors a systematic approach utilizing factors or "shared characteristics" of individual stocks (and other assets such as bonds) that have a historical record of superior risk and return performance.

These factors can range from individual characteristics such as the company's sales (revenue indicated on the company's income statement) or debt (total liabilities indicated on their balance sheet) to their performance in macro environments such as inflation or economic growth. A *factor* is a trait or characteristic that can explain the performance of a given group of stocks during various market conditions.

There are two main categories of factors: style and macroeconomic factors. (Both of these are covered later in the section "Introducing the Factor Groups.")

>> *Style factors* seek to identify the relevant characteristics of the individual securities (sometimes referred to as *microeconomic* traits or characteristics). Examples are the stock's volatility, market size, and valuation.

>> *Macroeconomic factors* refer to the general market's environmental and economic aspects. Examples are GDP (Gross Domestic Product) growth and inflation (for more details, see chapter 11).

Introducing the Factor Groups

There are two main category types of factors: *style* (sometimes referred to as *microeconomic*) and *macroeconomic*. Style factors are associated with the company (or investment vehicle) itself while macroeconomic factors are about the company's economic environment. In both cases, the factors act as drivers for the returns (for the company's stock appreciation, for example) for that particular asset.

Style factors

Style factors take into account characteristics of the individual asset such as its market size, value and industry/sector, volatility, and growth versus value stocks. Style factors help to explain or identify characteristics that drive that asset's price performance in the marketplace.

These factors are also referred to as microeconomic because they are an individual security or asset that drives its performance as a singular member or participant of the overall market and economy.

Value

Looking at value means typically looking at the company's fundamentals. The fundamentals are the most important financial data of the company such as the company's sales and net profits, balance sheet (assets and liabilities), and important ratios such as the price-earnings (P/E) ratio.

Looking at public companies (as through their common stock) through the lens of value factors is one of the most important factors because value investing has survived and thrived ever since they were initially codified by the work of Benjamin Graham during the Great Depression years. (For more details, see Chapter 6.)

TIP

Value investing is a very important discipline for those seeking a safer, long-term approach to stock investing success. Many aspects of it are covered in *Stock Investing For Dummies* (written by one of the co-authors of this book) because value investing strategies (and their relevant factors) should be a prime consideration for long-term investors. *The Intelligent Investor: The Definitive Book on Value Investing* by Benjamin Graham — known as the "father of value investing" — is well worth reading, too.

One of the most important reasons to embrace value as a primary factor (especially for beginning investors) is the emphasis on stocks that are undervalued, which makes them safer than other stocks. Undervalued means that all the key fundamental financial aspects of the company (such as book value or the price-earnings ratio) generally indicate that the price of the stock is not overpriced, meaning that you will not pay an excessive stock price versus the value of the underlying company and its intrinsic worth. The reason becomes obvious in market data; overpriced stocks are more apt to decline more sharply in a correction or bear market versus reasonably priced stocks.

The bottom line is the fundamentals of a stock mean a safer bet and a better chance at long-term price appreciation.

Size

The size of the asset, in this case public company, is a reference to its market size based on market cap or capitalization (total number of shares outstanding times the price per share). The most common cap sizes used are small cap and large cap. If you're seeking growth, lean toward the small-cap factor.

Large-cap assets may be safer but typically don't exhibit the same growth or price appreciation relative to the small-cap stocks. The historical data generally bears this out.

Quality

Quality is certainly joined at the hip with value. This factor should definitely be among your top three considerations — especially if you're more risk-adverse as a long-term investor.

Quality is a reference to the financial strength of the company and you would see this through factors such as low debt-to-asset ratios, a high return on equity, and stable earnings growth.

Dividend

Dividends are payouts to shareholders from the company. They are typically paid quarterly and are a sign of long-term financial health when the company has been paying dividends over an extended period of time (years and decades), and these dividends are paid reliably and are increased over time.

Dividends should be among the prime factors considered, especially if you seek income and also want to reduce risk and volatility. Dividend payouts are typically seen as a tangible expression of financial strength and during times of market decline and stress, dividend-paying stocks tend to rebound well.

Additionally, the long-term market studies strongly point out that dividends over an extended period of time tend to match or exceed the rate of inflation so this factor tends to add the bonus feature of dealing with inflation (a macroeconomic factor).

Growth

The growth factor highlights the measure of change in sales and earnings by the company in relation to its group (such as in individual industries or sectors). Is the stock growing better than its peers? If so, this factor should be considered.

As the historical market data suggests, companies with growing sales and revenue show stronger relative stock price appreciation, since investors notice the growth and buy up the stock.

Volatility

Market research over an extended period of time suggests that low-volatility stocks tend to earn a better return over the long term compared to high-volatility stocks. Given that, this factor will be beneficial.

TIP

A useful indicator to look at is beta, which is listed at many popular financial websites for a given stock. The beta indicates how much more (or less) a given stock is volatile versus the general market (based on recent market trading data).

For beta, the stock market itself is assigned a value of 1. A stock with a beta that is less than 1 is less volatile than the general stock market while a stock with a beta greater than 1 is more volatile than the general stock market. A stock with a beta of 1.2, for example, is considered 20 percent more volatile than the general stock market. A stock with a beta of, say, .9 is 10 percent less volatile than the general stock market.

A good example of a stock that has low volatility would be a large-cap public utilities company. A good example of a high-volatility stock would be a small-cap technology firm. If you're a retiree, you would most likely benefit from this factor to ensure getting low-volatility stocks.

Momentum

This type of factor is a better consideration if you're an experienced investor and/or speculator seeking short-term results.

Momentum is the reference to how well the stock's price has moved upward in a given period of time (such as six months or a year) versus its peers in that particular category. Some short-term focused investors and speculators believe that if a stock is performing much better in a bullish trend (stock market prices are trending upward) that it will continue to do so in the near term. In that case, it would provide superior short-term gains versus its peers.

WARNING

Although the momentum factor certainly bears this out, long-term investors should be wary. Just because a particular stock exhibits above-average upward movement, it doesn't mean it will stay that way. It also doesn't mean that the stock is an appropriate selection. In the past, there have been many poor-quality stocks that have exhibited great momentum in the short term but then declined significantly.

Internet and high technology stocks exhibited powerful momentum during 1999–2001 but had stomach-churning declines during late 2001 to early 2002. Some went bankrupt.

Macroeconomic factors

You could compare stocks and the stock market/economy to fish in a pond. You can analyze the fish and choose great fish (using, for example, style/microeconomic factors). But you should also analyze the pond (macroeconomic factors). You could choose the greatest fish in the pond, but what if the pond is polluted? Then even the great fish will underperform (putting it mildly). Shrewd investors will find a different pond.

For investors, the U.S. economy and stock market represent the "biggest pond" on the global financial scene. So if you're going to participate, you should understand the good, the bad, and ugly of this marketplace. (Chapter 11 goes into more detail).

Economic growth (GDP)

Gross Domestic Product (GDP) is one of the most watched economic indicators by investors and non-investors alike. It's a broad measure of the *economic output* (value of products and services) in a given timeframe (typically a calendar quarter or year) by a nation's economy.

When GDP is growing, companies (and their stocks) are doing well. In fact, when the economy is growing and doing well, the stock market tends to outperform other markets (such as the bond market). Factors tied to economy growth such as GDP offer profitable guidance for investors.

Given that, the major investing sites regularly report this and related economic data so that this factor helps investors optimize the returns in their portfolio.

Inflation

Inflation is a key factor. Most folks look at *price inflation* (the rising price of consumer goods and services). However, price inflation is not a problem. It's a symptom. Many people don't understand the cause of inflation (including many government officials and economic policy makers unfortunately).

The cause is *monetary inflation* (the overproduction of a nation's currency supply) that precedes the price inflation. When too much money is created and when that supply of money is chasing a finite basket of goods and services, then the price of these goods and services will rise. The goods and services didn't become more valuable the *currency* lost value (due to overproduction).

A complicating factor is the supply shortage issues during late 2021–2022 that augurs in cost-push inflation. When shortages occur (supply issues) and consumers contain to purchase the products in question (demand), the price inflation is further exacerbated.

In early 2021, when the federal government and the Federal Reserve were increasing the money supply (by spending trillions of dollars), this was the cue for alert investors to consider the inflation factor. This factor would have guided portfolio managers toward securities that would have outperformed in an unfolding inflationary environment.

Interest rates

In early 2022, the Federal Reserve (America's central bank) is (and likely will be) raising interest rates. Interest rates are essentially the price of borrowed money, and a factor on interest rates is key to making more optimal choices in your portfolio.

In general (and all things being equal), low interest rates are good for the economy while high (or rising) interest rates tend to be negative. Because so much economic activity (both business and consumer activity) is tied to credit (business loans, credit cards, home mortgages, and so on), rising interest rates tend to dampen or diminish economic activity while low or decreasing rates tend to do the opposite.

Given that, factors tied to interest rates can help you avoid stocks (and bonds) that would be harmed by rising interest rates so that your portfolio can continue to perform satisfactorily.

An Example of a Factor-Based Portfolio

You probably wonder how using a factor-based portfolio may differ with a traditional (or non-factor) based approach.

For decades, one of the simplest portfolio construction was 60 percent stocks and 40 percent bonds. After that simple diversification of two different asset classes, there may be diversification with each asset class.

The stock portion may have a mix of large-cap stocks (stocks with a market valuation, for example, exceeding $50 billion), mid-cap stocks (stocks in the $10–$40 billion range),and small-cap stocks (stocks with a market valuation under $10 billion). The bonds may be a mix of investment-grade corporate bonds.

The factor-based approach would make portfolio choices based on investment characteristics that have performed better than a random mix of securities. The stocks would be selected based on style factors such as value and quality so that selections are more optimal given the general market conditions at that time. If the general market was experiencing inflation, then inflation factors would be used to select stocks that perform better than average in an inflationary environment. The inflation factor is a macroeconomic factor described earlier in this chapter.

The bonds portion of the portfolio would also be viewed through the prism of appropriate factors. If you're seeking safety, low-risk factors, such as short bond maturities and high bond ratings, limit your market risk.

The Upside and Downside of Factor Investing

Diversification is a rock-solid never-ending part of the foundation of successful investing (especially stock investing). Choosing the stocks of financially sound public companies (they have "good fundamentals") that are varied (diversified) among different industries is an important long-term consideration. Factor investing helps to take this approach to a more effective level by reducing risk and enhancing returns.

Factor investing may sound attractive because it has so much weight behind it from academic studies and market data research. But it's far from perfect because not all factors can work well consistently, as the market can change quickly and make one factor turn from a positive to a negative.

Take, for example, those investors who embrace the size factor in their approach. This factor puts much emphasis on small-cap stocks that may work well during a robust bull market, but you could get hammered during an unfolding bear market.

The other side is if you choose an approach that works well during a bear market but that leaves your portfolio underperforming during bullish times. The value investing factor, for example, may work out fine during a bear market or a sideways market but it won't be optimal during a roaring bull market when value stocks lag the performance of growth-oriented choices.

TIP

Have a mix of factors working for you. Just as diversification works well with different asset classes in your overall portfolio, a mix of factors work out better in the long term versus too much reliance on a single factor approach.

A portfolio approach with a single factor will make you look like a genius if that factor is shining bright but you will see negative returns if that factor is (temporarily) out of favor with current market conditions.

Factor Investing through ETFs and Mutual Funds

For some folks, dealing with constructing a portfolio with an optimal balance of factors may seem daunting. You can put a factor investing strategy in place by choosing funds that adhere to factors. Exchange-traded funds (ETFs) and mutual funds have emerged in recent years that make it convenient to do a factor-based approach. You can find EFT at www.etfdb.com and mutual funds at www.mutualfunds.com.

Chapter **2**

Why Use Factors?

Factors can help you build a portfolio designed for your unique risk tolerance, investment time horizon, and financial goals using characteristics that history shows lead to consistent outperformance. An *investment time period* is the timeframe you expect to hold an investment, usually short (less than 5 years), intermediate (5–10 years), or long term (more than 10 years).

In this chapter, we show you how factor investing provides a building block that gives you the best odds of reaching retirement and income goals successfully. It helps improve portfolio results and reduces volatility. Factor investing, done right, enhances diversification in a way that lowers risk without sacrificing returns, by placing your investment eggs in many baskets to help ensure positive results!

Following a Systematic Approach

In a nutshell, factor investing is about defining and following a set of proven guard rails that keep your portfolio on track. Using a factor strategy not only gives you better returns, but delivers them more consistently while also protecting you from the dangerous pitfalls and mistakes that get other investors in trouble.

Leveraging the power of a persistent strategy

Investors worldwide have always sought the secrets that would help them invest right alongside legendary investors such as John Templeton, Warren Buffett, Jesse Livermore, Benjamin Graham, and John "Jack" Bogle.

Investing systems and rules have come and gone over the years, because it turns out many of them worked only in specific markets and just for a few years. These strategies picked up on short-lived trends and rules in stocks that were true only for a limited time due to certain conditions unlikely to repeat.

When you're investing based on factors, you're interested in a *persistent strategy* — one that can deliver results in the future.

By figuring out the themes, characteristics, and properties common to winning investment, or *factors*, you can discover a set of rules to create higher-performing portfolios. But how do you even try to comb through the mountains of market data over the last 100+ years to find what works?

Well, it turns out that you're in luck! In the last few years, financial academics have been hard at work doing just that — distilling these factors into useful sets of rules that you can put to work in your portfolios today.

REMEMBER

Though nothing works 100 percent of the time, especially over shorter periods, factors are most effective when combined with other factors in a master strategy. This has the effect of loading the dice in your favor.

Saving time

Time is money, the old saying goes, and investors since the ancient Chinese rice traders have always looked for ways to save time by streamlining and systematizing their trading and investing decision processes.

We all have busy lives, jobs to get to, kids to take to after school sports, and a million other things. A factor investing strategy can help improve your life by helping you make best use of your time and energy.

Jim used factor investing to save time during the COVID-19 market bottom in March of 2020. He needed an approach that identified resilient stocks and funds most likely to benefit from a market rebound, while also giving clients confidence in the historical reliability of these stocks to survive and thrive the unprecedented economic and market downturn everyone was experiencing as the world rapidly went into social distancing, quarantines, and government-mandated shutdowns.

He came up with a multifactor portfolio for new clients using the same principles in this book that was both sophisticated and easy to understand. This strategy gave them the confidence to enter the depressed stock market and stay on board for what turned out to be a profitable 18 months for investing, with many portfolios doubling in value.

Using modern advances

As investors, you always want to look for ways to take advantage of advances and breakthroughs in the investment field. Two trends that have come together to move investing forward have been computers and history; specifically, better methods of market data analysis and greatly expanded historical datasets to feed those computers.

Modern computers and new ways of crunching market data are at the forefront of the growing interest and advances in factor investing. Just as important is the expanding dataset as researchers and archivists have combed through old ticker tapes, micro-fiche and ledgers to complete the historical dataset of stock prices and company data; in some cases, right back to the Buttonwood Agreement that pre-dated Wall Street.

What is the Buttonwood Agreement? It's a single-page document that started the New York Stock Exchange 230 years ago on May 17, 1792, when 24 merchants and brokers met under a buttonwood tree and put their signatures to a set of rules and safeguards for trading. The meeting was necessary to re-establish public confidence in markets after the infamous Financial Panic of 1792 that had caused mayhem earlier that spring.

Investing options were limited back then. The only stock available was in the Bank of New York, The First Bank of the United States, some insurance companies, and Revolutionary War Bonds issued by Alexander Hamilton to help pay off the War of Independence from British rule.

Today, you can also take advantage of databases, services, and perhaps even pre-packaged investment products such as funds and ETFs that attempt to apply factor methodology in a practical way to select investments based on current stock and bond metrics.

Luckily, technology has made factor investing far easier and more cost effective than ever, as we detail in later chapters.

This enhanced dataset provides a richer and more complete testing ground to ferret out meaningful factors and to test existing assumptions more fully. This is an advance that you can benefit from!

VISITING WALL STREET

By the way, did you know you can snap a selfie in front of the buttonwood tree outside the NY Stock Exchange? It's the only tree in front of a building on Broad Street, and it's right across the street from the famous "Fearless Girl" statue. Pro-tip: While you're there, look closely at the cobblestones on Wall Street. Running right down the center of the street are post markers made of square wooden pavers marking what was once a Dutch defense wall, which is exactly how Wall Street got its name. Interestingly, the wooden pavers are a nod to a soon-discarded attempt in the late 1800s to build quieter New York streets by replacing cobblestones with hardwood pavers.

Following proven guidelines that work

Even a broken clock is right twice a day, and, like a coin toss, any system can come up with a winner or two from time to time. As an extreme example, a rules-based system (factor) that consisted of "sell all U.S. stocks and buy bonds" may have worked very well as a factor from September 1929 until July 1932 but this was only due to the stock market crash that kicked off the Great Depression. Using this factor after 1932 would have been a recipe for disaster and decades of underperformance! The point here is that you're looking for guidelines that provide a more universal advantage, and are not dependent on a specific set of historical circumstances.

The best factors you're interested in work in many different markets, countries, and decades. They aren't just one-trick ponies that have shown results once or twice in history, perhaps by chance or due to unique circumstances. You want rules that operate more broadly and dependably.

Following a disciplined core strategy

The most successful investors have a disciplined strategy driving their success. Incorporating factors into your investing adds not just a methodology for investment selection but also discipline to portfolio activity as it helps you determine what to buy, sell, or hold, and gives you the confidence needed to participate in the long term.

Protecting against emotional investing

The emerging field of behavioral finance says that regardless of how you design your portfolio, the major reason for your success or failure is your emotion-driven actions. In other words, if you want to be successful at investing, you have to protect against emotional investing, which results in buying high and selling low, repeatedly.

The long-running DALBAR study, which has been updated annually since the inception of the 401(k) over four decades ago, proves that this problem is widespread and damaging to wealth building. Investors lack discipline (of course it's not you, just other investors).

What is DALBAR? Located in Boston, DALBAR is one of the nation's leading independent research firms committed to raising the standards of excellence in the financial services industry. It compiles and analyzes mountains of data on mutual funds, life insurance, and banking products and practices. It has also been behind the nation's leading study on investor behavior for the past 28 years.

One of its most followed publications is the annual Quantitative Analysis of Investor Behavior (QUIB) Report, which measures how investors have performed with their actual investment portfolios versus how the funds they hold have performed during the same periods. You might think that investor performance and fund performance are the same thing, but DALBAR consistently demonstrates a devastating investor performance gap due to investors shifting money among their investments (for example, from stock into more conservative bonds or cashing out at exactly the wrong times).

Compounded over the years, this performance gap is devastating, costing many investors literally hundreds of thousands — or even more — in retirement dollars they could have enjoyed.

For example, its 2021 study (www.dalbar.com/catalog/product) shows that this performance gap jumped to a shocking 1032 basis points for 2021. 100 basis points equals one percent, so this represents a lag of 10 percent for investors versus the performance of the average fund they were investing in. Obviously, despite the recovery from the 2020 COVID-19 market lows, many investors bailed (perhaps believing the recovery was too good to be true) and then got back in at higher prices in the fall, only to experience a downtrend and realize they had once again bought high without benefiting from the previous gains.

In short, DALBAR's extensive research shows that investors are their own worst enemies. The results, as shown in Figure 2-1, are sobering and hard to dismiss as the researchers used real-time data from millions of investor-directed 401(k) accounts. DALBAR has concluded that as much as two-thirds of the market return investors should have enjoyed were squandered to emotional investing — selling into fear after downturns, and buying into euphoria after upturns. The problem, of course, is that investors end up bailing near the bottom, when they've had enough pain, and buying again near the top of the market cycle, when they can't stand to miss out anymore. These mistakes get compounded over the years, and become even more damaging.

The results are similar in every annual update of the DALBAR study. In short, it turns out that most investors are doing exactly the opposite of what they need to do to build wealth. They are buying high and selling low.

REMEMBER

A factor-based approach helps you avoid becoming an emotional investor. A portfolio strategy based on factors (ideally a diversified combination of multiple factors) can provide discipline, and powerful protection against emotional investing by offering a portfolio with which an investor can feel confident riding through inevitable downturns on the way to new highs. Only historically persistent factors can provide this sort of assurance, enabling investors to achieve their financial goals and helping to make sure their emotions don't cause them to outlive their assets.

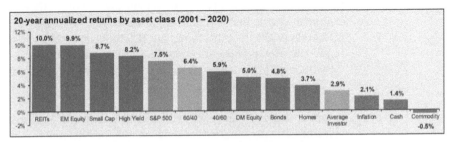

FIGURE 2-1:
DALBAR.

Source: https://www.maendelwealth.com/blog/rising-rates-let-the-game-come-to-you

Considering Reasons to Use Factors

There are other, perhaps not so obvious, reasons to use factors in your investment approach. Long-term investment success is measured by what you actually keep at the end of the day, and how comfortable the "ride" getting there was. After all, few of us desire a high return that comes at the price of high volatility and sleepless nights.

Keeping more of what you earn

You don't actually grow wealth by what you make in the market, but by what you keep! It's all too easy to forget your silent partner who's in the room every time you invest: the IRS! Unless you're investing in a tax-sheltered account such as a 401(k) or an IRA, the IRS wants a piece of the action, and if you ignore them, they will soon become a not-so-silent partner.

WARNING

Taxes represent a drag on the portfolio, or, if paid from some other account, your overall net worth, and this drag can really add up over the years. It's like a form of negative compounding. Chapter 20 shows you how to minimize your tax obligation.

A factor-investing approach can help reduce *turnover*, which is the buying and selling of portfolio holdings that can produce short-term gains (taxed the highest) or long-term gains that apply to positions held more than a year. It does this by identifying characteristics of outperforming stocks and bonds that typically don't change over short periods like a year, meaning that you are likely to be able to reduce the amount of short-term taxable gains, lowering your tax bill and letting you keep more of what your portfolio earns.

Used by professional money managers

Why do many professional money managers use factors? The short answer is because they work! Institutional and active managers have been using factors for several decades because investing in factors can help build better portfolios. Factors not only improve portfolio outcomes but can lower risk in at least two important ways.

» **Enhanced diversification:** A factor strategy builds less risky portfolios by enhancing diversification, which means you have more eggs in different baskets. It reduces the chance of a few holdings ruining the portfolio returns as can happen in more concentrated portfolios. A factor strategy doesn't rely on targeting trending stocks, but on identifying many holdings with winning characteristics.

» **Reduced volatility:** This may seem to be the same thing as enhanced diversification, but it's a distinct feature. It means that a factor portfolio is more likely to grow with less volatility than a similarly aggressive portfolio run without the benefit of a factor strategy. This means you can experience a smoother ride, which, besides the obvious benefit of a more consistent growth experience, can also improve outcomes dramatically because it effects investor behavior.

A less volatile factor strategy gives you confidence to stick with your investment plan in uncertain economic times that inevitably come and go. If a portfolio is so volatile that it scares you out of the market, the inevitable market rebound won't matter for you, as you won't be along for the ride. Factors can keep you on board with confidence.

Using the Two Models of Factor Investing

The quest to identify the most useful factors began half a century ago. The following sections take a look at the origins of systems that worked and still work today to help investors and portfolio managers.

Capital Asset Pricing Model

Capital Asset Pricing Model (CAPM) was developed in the early 1960s by Jack Treynor, John Litner, and William Sharp (the Sharp ratio is named after him). These three academics built on the previous work of Harry Markowitz who was studying the attributes of outperforming stocks looking for what characteristics they had in common.

The CAPM team studied investment managers who had outperformed the market, trying to determine whether their high performance was based on skill or chance, which is more difficult than it seems. (It's possible to have a random coin flip land heads up multiple times in a row by pure chance and it says absolutely nothing about the skills or methodology of the coin flipper.)

The CAPM used a one-factor approach to analyzing investment performance. *Market beta* was their term for comparing the risk of a fund or stock to the risk of the general market, which they called systemic or non-diversifiable risk.

Market beta measures the degree to which an investment tends to move with the wider stock market. A portfolio made up of all stocks (an example being the Vanguard Total Stock Market Fund) is considered to have a beta of one. A portfolio with less risk than the stock market would have a beta of less than one. A beta of more than one means more risk than the broader market.

CAPM assumes that the risk and return of any portfolio are only due to its degree of exposure to market beta.

One of the unexpected outcomes of this model was that it revealed many professional portfolio and fund managers were only beating the market by loading up on groups of higher beta (riskier) stocks rather than by their stock-picking skills. This was an important finding because many managers charged high fees for supposed stock-picking skills, when the outperformance could instead be attributed mostly to a factor to which exposure could be gained in much lower-cost ways.

One shortcoming of the CAPM model was that it also predicted that high-volatility stocks should outperform lower-volatility stocks. Although often true, it turns out that high-quality stocks (one of our favorite factors which we dive into later in this book) tend to perform better than predicted by the CAPM model.

The Capital Asset Pricing Model empowered the individual investor to save unnecessary fees and expenses, and was an early attempt at helping them realize that they could apply the same investing principles of investment legends themselves.

Figure 2-2 shows how CAPM helps investors manage and optimize risk and reward along a curve referred to as the *efficient frontier*.

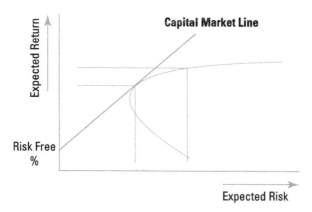

FIGURE 2-2:
Capital Asset
Pricing Model.

From 1927–2015 the U.S. market beta premium (calculated versus the riskless return on one-month U.S. Treasury bills) has averaged 8.3 percent. It has been positive around 66 percent of calendar years, and the odds improve the longer you invest. At the 20-year mark, the odds of outperformance are 96 percent.

To find out more about the CAPM, see https://corporatefinanceinstitute.com/resources/knowledge/finance/what-is-capm-formula/.

Fama and French 3-Factor Model

The Fama and French 3-Factor Model (FAMA) is a still widely used approach that builds and expands on the CAPM. In 1992, economists Eugene Fama and Kenneth French came up with a combination of three factors attempting to explain outperformance and identify stocks expected to do well in the future.

The factors they used were firm size, book-to-market value and excess return on the market. In short, by including the fact that value and small-cap stocks often outperform the market, they were able to create a better tool for analyzing portfolio performance. Eugene Fama and Kenneth French both were awarded a Noble Prize, and have claimed that their Fama–French 3-factor model explains over 90 percent of the returns of any diversified portfolio, compared with the average 70 percent given by the older CAPM model.

To find out more about Fama's and French's model, see investopedia.com/terms/f/famaandfrenchthreefactormodel.asp and www.chicagobooth.edu/faculty/nobel-laureates/eugene-f-fama.

Chapter **3**

Knowing Which Factors Are Worth Your Time

The simplest way to understand factor-based investing is that this kind of investing is about following a set of investing rules that have been defined, and then creating a diversified portfolio with that knowledge. Academics describe this as "quantitative characteristics shared across a set of securities."

Factors are the mechanisms that drive returns in stocks, bonds, and other assets.

Why should you care? Because factors can be combined and structured to build an investment portfolio to outperform the market over time.

It's not just about making money. There's another not so obvious reason you should pay attention to factors. Saving money! It's the other side of the wealth-building coin.

REMEMBER

Not every factor that looks good on paper is worth investing in. There are less than a dozen that stand the test of time and can be expected to help you win in the real world, net of all costs.

In this chapter, we discuss how you can decide which factors are worth being a part of your investment strategy, and those factors that probably aren't worth your money. (We devote subsequent chapters to each factor, so flip ahead if you're interested in a particular one.)

Putting You in Charge of Your Factor Investing Strategy

It may not be obvious to many people how disruptive and game-changing factor investing is to the long legacy of hot shot money managers that are to Wall Street what celebrities are to Hollywood.

You see, by isolating and identifying key characteristics that define outperforming investments, factor investing puts you on the same elevation as the professional money manager, giving access to a selection process once attributed to managers' exclusive stock-picking prowess. This holds out the promise of market-beating returns without having to pay high fund manager fees. The entire field of factor research has been a giant pain in the backside for overpriced money managers, even ones who have had market beating runs.

In previous decades, a successful fund manager was simply assumed to be performing due to his stock-picking expertise, and many assumed almost god-like status. Bookish academics have inadvertently undermined these market legends by demonstrating that, with very few exceptions, winning stocks shared key factors in common and these factors could be used in advance to pick a winning portfolio.

In fact: Currently, factor models can explain up to 95 percent of the differences between active managers (a tenet of the Fama and French Model; see Chapter 2), an attribute formerly ascribed mostly to manager skill. Factor investing offers the potential to achieve market beating returns without high manager fees, saving you money!

REMEMBER

Factor investing put the exclusive tools of professional money managers at your fingertips, but to work, you need to use them efficiently and with discipline.

Factor-based (or smart beta) strategies are gaining popularity and market share, competing with index funds (passive returns), and traditional manager (active) returns, as shown in Figure 3-1.

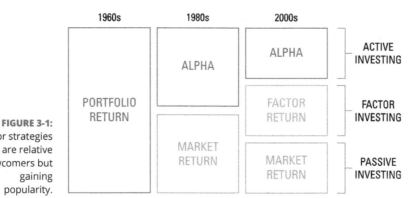

FIGURE 3-1:
Factor strategies
are relative
newcomers but
gaining
popularity.

Navigating the Factor Jungle

More than 300 factors have been discovered in recent years, but not all pass the feasibility test. Here's how you define a good factor:

>> Did it outperform (make money!) in the past?

>> Will it make money (net of costs) in the future?

>> Why does it work? (The answer to why helps you answer whether it will make you money, and also whether the effect might be already duplicated by another factor that already contains the elements of another factor.)

Chapter 1 covers a few factors that we follow and have found have worked in the past.

As factor investing gains popularity, it becomes even more important to do your own research and answer these three questions. You would think the academic spotlight now aimed at this field would make things clearer and better defined, and in many ways it is. What surprises new investors is what John Cochrane of the University of Chicago warned is becoming a zoo of factors. Factors are becoming so numerous and exotic that investors are confused by the sheer proliferation of discoveries (one hedge fund claims to use over 80 different factors in its stock pickings!)

TIP

Keep your strategy simple and focus on the proven factors, and the stocks, mutual funds, and exchange-traded funds (ETFs) that incorporate them, as we discuss in this book.

Avoiding the Factor Zoo

So why are there so many factors to choose from?

There are many reasons, but most of them break down to one of the following: A newly discovered factor works because of attributes that are already integral parts of an existing factor. Or, the factor is really a phantom result of poor statistical analysis and/or outdated or incomplete historical stock price databases. Answering the three questions in the previous section helps you determine whether a factor includes the right attributes.

Avoiding supercomputer factors

Supercomputers crunching numbers can be both a blessing and a curse. The details are beyond the scope of this book, but if you're interested it's worth reading more of what professor Cochrane has written about this. In short, the dangers of data mining and selection bias can cause very smart people to come up with powerful factors that aren't very profitable:

>> **Data mining:** The process of analyzing dense volumes of data to find patterns, discover trends, and gain insight into how that data can be used.

>> **Selection bias/survivorship bias:** Caused by choosing non-random data for statistical analysis; for instance, back testing a factor's historical performance against the pool of all existing small capitalization stocks inadvertently eliminates just as many stocks that are no longer trading as they've gone bankrupt or merged.

For example, Figure 3-2 shows a chart showing what percentage of stocks that were trading in the past are now delisted versus what percentage are still actively trading. Clearly, any factor would have to have outperformed in the real world that included these defunct stocks and not just when run against a database of currently existing stocks. Seems obvious in retrospect, but many factor discoveries have proven to be based on incomplete or biased databases. We talk about this a bit more in Chapter 8 with regard to small growth stocks.

REMEMBER

Computers are only as good as the data you feed them. A huge number of factors that seem to work on historical data models do not pan out in the real world for various reasons.

These factors are the product of powerful computers searching through enough data to find a situation where a new factor looks good by sheer accident and randomness. Of course, you want to avoid these factors because they don't have the predictive power for the future and won't bring you success in the future.

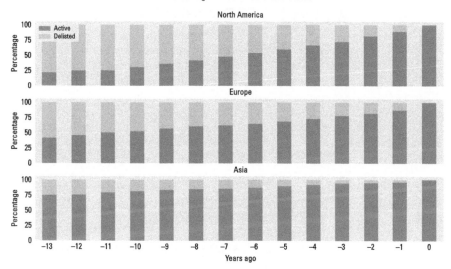

Percentage of Active vs Delisted Stocks

FIGURE 3-2:
Survivorship
bias: active versus
delisted stock
universe.

WARNING

The risk of using a factor from the factor zoo isn't just underperformance, but also the trading and management fees it costs you to carry it out. In addition, there's the opportunity cost to you had you done something more effective with your money!

Finding investable factors

Literally hundreds of factors have been discovered and analyzed in recent years (see the sidebar for some examples). Many of these factors work on paper, but to be useful for you in your investment strategy, factors need to clear a much higher bar.

Some factors only work in certain decades, or with a specific sector of the stock market. If a factor can't duplicate its outperformance in other decades and over long periods of time, it's not really investable.

An *investable* factor also needs to yield enough expected outperformance that it outearns the amounts you pay in costs, fees, and taxes:

>> All portfolios, no matter how efficiently run, have trading and operating expenses, and all investments have a buy/ask spread, meaning that you lose a little money simply transacting a buy or sell when it's needed to follow the rules of any particular factor.

A FEW FACTOR FAILURES

Could there really be hundreds of separate characteristics that predict higher returns? Here are some factors academics have announced that turned out to be either not real (meaningfully predictve) or just subsets of (or simply duplicating) other already known factors:

- Employee growth

- Maximum daily price return

- Overweighting illiquid companies

- Focusing on small-cap growth (turns out size factor works best with quality, and it's small-cap value that has outperformed).

Yale's Stefano Giglio and Chicago Booth's Dacheng Xiu have both done research on failed factors. You can see Xiu's paper at https://www.chicagobooth.edu/review/300-secrets-high-stock-returns.

REMEMBER

>> Unless you're holding your portfolio in a tax-sheltered account such as an IRA or a 401(k) (many now offer the ability to trade individual funds and stocks), there are potential tax costs for executing any strategy.

You especially need to account for taxes if you're using a high turnover factor strategy where gains are likely to be taxed at the less favorable short-term capital gains tax rate than the more favorable long-term capital gains rate. See Chapter 20 for more about your tax sitation, whether you're investing short term or long term.

When we distill these ingredients to their essentials, some basic rules emerge. These three things make a factor attractive:

>> **Doggedness:** The factor must show up through different time periods and not just one random decade or period. No one-trick ponies here. You want factors that persist for any investing period, given enough time.

>> **Prevalence:** The factor must demonstrate an advantage with various different countries and market sectors.

>> **Investability (actionable):** The factor must be able to be deployed cost effectively (costs include trading fees, taxes, and potentially time/research efficiency for more esoteric factors).

Factor outperformance is cyclical, yet hard to time. One factor is always leading the pack and your odds of guessing which one is negligble. Morningstar, a leading investment analytics company, has studied factor investing extensively and concluded that factor investing offers the promise of:

>> Improved absolute returns (more gains!)

>> Improved risk-adjusted returns (gains with less risk and a smoother ride than other approaches!)

>> Extended periods of outperformance followed by *droughts* (long periods of underperformance relative to whatever cap-weighted index you're trying to beat)

When using factors, you must stick with your strategy to earn the rewards! There will be times when you feel like bailing! It's best to wait for the historical outperformance of solid factors to materialize. Any attempt to time a factor approach requires skill and probably adds additional headwinds of trading costs and tax inefficiency (unless you're doing it in an IRA or tax-favored account).

TIP

Even the best factors experience periods when they underperform the market, and these are hard to predict. You need patience to let a factor work for you. You need to stay in it to win it! The key is, of course, to diversify factors in your portfolio.

» Understanding the pitfalls of market timing

» Using factors to beat the market

Chapter **4**

Beating the Market without Timing It

E ver since the advent of the first market investment indexes almost 140 years ago, active investors have used these benchmarks to gauge how well (or poorly) their portfolios were doing. These benchmarks are generally referred to as the *market.*

The Holy Grail of investing has been the goal of beating the market as represented by the well-known indexes ever since. Beating the market is naturally tied to the concept of *market timing* (moving investment money in or out of a financial market — or switching funds between asset classes, stocks, or investment products — based on predictive methods or emerging trends), because most investors conclude that to do better than the index they need to try to own more stocks that are going up and less stocks that are going down.

In this chapter, we review how investors typically have tried to beat the market and we show you how to use your factor investing techniques as a radically different (and possibly complementary) approach to beating the market.

Don't be intimidated by fellow investors who brag about market beating gains in one stock or another. This is common and can cause you to take undue risk to try something better. In reality, research repeatedly shows that as a whole their portfolios typically underperform the market (often drastically) net of taxes and expenses over the long term. A long-term factor-based approach is a much more reliable way to build wealth.

Beating the market outright is not necessarily the right measure of success for you. A more conservative portfolio that achieves the same (or even less) gains but with a lower risk is a winner too. Like everything else in investing, it ultimately depends on your timeframe, objectives, and risk tolerance.

Looking at the Indexes that Make Up the Market

We start off this chapter by examining what investors actually mean by the market. You get an introduction to a few of the indexes that comprise the market in the following sections.

A *stock index*, or *stock market index*, measures a stock market, or a subset of the stock market. It provides a benchmark to help you compare current stock price levels with past prices to calculate market performance, and your portfolio's relative performance to it.

The original index and its famous sister

When investors refer to the market, what they're really referencing is one of popular indexes designed to give a snapshot of how the universe of stocks is doing by tracking a selection of key stocks.

The Dow Jones Transportation Average (DJTA) is the oldest stock market index (created in 1884) and still in use today. Designed by Charles Dow, co-founder of Dow Jones and Company, it was comprised of eleven transportation companies; nine of them railways. He introduced the ground-breaking idea in a July 3rd "Customer's Afternoon Letter" to his top clients who for decades referred to this market index as "The Rails" due to its concentration in railroad stocks. Railroads were as exciting and game-changing then as the Internet, smartphones, CRISPR gene editing, and 3D printing are today, and equally transformational.

HISTORICAL PERFORMANCE OF THE INDEXES

Until recently, no one had calculated the Dow Jones Industrial Average going back to 1896, although data for the price index has been around for 125 years. One company, Global Financial Data, meticulously ran the numbers and concluded that, on average (including dividends), the Dow Jones Industrial Average returned 10.26 percent per annum between May 1896 and May 2020. You can see its fascinating index research online at www.globalfinancialdata.com.

You can contrast the DJIA with returns of 8.4 percent to the DJT, 9.7 percent to the S&P Composite, and 10.36 percent to the GFD-100 Index, which includes the top 100 stocks in the United States each year regardless of its sector.

Then twelve years later on May 26, 1896, Mr. Dow introduced a new index, the Dow Jones Industrial Average (DJIA), which is still regularly quoted as an indicator of U.S. stock markets and general economic conditions. Broader-based than the DJT, it was made up of twelve industrial companies and opened up at 40.94 points (try that fun fact on your investing friends!). The original companies it consisted of were American Cotton Oil, American Sugar, American Tobacco, Chicago Gas, Distilling & Cattle Feeding, General Electric, Laclede Gas, National Lead, North American, Tennessee Coal and Iron, U.S. Leather, and U.S. Rubber. All titans of American industry at the time. In 1928, the DJIA was enhanced to include 18 more companies, for a total of 30, which is why most DJIA charts go back less than a century.

The most popular index today

The S&P 500 Stock Composite Index was introduced in 1957 and is the most widely used indicator of U.S. stock performance around the world. In fact, for many investors it's virtually synonymous with the U.S. stock market.

Since its inception, the S&P 500 has gained an average of around 10 percent per year, as shown in Figure 4-1.

NOT JUST AN ACADEMIC EXERCISE

For most of modern investing history, the idea of beating an index was largely an academic exercise. Commissions on buying and selling stocks were expensive (think $1,000 for a $10,000 trade) making application impractical for the average investor until the advent of discount brokers in the mid-1970s.

This meant that, unless you were a multi-millionaire, there was really no way for you to invest in the index to begin with, and there were no funds or packaged investing products that would do it for you.

All of that changed when an upstart named John "Jack" Bogle pioneered the first index fund for retail investors in 1974. His now famous firm, Vanguard, gave investors the first efficient, full-invested (long only), and low-cost way to actually invest in the S&P 500 index.

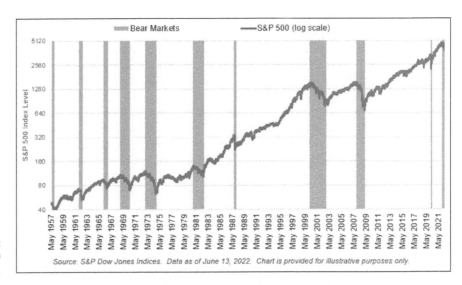

FIGURE 4-1: How the S&P 500 has performed.

Planning Your Market Strategy

From technical analysis to trend following, you can try to beat the market in many ways. That usually means attempting to beat an S&P Index Fund over a meaningful period of time.

Before you try timing the market, take a moment to gauge the potential reward you get for the time you invest in applying market timing. The best way to do this is to look at the exhaustive data meticulously gathered by academics over recent decades. Spoiler: It shows overwhelmingly that the vast majority of investors who try to time the market lose over the long term, and very often over the short term as well.

WARNING

Granted, you may have other reasons to time the market (other than long-term outperformance) such as pursuing peace of mind (going to cash so you can sleep at night) during uncertain economic times or times of conflict and war. It's often a losing game, though, so it's one you should approach with caution.

Nothing illustrates the challenges of trying to beat the market through market timing (moving strategically between cash and stocks) than what happened in the stock market when Pearl Harbor was bombed in 1941.

What do you think would have happened if you *took cover* (cashed out) your investment portfolio after hearing news of the unprecedented Japanese attack on Pearl Harbor, knowing it meant the start of a new World War?

It's worth considering, in light of current global conflicts and uncertainty. Would you have gone to cash for a few months or even years?

Barton Biggs, in *Wealth, War and Wisdom,* analyzed stock market behavior during the key events of World War II and previous wars, and the results are truly fascinating as shown in Figure 4-2. (You can read more about Pearl Harbor and its effect on the stock market at www.maendelwealth.com/blog/the-pearl-harbor-market-bottom.)

Had you sold based on market timing after hearing of the bombing of Pearl Harbor, you would have missed the start of one of the greatest bull markets in history.

REMEMBER

Historically, without fail, the bias of the stock market has been upwards. Any time your portfolio is in cash or you're engaged in market timing, be aware that you're directly competing against the tendency of stocks to gain over the long term.

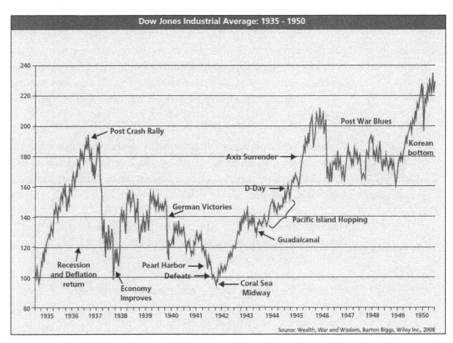

FIGURE 4-2: How World War II events affected the stock market.

Source: www.maendelwealth.com/blog/the-pearl-harbor-market-bottom

Beating the Market with Factors

There's a way to trounce the market over time without poring over stock charts every day or even worrying about whether the economy is booming or receding, whether it's a bull or bear market, or even one of those mystical corrections that commentators refer to when they have no idea what's actually going on.

You see, when you're market timing, you're trying to beat the market by capturing less of the downside and more of the upside of a stock or fund. Whether you're using chart analysis (technical analysis) or watching economic indicators (fundamental analysis), you're trying to make an educated guess of when a meaningful downtrend or uptrend is likely, and of course, you need to make that assessment before the trend has completed while there's still room to benefit from it.

Doing so is a very difficult thing to do, as the data shows time and time again. In fact, professional portfolio managers spend entire days attempting to outperform the stock market and tend to fail quite badly.

How bad? Well, about 95 percent of all mutual fund managers fail to beat their benchmark index over any ten year period, and those that do almost never beat it a second time over the following decade.

According to a 2020 research report, nearly 90 percent of actively managed investment funds failed to beat the market over the previous 15 year period.

It's tempting to time the markets but it's been proven over and over again that most people fail at it. Switching your holdings when you think the market is headed up or down typically doesn't work. If it did, the professionals would be beating the market more often. If pros can't do it consistently, you probably can't do it either.

Figure 4-3 shows a sample of the lucky few who beat the market over recent decades. Warren Buffett has been known to use factor strategies, whether deliberately or instinctively.

The World's Top Investors

Investor, Key Fund/Vehicle	Period	Average Annual Returns After Fees
Jim Simons, Medallion	1988-2018	39%
George Soros, Quantum	1969-2000	32%
Steven Cohen, SAC	1992-2003	30%
Peter Lynch, Magellan	1977-1990	29%
Warren Buffett, Berkshire Hathaway	1965-2018	21%
Ray Dalio, Pure Alpha	1991-2018	12%

FIGURE 4-3: Pros who beat the market.

You take on several additional hurdles when attempting to beat the market through timing that work against you:

>> Increased trading costs (work against your returns)

>> Increased tax burden (long- or short-term capital gains)

>> Increased time commitment (you could be doing other things)

There's another danger to market timing. Being out of the market when things come roaring back. And if you think you'll have plenty of time to get back in on an uptrend, consider the fact that approximately 50 percent of the S&P's strongest days occurred during a bear market, and that historically, the best and worst days are often clustered together.

Figure 4-4 illustrates how an investor would have fared if they'd been out of the market during the best market days. Remember these tend to occur right in the middle of bear markets when everything in the world seems to be headed the wrong way, a time when you could easily have market timed your way to the sidelines.

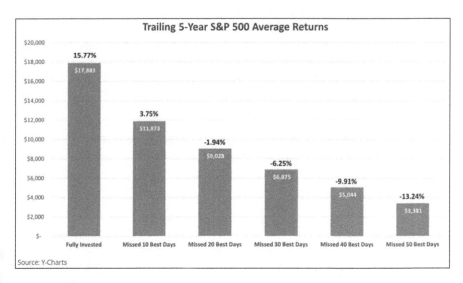

The S&P is up over 76 percent in the last 5 years and during that time, if you missed just 10 of the best days, you're barely beating long-term average inflation. Right now (early Summer 2022) with inflation reported at 9 percent, you'd be losing badly.

It gets worse. Miss any more than the 20 best days and you've lost money, especially compared to the opportunity cost of where you'd have been staying fully invested.

By using factor investing, you can ignore timing and focus on loading your portfolio with stocks that have factors that have outperformed historically.

By using a factor-based approach, you can:

>> Make efficient use of your time with a systematic approach to investments.

>> Reduce your vulnerability to volatility and trying to time it.

>> Remove emotion (powerful fight or flight reflexes) from your investing.

REMEMBER

Trying to beat the market through timing is not the only approach. Factor investing is a better way to do this, and has the added bonuses of freeing up your time, and likely reducing your costs and taxes as well!

2

Going Deep with Factor Strategies

Chapter **5**

Making Room for the Growth Factor

The growth and quality factors harness the prospects of a company's growth by examining sales, historical earnings, and projected earnings. Growth strategies, also called *capital appreciation* or *capital growth*, have been in use since the 1950s and are popular because they make intuitive sense to investors and money managers.

There are many variations on the growth and/or quality theme with long formulas and equations that can appear confusing and somewhat contradictory.

You don't want to ignore this powerful factor, as it has high explanatory power in identifying stocks that are expected to grow earnings, sales, or profit margins above average versus their industry sector or the market.

For the purposes of this chapter, we call it the quality growth factor.

The easiest way to understand quality growth factor is as a mix of company earnings profitability and quality. Specifically, you look for high quality firms that are consistently growing, consistently profitable (stable earnings), and have solid balance sheets without unsustainable levels of debt.

TIP

Investors often gravitate to either the growth or value camp, as each has investing legends as proponents. Our advice? Use both!

Seeking Profitability

Profitability is not exactly the same as profits. Rather, it measures an organization's profit relative to its expenses and is a measure of the efficiency with which it achieves those profits. We like more efficient companies because they achieve more profit as a percentage of expenses and assets than less-efficient organizations. This means high profitability companies can spend less to generate the same profit. This not only identifies companies with good management and business models, but can identify competitive advantages that are difficult for lesser companies to match.

A popular gauge of a company's profitability is high return on equity — a feature we're looking for in a stock when applying quality growth factor. *Return on equity (ROE)* is a measure of financial performance and how efficiently a company generates profits.

ROE is calculated by dividing net income by shareholders equity (a company's assets minus its debt):

$$\text{Return on Equity} = \frac{\text{Average Shareholders' Equity}}{\text{Net Income}}$$

The higher the ROE, the better the company is at turning its resources and assets into profits. Because shareholder's equity is the same as a company's assets minus its debt, ROE is also defined as return on net assets. A good ROE varies based on what's normal for the company's sector or industry.

ROE measures a corporation's profitability and how efficiently it generates those profits.

REMEMBER

Figure 5-1 shows that companies with higher ROE have historically outperformed companies with lower ROE.

One challenge in applying the quality growth factor is avoiding unintended exposure to high growth stocks that also have unusually high valuations. Right now (summer 2022), the quality growth factor has been outperforming for well over a decade, and many top stocks are near the top end of their historical price-earnings (PE) ratios even after the market pullback of recent months. Is the market revaluing even high profitability stocks, or will this trend persist? Could current conditions present a buying opportunity? Diversifying factors may be the answer.

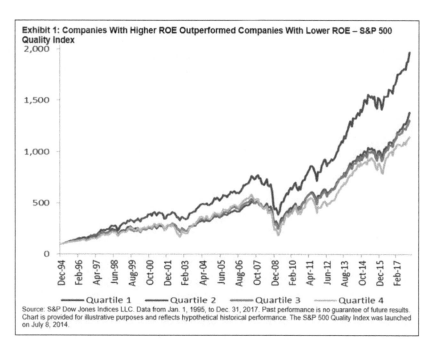

Exhibit 1: Companies With Higher ROE Outperformed Companies With Lower ROE – S&P 500 Quality Index

Source: S&P Dow Jones Indices LLC. Data from Jan. 1, 1995, to Dec. 31, 2017. Past performance is no guarantee of future results. Chart is provided for illustrative purposes and reflects hypothetical historical performance. The S&P 500 Quality Index was launched on July 8, 2014.

FIGURE 5-1: How quality growth factor companies perform.

THE HISTORY OF GROWTH QUALITY

Eugene Fama and Kenneth French's 2006 research paper titled "Profitability, Investment and Average Returns" demonstrated that firms with high profitability tend to continue to have high future returns. Then, in 2013 Robert Novy-Marx made a significant contribution to this field with a paper called "The Other Side of Value: The Gross Profitability Premium" that provided additional insights.

Incidentally, this research along with the research in other factors, helped explain some of the exceptional performance of legendary investors such as Benjamin Graham, Warren Buffett, and David L. Dodd who all used their own measures of profitability to identify winning investments. This further demystified the aura around great stock-pickers; illustrating that, to a large extent, they were methodically applying various factor metrics to their stock picks rather than simply being great market "timers" or simply having a nose for great stocks.

All of this underscores the idea that, by applying these same factors, and a whole lot of discipline, you can also build healthy returns.

It's important to try to avoid growth stocks that have overly stretched valuations, regardless of what the investing herd is doing (think Internet stocks in the late 90s). These stocks could pull back especially hard during a market downturn and hurt your portfolio's performance.

Looking for Stable Earnings

"It's far better to buy a wonderful company at a fair price than a fair company at a wonderful price."

—WARREN BUFFETT

High quality stocks tend to have stronger balance sheets, higher margins, and more stable earnings than low quality stocks. High quality stocks also tend to outperform their lower quality counterparts over a long timeframe.

Strategies based on profitability and quality are growth strategies and as such they combine especially well with value strategies, reducing volatility and smoothing out returns.

Growth has been outperforming value since around 2006. This is a long period of time and has demoralized pure value investors. As Figure 5-2 shows, however, value was an outperforming strategy for decades between 1926 to 2006. Analysts disagree on what accounts for this, and generally conclude that value will once again have its day leading the pack.

In the last 16 years, the market has been dominated by growth stocks. Value has underperformed. Yet, a glance at the long-term historical chart in Figure 5-2 is a reminder that value has actually had many periods of outperformance.

It's too soon to tell, but a new value outperformance cycle may have already started. Since the pandemic in 2020, the rate of outperformance of growth versus value has slowed. This may be an early indication that a new value cycle is starting.

Over the very long term, all the factors we identify in this book should help your portfolio outperform. The risk is really your patience and ability to weather periods of underperformance while other people are making money and who seem to be outperforming in the short term.

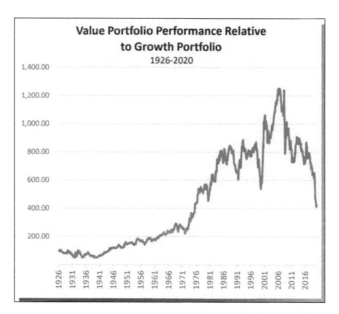

FIGURE 5-2:
Growth versus value since 1926.

Again, we don't recommend making a huge bet either way. Research has shown that timing factor strategies is even more difficult than timing the general market and that, while all of them should do well over time, combining factors is the best way to make sure you get steadier returns that prevent you from falling victim to your emotional brain's need to take action (such as switching stocks or cashing out).

Figure 5-3 illustrates the relative performance chart of value versus growth (downward sloping line) since 1994 as well as growth versus value (upward sloping line). The charts are inverses of each other and clearly show why we don't recommend using value factor alone. The last time it outperformed was after the financial crisis (between 2000 and 2007) fifteen years ago!

Appendix A and Appendix B include many resources that help you screen for quality growth factor to build a portfolio of individual stocks, as well as exchange-traded funds (ETFs). There is also growing evidence that there are efficiencies to be gained from using EFTs that employ growth quality factor as part of a multi-factor approach or a modified factor tilt approach.

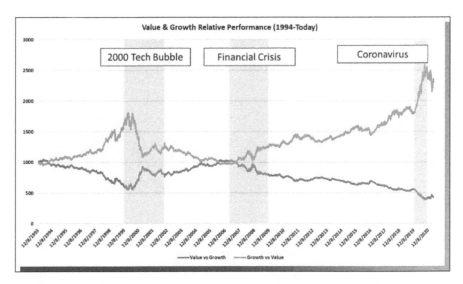

FIGURE 5-3:
Growth versus
value since 1994.

Staying Vigilant for Non-Quality Growth Stocks

Of course, as investors it's important to stay vigilant for elements that could rapidly erode quality earnings. Many investors in recent years have had to learn this time-honored lesson for themselves. The modern world changes faster than ever, and new technologies can make whole industries obsolete. If you're over 30, you probably remember going to Blockbuster (a former quality growth stock) for DVDs and videotapes before high speed Internet and streaming media services revolutionized the industry.

More recently, video gaming companies such as GameStop have hit similar challenges.

Financial fraud is another aspect of modern life that rears its ugly head when least expected. Theranos and Enron were both quality earnings leaders that turned out to be engaging in fraud of one kind or another. Theranos CEO Elizabeth Holmes was not so long ago lauded as the world's youngest self-made billionaire and now faces up to 20 years in prison for promoting a fraudulent medical testing product. Anyone owning the stock as this came to light had a very painful rollercoaster ride downwards, often compounded by the disbelief that kept investors from taking action and the company's PR attempts at minimizing the story.

Enron, one of the biggest so-called success stories of recent decades and a stock that would have topped any quality factor list, blew up seemingly overnight due to its reckless use of derivatives and special purpose entities, and shady accounting practices designed to hide losses and make earnings appear far better than they were.

TIP

Besides vigilance (knowing what you own), diversification is the key to minimizing the damage from these sorts of events. Of course, most factor funds or factor ETFs maintain a discipline of holding 50–100 stocks or more as part of their operating parameters.

SUCCESSFUL COMPANIES THAT WENT BANKRUPT

These former top Wall Street darlings would have topped any quality growth factor list at some point, but ended up failing (through bankruptcy or going out of business). Dozens of other casualties of recent decades could have put a dent in any portfolio not closely supervised or diversified.

- Blockbuster (1985–2010)
- Polaroid (1937–2001)
- Toys R Us (1948–2017)
- Pan Am (1927–1991)
- Borders (1971–2001)
- Pets.com (1998–2000)
- Tower Records (1960–2004)
- Compaq (1982–2002)
- General Motors (1908–2009)
- Kodak (1889–2012)
- BlackBerry (1984–present; still in business, but not the quality growth business it once was)
- Enron (1985–2007)

Employing a Low Turnover Strategy

Quality growth factor has a potential advantage as a low-turnover strategy. Because individual stocks with high earnings quality tend tend to continue to be well managed, their advantage can persist for long periods of time.

"Winners tend to keep on winning" is an aspect this factor has in common with the momentum factor (see Chapter 7). The difference is that, unlike momentum that persists for 1–18 months (by most measurements), quality growth factor can persist in a stock for many years. Take Apple, Google, or Amazon, for example!

What this also means is that holdings of a quality growth factor strategy don't typically change or turn over that much year to year.

A low-turnover strategy has lower transactional costs, and tends to also be more tax friendly as most of the gains are at the more favorable long-term tax rates rather than at the ordinary income rate applied to holdings held less than a year and a day.

REMEMBER

If you're investing in a non-retirement account, be aware of tax implications of various factor strategies. Consider holding lower-turnover factor strategies in your taxable investing accounts and high-turnover (potentially high tax) strategies in your IRA or other tax-qualified accounts.

For more about your tax situation be sure to see Chapter 20. There's no free lunch in investing, but taking advantage of the IRS allowing you to compound wealth tax-free comes pretty close!

Chapter **6**

Value Investing with Factors

Using valuation factors for your long-term wealth-building pursuits is very advantageous for you. The essence of the strategy is to buy valuable companies that are cheap stocks.

At the core of valuation is two things: net profits and assets. If a company has plenty of both and you can acquire it with as low a stock price as possible, then you reach valuation nirvana.

In this chapter, we show you how to find those stocks that have the value factor, which includes a company's true value, the company's expectations, value assets (market and book), and other ratios (such as price-earnings and price-to-sales).

Paying for Value

The most important reason that a stock has value is whether the underlying company can earn a profit — and earn that profit consistently. Consistent profit is the most important feature of a valuable company.

When the company is profitable, everything is humming. Its bank account grows, its employees keep their jobs, its vendors see their bills getting paid, and government tax collectors are happy with its slice of the net profit. The company is surviving and thriving and its profitability means that the company can expand and continue to do well. Investors are then rewarded with appreciating stock prices and dividends that keep coming in, along with the prospects of increased dividends in the future.

So net profits (earnings) and consistent net profits (earnings year-in and year-out, quarter-in and quarter-out) bode well for the company and the company's value, which makes value investors happy.

REMEMBER

The great value investors (such as Warren Buffett and John Templeton) focused on companies and not on the stock. They would look under the hood and find what strengths the company had that the marketplace was ignoring. They would look at the company's weaknesses to see whether they mattered.

Stock versus company

To truly profit with a value stock, you should look out for a profitable differential between the company's true value versus the price of its stock.

One of the most important observations you can make is that every public company has a dual personality. The stock exists in the buy-and-sell-or-hold realm of the stock market — its stock price. But the underlying company itself operates in the real world as it seeks to make a profit producing whatever goods and/or service it offers — its true value.

This dual personality can also explain the seemingly irrational behavior of the stock itself. How often have you seen a company that seems to be doing just fine yet the stock is tanking? Or even more puzzling, hearing that the company is experiencing massive losses, yet its stock is sharply up that day?

People buy today (either good or bad stocks) due to what they *expect* will happen to the underlying companies (and by extension, their stock prices) in the near future.

Exceeding — or not — expectations

The number one reason why investors, traders, and speculators buy (or sell) a given stock can be explained in a single word: expectation or what we call the big "E."

When a solid profitable company reports seemingly good earnings during that particular *earnings season* (the period of time after a given quarter when the company reports vital numbers such as their quarterly earnings or net profit) that the financial media touts so often, imagine the surprise if the stock's price goes down. What gives?!

Perhaps the stock's underling company was expected to earn $2 per share but the finalized earnings number comes in at $1.50 per share. You may say (plausibly) "Great! Nice profit!" But the financial media scuttlebutt may be along the lines of "The company has disappointing earnings. The earnings per share came in sharply lower by 25 percent!" This negative spin affects behavior. Those who held the stock may sell all or some of their holdings because they may be convinced to expect a pessimistic outlook for the company's prospects.

A similar dynamic could occur with an entirely different situation; when you see a company with losses having its stock go up. Imagine a company reports a loss of $3 per share, yet the stock goes up. Why did the stock go up? The investment company and the financial pundits expected the stock to have losses of $5 per share but were pleasantly surprised to see the actual losses on a per-share basis come in 40 percent or less.

In this case, observers feel that shrinking losses bode well for the company's future. Expectations become more positive. Again, whether the company is doing well or not now affects investor expectations for the future.

TIP

If you're a long-term investor, don't get twitchy or too nervous or too optimistic given a company's short-term prospects for its stock price. Every company has a hiccup with its short-term operations.

Every stock seems to zig when you expect it to zag. The irrationality clears up over time. Long term, the stocks of fundamentally solid and profitable companies zag upward. Meanwhile, the stocks of troubled and unprofitable companies zag downward. Understanding the difference means focusing on value and the relevant value factors.

Analyzing the Fundamentals

The value investor utilizes fundamental analysis. Long-term investing is about the fundamentals, meaning the company's financial data (sales, profits, assets, liabilities, net equity, and so on) and its prospects in the market and sector/industry.

As a factor-based value investor, you should look at the most important fundamentals, which means the ones that offer consistent performance given decades of data showing what works for long-term success.

Fundamental Analysis For Dummies, 2nd Edition, by Matt Krantz, (published by John Wiley & Sons) provides some great insights on all the essential company financial data and the most useful ratios and analytical guidance.

TIP

No single ratio is a sure-fire sign (good or bad). Use multiple ratios to gain a more accurate picture of the company's standing.

Understanding different types of value

Public companies (and their stocks) have value in similar ways to other assets, such as cars, houses, and even groceries. If you regularly buy chicken at the supermarket, you know when it's a good deal, when the sale is worth it, or when it's too expensive. If you thought chicken was a great deal at $4 a pound, then you know it is a screaming buy at $3.25 a pound. In both cases, the chicken was the same, but the price was different.

If you bought chicken at $4 last week, and this week it's on sale for $2.99 per pound, you don't lament your purchase by saying "Oh no! The chicken I own that is currently in the freezer just lost a third of its value! I better sell!" Of course not. But that is what many investors do with stocks. If a stock's price goes down, it doesn't necessarily mean the underlying company's value goes down. It only means the price went down. Obviously if the company is suddenly in trouble, the price drop is justified and you would consider selling your holdings in that company.

Conversely, if you see that chicken is now selling for $40 a pound, you definitely wouldn't buy (unless you're a starving millionaire on a desolate, uncharted island) because the price isn't worth it. The price is much higher than the value of the underlying chicken (or whatever asset being considered).

Many stocks' prices have gone down in recent years due to factors not tied to the company's financial health. In 2008, many stocks crashed, but value investors didn't panic. They surveyed the wreckage to see what fundamentally sound and profitable companies were on sale with stock prices lower than the company's intrinsic (or book) value.

There are different ways to measure a company's value. Two of them are market value and book value.

Market value

When you hear that public company XYZ's stock is $50 per share, that is market value. In other words, what is the market (stock market) willing to pay for a single share of XYZ's stock? To figure out the total market value for the stock, you simply multiply the total number of shares outstanding of the company by the market price per share.

If XYZ had 10 million shares at $50 per share, then XYZ's total market value is $500 million (10 million shares times $50). This value is also referred to as *market capitalization* or simply "*market cap.*" In this instance, XYZ is a small-cap stock because its total market value is under $1 billion. (More on market size in Chapter 8.)

REMEMBER

Market capitalization matters in your investing pursuits. Small-cap stocks may have good growth potential but they can be riskier than their larger counterparts. For added safety, many investors seek large-cap stocks (companies worth more than $100 billion). There are also mega-cap or ultra-cap stocks for companies worth more than $500 billion and some companies have even crossed the trillion-dollar mark.

Intrinsic (book) value

Book value, also referred to as *intrinsic value* or *accounting,* looks at a company's value from the classic balance sheet perspective of total assets less total liabilities equals net worth. In the world of stocks, *net worth* is referred to as *net equity* or *stockholders' equity.*

With book value, you tally all the company's assets ranging from cash in the bank to accounts receivables to real estate and equipment. The breakdown is also between tangible assets (equipment and vehicles, for example) and intangible assets (such as goodwill and intellectual property).

The total liabilities include short-term loans and long-term debt (such as mortgages and bonds). The net equity would be what is left should all the assets be liquidated and all the liabilities paid off.

Looking at the important numbers

The advantages of value investing become apparent as you see how certain stocks do well in bad economic times when many other stocks are hammered.

If a stock is cheap and the company is sound then the reasoning is that the stock couldn't fall much further and certainly wouldn't fall anywhere nearly as bad as the overpriced stocks of growth companies that would be hit harder in bad economic times.

Price-earnings ratio

The first number to focus on is one that some investors feel is the single most important and is its own value factor.

The price-earnings (P/E) ratio is a good number to look at on a major financial site. It tells you whether the stock price is a good deal or it's too pricey.

Understanding the P/E ratio is important. It's one of the few ratios that tie the underlying company directly to the stock price. It helps you make a rational judgment about the stock's true value.

The P/E ratio is calculated by taking the price of the stock per share (P) divided by the net profit of the company per share (E). If a stock is $20 per share and its net earnings are $1 per share, then the P/E ratio is 20 to 1 or just simply "20". The P/E ratio is also referred to as the *earnings multiple*.

As a very general rule, here is how you can evaluate the P/E ratio:

>> A low P/E ratio is below 20. It indicates a good value and relatively low risk.

   A low P/E ratio is not automatically a good thing. Some stocks have a low P/E ratio due to a company's poor performance, so look at other factors to augment the P/E ratio in your analysis such as sales and earnings growth over multiple periods (such as the most recent three years).

>> A medium or average P/E ratio is in the 20–35 range.

>> A high P/E ratio is above 40, and may indicate an overpriced security.

>> A P/E ratio of 100 or more is wildly overpriced.

If a stock has no P/E ratio or "N/A" or a negative P/E ratio, be very careful as it likely indicates the stock of a company either has no earnings or (more likely) losing money. If you invest in a stock that is losing money, then you're not investing. You're speculating.

Remember that the P/E ratio is not a strict, uniform measure across all types or categories of stocks. High P/E ratios (such as 40 or more) are considered either normal or acceptable for growth stocks. Some companies are known for low P/E ratios (such as utilities) so make sure that you find out what the average P/E ratio is in that particular industry before you judge whether a P/E ratio is too low or too high.

Price-to-book ratio

The price-to-book (P/B) ratio compares the value of the company itself from a balance sheet point of view and compares it to the company's market value or market capitalization.

P represents the market price and B represents the book (balance sheet) value of the company itself. If XYZ has a market cap of $10 million and a net equity of $5 million, that's a P/B ratio of 2.0, which is fine. In good economic times, a P/B of 2 or 3 or as high as 4 isn't an issue.

The higher the P/B, the higher the market is pricing the stock relative to the company itself. Be wary that a stock is overpriced by rising P/B ratios.

Lastly, in bad economic times coupled with a slumping stock market, the P/B should be lower than 2 (or 3) indicating more equitable value between the market capitalization and the company's book value.

Price-to-sales ratio

Another valuation method is the price-to-sales (P/S) ratio. It compares the market capitalization with the annual sales or total revenue. If the company has a market cap of $12 million and sales of $6 million in the most recent 12 month period (typically either a calendar year or the most recent four quarters) then the P/S (or PSR) ratio is 2.0.

Usually the market capitalization number would be greater than the sales total but again, watch for how high it is. A P/S ratio of 2–5 is much safer than a higher one. A P/S ratio that's double digits or higher is a very negative sign and signals extreme overvaluation.

Chapter **7**

Banking on Momentum with Winners and Losers

Momentum investing refers to buying stocks and bonds that are trending up faster than other stocks and bonds, while avoiding or selling those that are going down, regardless of valuation or other fundamentals of the underlying company. You're basically capitalizing on their momentum in the marketplace.

The momentum factor is a brazen attempt to only buy stocks that go up in value. If they're not trending up, you don't buy them. And conversely, in a more advanced implementation, you can also sell short stocks that are trending down.

Momentum is in some ways the black sheep of the factor family as it contradicts what investors think they know about investing — buy low and sell high and don't chase performance, which are two maxims most investors learn first.

The common sense ideas that it's better to buy at a lower price than a higher price and that last year's winners are unlikely to repeat their lead have a good dose of truth to them. Investors like Warren Buffett have made fortunes with this sort of value-based approach. Paradoxically, these things that everybody knows are also the reason many use to resist using the momentum factor when selecting investments.

But in this chapter, you see that the momentum factor actually plays quite well with the other factors and helps you diversify your portfolio — something that, in turn, helps you with your long-term factor-based investment strategy.

Defining Momentum

The momentum factor is predicated on the idea that once certain trends are in place they tend to continue longer than expected. The simplest way to think of the momentum factor is by leaning into what's working and leaning away from what's not. Think of how you pick which movie to watch. You most likely will pick one with an actor, director, or writer that you've enjoyed in the past. You're banking on the trend that you'll continue to enjoy movies those people are involved in.

Using the momentum factor is the same thing: You're banking (no pun intended) on the idea that winning stocks tend to keep winning over the short to medium term. By allocating funds to stocks that have performed well and underallocating to or avoiding stocks that have not been performing well, you're attempting to tap into these trends.

The psychology of the momentum factor

Of course, most investors tend to take gains off the table too early out of fear that those gains will evaporate, and they hold onto losing positions in the (often misguided) hope that the stocks and bonds will bounce back. And then, if they do rebound, most investors rush to sell them at breakeven prices because they think "I've finally got my money back."

Emotions and the psychology of the human brain, driven by fear and greed, and fight or flight, get in the way of smart decision-making. While these reflexes certainly kept our cave-person ancestors safer from wooly mammoths and saber-tooth tigers, they're not a helpful way for you to run a long-term wealth building strategy.

Letting profits run and cutting your losses is a better and more rational strategy, but much more difficult psychologically, to execute in practice. This is where incorporating a momentum strategy can help you systematize and automate the investment process so that you don't give the cave-dweller part of your brain the chance to mess up things.

REMEMBER

The momentum factor helps you fight what the emerging field of behavioral finance calls the *disposition effect*, where investors hang on to their losers too long and sell their winners too soon. The more rational (and mentally difficult) strategy is cutting losers short and letting profits (winners) run.

Types of momentum

There are two different types of momentum:

» **Cross-sectional** measures relative performance versus the returns of other stocks or bonds in the same asset class. It compares the performance of one asset versus another.

» **Time-series** is also known as *trend following* and focuses on measuring the trend or performance of an asset versus its past performance.

TIP

Time-series momentum factors normally have higher turnover, which makes them less tax-efficient. These stocks are ideal for individual retirement accounts (IRAs) or other tax-advantaged accounts.

Exploring different momentum strategies

The approach you take for the momentum factor needs to keep costs below the momentum premium you expect to make over simply investing in the index via an index fund, or your effort is wasted. You need a timeframe where you evaluate funds and decide how long you want to evaluate:

» **Use a look-back time period.** Any momentum factor strategy (including exchange-traded funds [ETFs] that implement a factor strategy or tilt) has to includes a look-back time period (or snapshot window) for determining what's been doing well.

» **Different lengths of look-back perdiods have pros and cons.** For example, while a shorter (say, quarterly or even monthly) window may pick up trends earlier (including momentum stocks that have lost momentum), implementing those changes more frequently will add incremental costs in terms of trading fees and taxable gains in non-IRA accounts that a longer snapshot window approach would not.

» Likewise, a strategy that updates a portfolio less frequently, say every six to twelve months, reduces trading and tax costs, but may come at the cost of being less responsive to trends.

TIP

One advantage to implementing your own momentum strategy is that you can decide how long or short your snapshot window is, and you can update your portfolio more frequently than ETFs and funds do. It also gives you more control over taxable gains. For example, if it's late December and you know you'll be selling highly appreciated holdings that have lost momentum, you can delay the update a week or two into the following year to postpone the impact of having to pay any capital gains taxes another year. Flexibility can be an attractive aspect of running your own strategy.

Looking at a momentum example

A momentum ETF, MTUM, launched in 2013. Figure 7-1 shows how it performed compared to SPDR S&P 500 Trust ETF (SPY), one of the most commonly used U.S. stock benchmarks EFTs, from 2013–2020. Seven years after its launch, $10,000 invested in MTUM would have grown over $3,700 — more than the very same amount invested in SPY at the same time.

FIGURE 7-1:
A snapshot comparison between a momentum EFT and a benchmark ETF.

The reason we're looking back only from 2013–2020 is to illustrate an important point about implementing any momentum strategy: You need to be aware of the length of the look-back period a momentum fund is using to determine momentum.

This particular fund uses a long look-back period. At the time, the look-back period for this ETF was six months. As the market began its sharp dip during the COVID-19 pandemic, MTUM would be picking its next stock additions based on how it had done the last six months of 2019, not on how it had performed in the first month or so of the downturn, which would have reduced the ETF to only those stocks that were holding up well in the pandemic. Investors who were aware of this knew they could expect a worse than average performance in a market downturn compared to a fund using a shorter look-back period. This is exactly what happened as shown in Figure 7-2.

The problem was that the holdings that had done well in 2019 were now falling even harder than the market. Holding a fund that bases its selections on such a long snapshot is not easy. (Whether selling at that time was the right action to take depends on risk tolerance and time horizon. This ETF's momentum methodology may well outperform in the years ahead.)

Figure 7-2 shows how MTUM's performance compares to VOO (the Vanguard S&P Index ETF) in 2021.

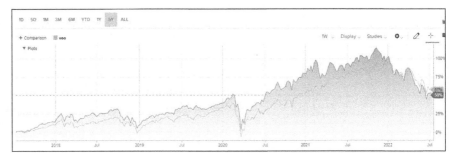

FIGURE 7-2:
How one ETF compares to another in 2021.

It's important to remember that the momentum factor is still a hotly debated factor in financial circles. Exactly why it works and how best to implement it are very much active areas of inquiry. Yet almost every trading desk, hedge fund, or private money manager utilizes momentum factor in their daily investing operations. It's a big deal.

WARNING

Momentum has been one of the most successful factors over the last 10 to 15 years, but it's important not to chase the momentum factor at the expense of neglecting other factors. Investors have a tendency to keep adding to what's working, leading to massive portfolio overweighting in a popular or trendy factor. Factors work best when combined with other factors in a factor-diversified portfolio, as each will contribute periods of outperformance. So diversify your factors and stay disciplined!

MOMENTUM FACTOR RESOURCES

To learn more about the history and development of these successful momentum models check out the following resources. Be sure to see Appendix B as well for specific mutual funds and ETFs and closed end funds to explore further.

- `https://www.jstor.org/stable/2328882?origin=JSTOR-pdf`

  Read the paper that brought momentum to mainstream money management. Jegadeesh and Titman's ground-breaking 1993 published paper on momentum: "Returns to Buying Winners and Selling Losers: Implications for Stock Market Efficiency" (*The Journal of Finance*)

- *Quantitative Momentum: A Practitioner's Guide to Building a Momentum-Based Stock Selection System*, 1st Edition (Wiley Finance)

  This book details the ways in which momentum stands on its own as a stock selection strategy, and gives you the expert insight you need to make it work for you. You'll dig into its behavioral psychology roots, and discover the key tactics that are bringing both institutional and individual investors flocking into the momentum fold.

  Systematic investment strategies always seem to look good on paper, but many fall down in practice. Momentum investing is one of the few systematic strategies with legs, withstanding the test of time and the rigor of academic investigation. This book provides invaluable guidance on constructing your own momentum strategy from the ground up.

- `https://seekingalpha.com/article/4006642-understanding-momentum-factor?`

  This popular article from the website Seeking Alpha is Part 5 in a series about smart beta ETFs and details how stocks that have recently risen or fallen in price will continue that trend over the medium term.

Making Money by Short-Selling Downtrends

Though not for the faint of heart, money can be made on downside momentum too! Just as an uptrend in motion tends to stay in motion (within certain parameters), a downtrend in motion tends to stay in motion too.

Short-selling involves borrowing stock shares that you think will drop in price, selling those shares, and then buying them back at a lower price, thus returning them and finishing the transaction. You profit the difference between the sell price and the buy price.

REMEMBER

A stock that screens exceptionally poorly for quality or value and might be expected to decline,may be well suited to a trend-following metric such as momentum.

Profiting from stocks with downward momentum

Short-selling is a way to profit from a downtrend. The downward trending stocks are your best candidates for short-selling. If everything goes right, you make money by selling short when the persistent downward momentum starts, and cover the trade once the stock falls further down, and ideally when the downward trend is ending or losing momentum.

TIP

ETFs are treated as stocks on exchanges, and are allowed to be sold short (unlike mutual funds which cannot be shorted), depending on your broker's specific policies.

How short-selling works

Short-sellers hope to make money by selling shares of a stock or ETF at a higher price today and using the proceeds to buy back (cover) the trade at a lower price sometime in the future.

Figure 7-3 shows a simple example of a successful short trade of a market index ETF. In this scenario an investor sold short 100 shares of XYZ stock at $20/share and closed the short when XYZ was trading at $10/share, pocketing the difference for a profit of $1,000.

The risks of short-selling

WARNING

Short-selling stocks comes with significant risks and is only something you should attempt when you have experience with selling. Overlaying momentum factor to decide which stocks to short can certainly provide a solid approach and guidance, but as always, there are no guarantees in investing.

>> Because you only make money on a short-sell when the stock drops, the risk to you is that the price of a stock can increase instead of drop.

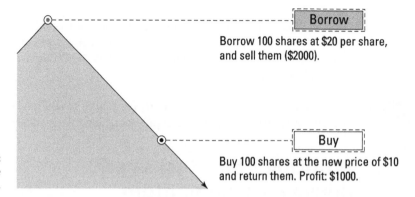

Borrow

Borrow 100 shares at $20 per share, and sell them ($2000).

Buy

Buy 100 shares at the new price of $10 and return them. Profit: $1000.

FIGURE 7-3:
A short trade
of an ETF.

>> It's important to remember that a stock can only drop to zero but, because a stock can hypothetically increase indefinitely, there's an element of asymmetric risk and unlimited loss potential, unless you also employ a stop-loss order strategy while entering the trade. (See Chapter 10 for stop-loss orders.)

>> There is also a chance that this kind of trend reversal (perhaps driven by an earnings surprise or sudden takeover bid) drives existing short-sellers to panic and buy back their positions, causing what's known as a *short squeeze*.

Figure 7-4 shows the risk/reward potential of any short-sell trade.

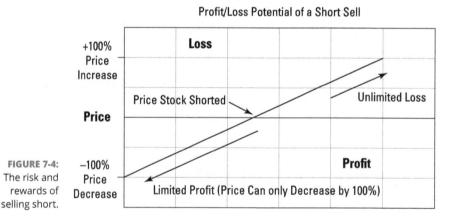

Profit/Loss Potential of a Short Sell

FIGURE 7-4:
The risk and
rewards of
selling short.

INVERSE ETFs

One exciting new tool for investors looking to make money on the downside is the expanding list of inverse ETFs that effectively allow you to sell short by going long (buying) shares of their fund. You purchase these ETFs just like any other ETF, but they are designed to perform the opposite of the index or basket of stocks they track. An inverse S&P Index Fund ETF would be expected to go up by the same amount the market goes down on any given day (the reverse applies too, of course!). The risk management advantage is that when you purchase an inverse ETF, your risk is limited to the price paid for the fund, unlike when shorting a stock. Also, purchasing inverse ETFs can be done with a regular brokerage account and does not usually require a margin account. The obvious disadvantage, in terms of seeking a tool to apply the momentum factor, is that there are not yet any inverse ETFs designed around holding a basket of stocks with high downward or negative momentum characteristics.

Minding the costs of short-selling

Shorting stocks (other than using inverse ETF's) also requires you to have a margin account, which comes with interest rates and minimum equity requirements, so be sure that you're fully informed before attempting to capture downward momentum in your portfolio. Your broker (whether discount or full-service) charges interest for loaning the stocks you short, and each broker has different margin rate tiers or rates that depend on the amount loaned (the larger the amount, the lower the rate). These rates are also subject to periodic rate increases or decreases due to prevailing interest rates. So, if you hear that the Fed has raised interest rates, expect margin rates to rise incrementally as well. (We discuss margin in Chapter 10.)

Another potential cost occurs if you decide to short a hard-to-borrow stock where the broker has difficulty locating enough shares to lend. These stocks come with a higher than normal fee, and varies depending on the broker.

Finally, you don't collect dividends on the shorted stock (assuming it pays any). In fact, you owe the dividend payments and must pay them to the lender. This can be considered an additional expense, especially when shorting a high-dividend stock.

TIP

Several momentum factor ETFs are reportedly on the drawing boards that would use both negative and positive momentum in their strategies. If they're launched and approved, you might consider letting them do any short-selling for you.

Knowing the Potential Limitations of the Momentum Factor

Every strategy and factor has its limitations. The momentum factor is no exemption.

Expecting higher volatility

While momentum has outperformed in the long run, the leading momentum ETFs and sector rotation ETFs have failed to beat the broad market in 2020–2022. Investors who favor indexing have done better owning the S&P 500 ETFs from SSgA (SPY), iShares (IVV), or Vanguard (VOO), or the broad market ETF (VTI), than by owning the momentum ETFs. To be fair, the momentum ETFs, for example, ticker MTUM, only underperformed due to dropping more than the market since November of 2021 at which point it was almost 22 percent ahead of the index, which places its current three-year performance below that of the index.

Figure 7-5 shows the chart of some of the leading momentum factor ETFs versus VOO (the Vanguard S&P 500 ETF) from July of 2019 to July of 2022. You can see that after beating the index and peaking around November of 2021, most of them pulled back harder than the index during the market correction since.

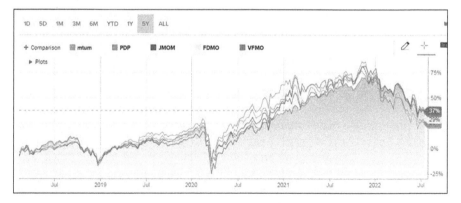

FIGURE 7-5:
How momentum
factor ETFs
have fared.

Stocks with the momentum factor tend to be more volatile than the general market, so this is not unusual or even unexpected. In fact, it likely represents a good opportunity to buy (or rebalance) into momentum as it will likely make up the difference and resume outperformance in the coming market cycle. Rebalancing entails skimming the excess profits off your outperformers and adding those profits to the lowest performers.

WARNING

For factors like momentum to work in your favor, you need to accept that there will be periods of underperformance on the way to long-term outperformance. Realize there will be some volatility, especially in downturns, and either have an effective profit-taking strategy or have patience and only commit long-term money you know you can leave working for you. This is no place for the rent money, or even the money you're saving for your next car or boat. Think four or more years, at a minimum.

Paying higher fees and taxes

Momentum factor, by definition, implies a high-turnover strategy. Stocks that lose momentum have to be kicked out and that means trading costs and often capital gains.

Some momentum ETFs have found innovative strategies or arrangements to minimize trading costs and to maximize offset of capital gains and losses annually to reduce potential taxes. Be sure to dig into the details of each ETF. The fund prospectus is a great place to start.

The key is to make sure that however you implement momentum in your investing approach, the expected benefit of the approach persists after factoring in these two drags on performance.

Choosing a Momentum Approach

Here are some of the most common momentum approaches to give you an idea of the variability possible. Who knows? With some diligence and thought, you may be able to discover your own winning approach.

- » **Relative:** Calculate distribution of relative returns versus every other stock in the chosen stock universe and use that data to design optimal portfolio.

- » **12-2, 12-1, 12-0:** Formed by looking solely at absolute returns, these are the original momentum portfolios.

- » **One Year High:** A portfolio of stocks that have hit one-year highs recently or within a certain window.

- » **Acceleration:** Based on ranking stocks on their performance over the last six months versus their preceding six-month returns to that.

>> **CAPM-α:** Based on ranking stocks on their α over an index.

>> **Sharpe Ratio:** Rank stocks by their Sharpe Ratios, which compares the return of an investment with its risk. Sharp ratios above 1 are desirable offering excess returns relative to volatility.

>> **Residual Idiosyncratic:** Rank stocks based on whatever is left unexplained by the FAMA/FRENCH 5-Factor Model. (See Chapter 2 for more about this model.)

>> **All Time High:** A portfolio of stocks that have hit all time highs recently, usually the preceeding 4–8 weeks.

REMEMBER

While momentum is now a well established factor investment strategy, it's not necessarily an easy one to implement or to stick with. Differences in how momentum is implemented in a portfolio can have a significant impact on performance and outcomes.

Chapter **8**

Sizing Up a Stock's Size

E ver since the landmark 1993 paper by Eugene Fama and Kenneth French (see Chapter 2), the so-called small-cap effect has been known as one of the pillars of factor-based investing among the academic investing community.

Size factor was the original factor and the first actionable research that challenged the dominant Capital Asset Pricing Model (CAPM). CAPM dominated academia in the 1960s and still provides a framework for modern finance. The small-cap premium or unanticipated outperformance of small-cap stocks was the first market anomaly where the extra return wasn't explained or predicted by the established risk/return model.

In this chapter, we discuss how the size factor has turned out to be a little shaky, with a lengthy period of underperformance of small-cap stocks, as well as promising refinements that make the size factor worth being a part of your investment strategy.

Defining the Size Factor

Also known as *small minus big (SMB)*, the size factor refers to the long-studied phenomenon that small-cap (market cap of less than $2 billion) and mid-cap (a market cap of $2 billion to $10 billion) stocks generally outperform large-cap stocks (market cap of $10 billion or more).

The size factor is less persistent than other factors such as value and momentum but it's an affordable factor to implement and shows pervasiveness widely across financial markets. Increasingly, research shows size is most powerful and best pursued in combination with other factors.

Don't be fooled into equating the size factor with the price of a stock — a common misconception.

Size factor is the amount of shares multiplied by the stock price. For example, say you have expensive stock of a company that prints 3D houses (THRD) trading at $400/share and a cheap stock of a company that smelts steel (STL) trading at $19 share.

The price alone tells you nothing about whether they're large or small-cap stocks. To know the market cap of a company, you need to know the amount of shares outstanding and multiply it by the stock price.

In this example:

Company	Current Stock Price	# Shares Outstanding	Market Cap
THRD	$400	$2 million	$800 million
STL	$19	$600 million	$11.4 billion

In this case, the cheap stock STL is a large-cap stock (above $10 billion market cap) and the expensive stock THRD is a small-cap stock (market cap below $2 billion).

THRD, the $400 stock, is a candidate for a small-cap size factor portfolio, while $19 STL isn't.

Size factor (or small-cap factor) is based on the idea that stocks with a lower market value (mid and small caps) realize higher returns over time than large caps or stocks with a higher market value.

Timing with the size factor

Although the size factor has faced some criticism in recent research, when carefully defined and used within a broad multifactor strategy, it still proves to be an important source of outperformance.

Criticisms have largely centered around the original datasets first used to identify this factor, and seeming inconsistencies between its real-world performance versus expected performance. We explore this criticism in the next section "Exploring the Cons of the Size Factor."

The solution, surprisingly, is to use a finer screen to minimize small-cap growth stocks when using size factor as they actually deliver poor growth relative to small-cap value stocks, and are more volatile as well. (This unsavory combo of lower appreciation with higher volatility has earned small-cap growth stocks the nickname of *the black hole of investing*.)

From 1927 to 2015, the U.S. *size premium*, calculated by subtracting the average annual return of large-cap stocks from the average annual return of small-cap stocks, was 3.3 percent. Right now, small-cap and value stocks have underperformed for approximately the last decade (2010–2020), which isn't abnormal. Historically, underperformance has happened many times and can be expected to occur again in the future. If anything, size factor's time may have come. As Figure 8-1 shows, small caps are at their lowest valuations in twenty years. Loading up on some additional small-cap value exchange-traded funds may well prove to be a winning strategy over the coming decade. Overall, the best strategy for success is to combine factors.

Charts in Focus: Small Caps
Small Caps at Lowest Valuation in 20 Years

S&P SmallCap 600 Index/S&P 500 Index,
12-Month Forward Price/Earnings Ratio

Source: Bloomberg as of Sept. 1, 2021

FIGURE 8-1: The small caps at their lowest valuations in 20 years.

TIP

Market cap is calculated by multiplying a company's total number of shares by the current stock price. For example, a company with 10 million shares selling at $100 would have a market cap of $1 billion.

Exploring the Cons of the Size Factor

In this section, we explore the two main issues that make people question the veracity of the (small-cap) size factor:

>> Deficiencies in the original historical database

>> Apparent failure to perform versus academic expectations

Deficiencies in the database

The size factor was noted by Rolf Banz in 1981 using data from 1936 to 1975 to identify what he called the *size effect*. He, like most other students of Eugene Fama, used the University of Chicago's CRSP database as the backbone for his work.

The CRSP database is constantly being updated and corrected, especially for negative events; for example, delistings that had not been properly noted previously. An enterprising researcher named Tyler Shumway upset the market when he identified a huge set of additional delistings of stocks that ceased trading before investors had a chance to sell them. He found that the CRSP files were missing thousands of historical delistings for bankruptcy, insufficient capital, and other unannounced performance-related reasons where no delisting was officially filed.

You can read the fascinating 1997 *Journal of Finance* article, "The Delisting Bias in CRSP Data" by Tyler Shumway if you're interested. You can download it for free at https://www.jstor.org/stable/2329566.

Once the findings were accepted and the CRSP database updated, all the previous findings regarding small capitalization stock outperformance had to be recomputed and re-analyzed.

With the newly corrected data, the outperformance for small caps was much less convincing. In fact, even the original discovery research no longer showed a convincing effect that could be captured and used to improve investor performance.

Tossing out the small-cap growth stocks

In 2015, Fama and French, flying to the defense of their disputed original factor, sorted the data and found that the subset of small-cap growth stocks were, paradoxically, responsible for most of the statistical and sporadic underperformance of small-cap stocks as a whole. It was in a subset, small-cap value stocks, where outperformance can be found.

Once they removed small-cap growth stocks from their analysis, the size premium reappeared and, for academia, the size factor is now one that you can profitably use in your investment strategy.

WARNING

It turns out that small-cap growth stocks tend not to be very profitable. If you use a small-cap fund or ETF to gain exposure to size factor, make sure it has a methodology in place to avoid unprofitable small-cap growth stocks.

Just as important, the new methodology now shows significance in many different markets around the world, whereas previously it was mostly limited to the United States.

Backing them up was a study that underscored that size factor matters, in a bigger way than thought previously, but only if you kick out the junk — the stocks of low quality companies that, in the small-cap universe, tend to show up in the small-cap growth category.

Clifford Asness, Andrea Frazzini, Ronen Israel, and Tobias Moskowitz shored up the updated research with their 2018 paper in the *Journal of Financial Economics* with the somewhat cheeky title "Size matters, if you control your junk."

For those confused by the discrediting of size factor in financial news in recent years, they concluded that the size premium has been accused of having a week historical record, performing much less well than other factors, being seasonal and inconsistent over time. However, when they adjusted the factor to control for quality by eliminating low quality (for example, earnings and balance sheets) stocks from the mix, performance improved drastically to a level on par with other established factors, and the seasonality and unpredictability disappeared.

This result held true for the stocks of 30 different industries and 24 international markets that they studied. Low quality junk was correlated with and could be largely eliminated by simply removing small-cap growth stocks. The small-cap value premium or size factor is absolutely real, provided you exclude non-profitable small-cap growth stocks.

This was a surprise for investing academia because it had previously been (falsely) assumed that small-cap growth stocks had more risk and therefore investors would be compensated for taking on that risk with additional returns over time.

REMEMBER

Research shows that size factor works best when combined with other factors such as value and quality. Rather than use it as a standalone factor, think of it as enhancing the returns of other factors.

Considering the timing

Using size as the only factor may appear to go against everything we've said about combining factors.

Generally, diversification is the sure way to long-term investing success, whether it's diversification of assets, stocks and bonds, or investing factors.

But, because evidence from funds that follow the size factor clearly shows, many investors move in and out of this strategy, perhaps more than any other factor. They're probably mostly driven by emotion, or simply getting bored of waiting for the performance premium to manifest, and moving on to other opportunities. Regardless, if you're going to time the market, why not try to do it deliberately and with a strategic overlay to your actions rather than by gut feel or emotion? Check out Chapter 4 where we offer more advice on market timing.

Dealing with sensitive bull and bear markets

Small-cap stocks tend to be especially sensitive to economic downturns and expansions, and the reasons are fairly obvious. All companies start out small, and for a growing company with big dreams, financial conditions such as the cost of borrowing funds for expansion and the appetite of Wall Street for shares of untested companies issuing new stock to raise capital can make or break them.

REMEMBER

During downturns, small-cap stocks tend to underperform because they have fewer buffers to survive economic shocks compared to their larger brethren.

For these and other reasons, size factor often comes with increased volatility rather than other factors. This, in addition to the normal historical ebb and flow of outperformance among various factors, means that investors who employ a strict buy and hold approach to size factor can experience some very tough years when it seems like almost anything else is outperforming them.

Most investors eventually give up on this approach and move on to another one, which defeats the purpose of factor investing and can sabotage wealth building.

The solution is to either use size factor as part of a long-term cocktail of factors, or, if used alone, time it with the market. (See Chapter 4 for that strategy.)

Small companies, and therefore size factor, outperform during times of economic recovery and expansion as shown in Figure 8-2. Buying small-cap stocks after an economic contraction or recession and holding through the period of economic recovery and selling as the expansion peaks would be the most profitable approach.

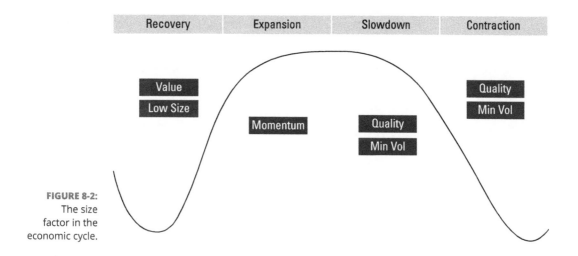

FIGURE 8-2:
The size
factor in the
economic cycle.

Using Size Factor with Funds

Finally, many funds and ETFs attempt to capture size factor effectively, including some new entries that have filed for approval to be launched in coming years.

Appendix B lists many ETFs in this category.

Always be sure to read the prospectus (or, if it puts you to sleep, at least the summary pages) looking for the actual methodology used by that particular fund. Is it strict about staying with small caps? What happens when a stock outgrows the small-cap classification? Do they have an active methodology to identify and minimize or eliminate pesky unprofitable small-cap growth stocks?

How do they pursue their chosen factor or factors while minimizing fees and trading expenses? What does it cost you to own the fund? Find out! It's your money you're investing.

If you keep on top of your invesments, you keep more of what the market offers. This applies as much to keeping up with new factor research as being aware of what the investment products and platforms you chose are costing you. After all, you want to keep your profits and benefit from them — not to have them drip and erode away through expenses and taxes.

Chapter **9**

Dividend Income Using Factors

N o book on stocks and exchange-traded funds (ETFs) is complete without a chapter on a powerful feature of stocks: dividends.

In this chapter, we show you to how take advantange of dividends, and how you can build your portfolio in the near term while providing future income that can meet or exceed the rate of inflation in the years that you will need inflation-adjusted income (such as in retirement).

Getting Started with Dividends

Dividends are different compared to another source of investor income (interest). While interest is a payment made by a debtor to a creditor, *dividends* are a payout from typically a public company to its owners (shareholders).

When you hear someone use the phrase *stock dividends* or say something like "my stock pays a dividend" remember that stocks don't pay dividends; the underlying company does. Dividends come from the company's operations (for example, net profits).

If you're receiving dividends from a company that is losing money (net losses as an example) and the only reason is because you want (or need) the dividends, then strongly consider selling the stock and use the proceeds to find a more financially sound company that pays dividends. If you're using value factors, you can avoid companies that are losing money and in danger of cutting or cancelling their dividend payouts.

Gaining dividend benefits

The most obvious benefit of dividends is that it can be reliable passive income for you that comes quarterly (and some securities pay a monthly dividend). But here are other benefits to keep in mind:

>> **Inflation:** Many long-term studies have shown that annual dividend payments tend to match or exceed the rate of inflation. This can augment your fixed-income investments (such as bonds).

>> **Tax:** The dividends from most stocks and stock-related ETFs and mutual funds typically are considered qualified dividends, meaning that these dividends can qualify for a lower tax rate. (See Chapter 20 for details.)

>> **Reinvestment:** You can revinvest dividends by buying more of the underlying stock, ETF, or mutual fund to keep your holdings growing in value over time. (More on this in the "Reinvesting Your Dividends" section, later in this chapter.)

Using value factors for dividends

For finding and analyzing great dividend stocks, consider not only the points and resources covered in this chapter but also the value factors covered in Chapter 6 and also consider using the stock/ETF screening tools covered in Chapter 15.

The value factors that help you buy strong companies as cheap or relatively inexpensive stocks can help you in your dividend pursuits. The price–earnings (P/E) ratio, for example, is a very useful tool in analyzing stocks that have the earnings power to be a reliable dividend paying company. See Chapter 6 to find out more about P/E ratios.

Understanding the Difference Between Dividend Amount and Dividend Yield

What gives you a better return on your money from a yield point of view: a $20 stock providing you a $1 dividend or a $100 stock with a $5 dividend? In this case, neither. Both have a 5 percent dividend yield. Understanding yield is important if you want to make the most dividend income for your stock-buying money. The *dividend yield* is the calculation of how much dividend income you're getting from a stock purchase quoted as a percentage (%). It's a great way to compare income from a variety of sources (such as different stocks, different investments, or from a bank account).

The dividend yield is calculated by

> Annual dividend per share divided by current share price

If you bought a stock today at $50 per share and the expected dividend for the next 12 months is a total of $3, then your dividend yield is

> $3 annual dividend divided by $50 share price = 6 percent.

Is that a good dividend yield? Yes. It's higher than the stock market average (roughly 2 percent) but remember to check the dividend payout ration (DPR) to see whether the dividend is safe. See the next section for more on DPR.

REMEMBER

Whenever you check a stock at the financial sites or the newspaper's financial pages, the dividend yield quoted is as of that moment or that trading day only.

Say that you bought stock for $40 per share with a a $3 annual dividend a year ago. The stock is now trading at $50 per share. So, although today's yield is quoted at 6 percent, your particular yield is different because you bought at a different share price and a different time. When you bought the stock at $40 per share, you locked in a yield of 7.5 percent.

Say that the dividend is increased from $3 per share to $3.50 per share, and the stock is trading at $55. Anyone buying that stock at $55 and getting $3.50 dividend per share would be getting a yield of 6.36 percent. Your new dividend yield is 8.75 percent — 3.5 annual dividend divided by $40 — that's a good thing!.

As dividend payouts grow, your true dividend yield (based on the original cost of your stock purchase) grows as well, which bodes well for the foreseeable future provided the company's fundamentals (including its value factors) continue.

REMEMBER

If the underlying company is strong (see Chapter 6 for ways to find out) and its stock goes down temporarily, it can be a buying opportunity but not a reason to be concerned. When the stock goes down and you have designated your dividends to be reinvested in the company's stock, this means you buy the stock at a lower price, giving you more stock, which means expanding your dividend income. The only reasons to sell your stock is if you need the money or if the underlying company is no longer meeting your criteria (ceases to perform according to their chosen factors or ceases to be a strong company).

Knowing the Dividend Payout Ratio

Getting paid dividends is great, but what is better is that you keep getting dividends well into the future. Just because a large corporation is making these dividend payments, don't assume your dividend payout is safe until you look at the fundamentals tied to the dividend being paid. To do so, you need to look at the dividend payout ratio (DPR). The *DPR* is the ratio of the dividends paid by the company relative to the company's net earnings (or net profit).

The DPR helps you see whether your dividend is safe. The DPR formula is

Dividend per share divided by the earnings per share

Say the company is paying an annual dividend of $3 per share. Assume that the company's earnings (or net profit) are $4.50 per share. Here's the DPR formula:

$3 dividend per share (DPS) divided by $4.50 earnings per share (EPS) = 66% DPR

Generally, a DPR of 80 percent or less means that the dividend is safe. The dividend amount being paid is less than 80 percent of the net income or earnings per share. There is ample income to cover from the net earnings to comfortably pay the dividend amount.

WARNING

A DPR above 90 percent is an issue. A DPR above 100 percent is in the danger zone. In other words, if the dividend is much greater than the company's net earnings, then the danger is that the dividend could be reduced. In some cases when companies are losing money, the danger is that the dividend could be cancelled altogether.

The bottom line is that if that dividend is necessary to you, get very familiar with the DPR and always make sure that the dividends being paid are less than the earnings and preferably that the DPR is lower than 80 percent.

There are exceptions to this rule. Some types of securities are structured to provide dividend payouts of 90 percent or more to gain tax advantages. A good example is the real estate investment trust (REIT). A DPR of 90 percent or slightly higher is acceptable, but if the REIT has a DPR much higher than 100 perceent, be concerned and check the REIT's fundamentals to see whether there are financial difficulties (such as too much debt).

Checking Dividend Growth

If you're investing in stocks for current dividends, that's great but you should check to see whether this particular stock or ETF has shown good dividend growth in recent years. *Dividend growth* is a company's long-term record of consistently paying dividends that tend to increase annually and reliably over many years. Some companies have shown consistent dividend growth over decades. It's a good gauge for what kind of dividend increases can occur in the coming years.

TIP

Definitely check the dividend growth if one of your goals is to have substantial dividend income in the future.

To check for past dividend increases, go to Nasdaq (www.nasdaq.com). Search for a stock or ETF and then click the Dividend History link at the left. You can see every dividend payment made, the amount, the date, and so on for the last ten years. This past performance gives you a strong picture of that particular dividend payer. A strong past performance in dividend payouts and dividend increases tends to continue.

Getting Paid by Your Dividends

Most dividends are paid quarterly, but some are paid monthly. You should be familiar with the key dividend dates for the stock(s) you're invested in. Here are the key dates:

>> **Declaration date:** This is when the company announces the amount of the dividend and when it gets paid.

>> **Date of record:** This is the date that you should officially be recorded on the company's shareholder records to qualify for the dividend.

>> **Ex-dividend date:** When you buy stock to qualify for the dividend, you must buy at least two business days before the date of record to give time for the

trade to be settled. If the date of record, for example, is Wednesday, July 5th, you must have purchased that stock by Monday, July 3rd to qualify for that dividend payout. If, for example, you buy on Tuesday, July 4th, you will not be on the books.

>> **Payment date:** This is the actual day the payment is either mailed (by paper check) or is electronically sent to your bank account.

To find the dividend dates for your stocks, you can look them up at the sites listed in the resources sidebar.

Reinvesting Your Dividends

One of the best ways to grow your wealth faster is to have your dividends reinvested in the stock of the underlying company. Today, that is easier than ever before. In the following sections, we discuss two ways you can do just that.

TIP

Having your dividends reinvested takes advantage of a popular approach referred to as benefits of dollar cost averaging. This approach works well over time to build your wealth. The concept is that regular payments will buy less of the stock when the stock price is higher and more of the stock when the price is lower.

If you have long-term holdings in quality, dividend payers and there is a bear market or correction in the near term, the reinvestment means that you will pay your stock at a lower cost and simultaneously garner a higher dividend yield with that same stock.

Dividend reinvestment through your broker

There are many benefits to maintaining a stock brokerage account and one of them is automating the act of dividend reinvestment. Although every broker does this a little bit differently, it's not difficult to do.

The next time you're in your brokerage account, go to your positions summary and find the area for dividend management. You can opt to either have the dividends credited to your account or to be reinvested in that given stock or ETF. Some brokers even have a feature to have all dividends reinvested so that you can automatically have each security's dividend reinvested in that given security.

Whether you have one stock's dividends reinvested, some, or all, you can always discontinue it later. So the decision is easy: Reinvest the dividends when you don't need them and change the option later when needed.

Using dividend reinvestment plans

One way to build wealth is to have a dividend reinvestment plan (DRP). Most stocks that pay dividends tend to have a DRP. To make sure, go to the company's website to confirm (and sign up). Over 1,000 (and counting) dividend-paying companies have a DRP. Each DRP is different in small ways but virtually all of them have two primary features:

>> Dividends are reinvested.

>> You can send in optional cash payments to the account and buy more stock typically without commissions or other transaction costs.

Additionally, most DRPs can qualify to become individual retirement accounts (IRAs) giving you long-term tax-advantaged benefits.

Projecting Dividend Income

What type of income are you looking for with your dividend pursuits? $2,000 per year to help augment your lifestyle (such as paying for that nice vacation?) or do you seek dividends to fully or partially fund your future retirement income?

It's always a good idea to plan your financial future and do estimates of what your future income needs may be. Say you will retire in five or ten years. Find out what your potential Social Security income will be (go to ssa.gov to do an income estimate). Say that you will get $25,000 annually in Social Security at retirement time. But in your income and expense projections, you find that at retirement time you will need approximately $30,000 of annual income to be somewhat comfortable. How do you handle the $5,000 income shortfall? You need to re-position the securities in those accounts for income — in this case, dividend income.

Here is where dividend growth strategies can fill in the shortfall. Many dividend opportunities in today's stock market can earn a dividend yield of 3.5 percent, for example. Consider the following formula:

Amount of income needed divided by dividend yield equals stock or ETF amount to purchase

Now plug in your numbers:

$5,000 needed divided by 3.5 percent yield = $142,857

In other words, if you buy approximately $142,857 of dividend stocks between now and your retirement earning 3.5 dividend yield, you would achieve your minimum income goal at retirement. Keep in mind that if the dividends are growing, then you could acquire less than the target amount and still reach your goal. This is, of course, a simplified example but hopefully it gets you thinking. Your best bet is to seek a financial planning professional to assist if necessary.

Where to find good dividend payers

Every sector of the economy has different features and characteristics and the same can be said of these sectors from a dividend point of view. If you were looking for great dividend payers, some sectors offer better opportunities than others. Here are some common sectors for good dividends:

>> **Utilities:** Gas and electric utilities are well known for having great dividend payers.

>> **Consumer staples:** Food and beverage companies, for example, tend to pay higher than average dividends.

>> **Financial and banking sector:** Another sector known for good dividends.

>> **Real estate:** Companies such as those categorized as real estate investment trusts (REITs) pay solid dividends.

TIP

ETFs and mutual funds have many great dividend-income opportunities. For example, you can go to the ETF database site (www.etfdb.com) and search for *dividend* or *dividend yield* and you can find dozens of solid, dividend-paying ETFs. Some of them pay monthly dividends. For more information on ETFs, check out Chapter 16.

TIP

Another great source of solid dividends and a greater measure of safety as compared to common stock is preferred stock. A great way to invest in preferred stock is through an ETF. To find preferred stock ETFs, go to sites such as ETF (www.etf.com) and search for *preferred*.

DIVIDEND RESOURCES

To learn about dividends and strategies to enhance your dividend income, check out these resources:

- Dividend.com (www.dividend.com)
- Dividend Hunter (www.dividendhunter.com)
- Dividend Channel (www.dividendchannel.com)

All three of these provide comprehensive data, analysis, and news about dividend-paying stocks. For dividend ETFs, check out the resources in Chapter 16.

3

Using Factor Investing in Your Portfolio

IN THIS PART . . .

Using brokerage orders to complement your factor investing.

How macro factors help your stock investing approach.

Following the time-tested buy low, sell high rule.

Adding international stocks to your portfolio using factors.

Time your approach with technical analysis.

Finding opportunities with stock screening tools.

Chapter **10**

Using Brokerage Orders with Factor Investing

When you're implementing your factor investing approach, you likely do it in a stock brokerage account. But while you're using your account, take a look at what the brokerage firm offers you that can enhance your success and minimize any potential losses.

No approach in the stock market (or any market really) is foolproof. As an investor, you should use all the tools of the trade to minimize the risk of investing. One of those tools are brokerage orders.

Brokerage orders certainly mean the obvious — they are the actual transactions you implement in your brokerage account to ultimately buy and sell securities for your portfolio. In this chapter, we show you how to use them properly, which can add discipline, predictability, and flexibility to your factor investing approach.

Understanding the Types of Brokerage Orders

Brokerage orders are generally sorted into two main categories: condition-related orders and time-related orders. We could make the case for a third category that's a combination of orders, which can create a set of two or more orders simultaneously from the two main categories but we stick to the two main categories in this chapter.

TIP

Most brokers have tutorials at their website and you should learn from them. Master even a few and you can save many positions from dangerous market events.

The following sections talk about the different types of orders and what kind of category they fall into.

Of course, always check with your broker what orders are available to you and the how and why of each one.

Condition-related orders

Just as the name indicates, this type of order is executed only when a certain condition is met. Instead of being subject to the whims of the market and settling for a price that the market sets, you take control and only buy (or sell) at your desired price.

The market will usually have you settle for buying at a higher price or selling at a lower price. Most investors (and speculators) should use condition-related orders whenever possible.

Limit

A good example of a conditional order is the *limit order*. Say for example you want to buy the stock of the public company Hokey Smoke Inc. (HSI) at $30 per share. You enter the order as, say, "buy 50 shares of HSI at a limit order of $30."

If HSI goes down to $30.01, then the order isn't executed because the stock didn't specifically hit the $30 price. If the stock goes to $30 or lower the order is triggered and then filled.

The limit order actually hits at the specific price *or better*. That's right; you could end up buying that stock at a slightly better price especially if the market is moving fast (or volatile) at the time of the trade. In this case, you could end up buying the stock at $29.99 or $29.98 or even lower. The reasoning here is if you like the stock at $30, you would really like it at a lower price.

You can also use the limit order when you're selling your stock (or other security). Say you did buy HSI and time has passed and that stock's price is now $50 per share and you're ready to sell it. In that case, you enter a limit order to sell it at $50 or better. In this case, if the stock is at $49.99 (or lower), then the trade isn't executed.

However, if the stock is doing well that day and it's rising, the odds are good that you will get your $50 per share sold and maybe higher (such as $50.01 or better).

Make a limit order your first consideration when buying (or selling a stock). When the market is calm (not volatile or extreme), you should generally be successful in getting your price. Buying a stock of a company you want in your portfolio at the lowest possible price is part of your overall success. And when the time arrives, selling the stock at the highest possible price (again, achieved with limit orders) is also part of your overall success.

Market

This is the simplest and most immediate order that you can do. A market order is a brokerage order to buy (or sell) a particular security (stock, ETF, for example). This happens when you submit your order to buy (or sell) immediately regardless of the price at that given moment.

Market orders come in handy during extreme events, such as when markets fall over 1,000 points in a day (2022 has seen a few periods like this). Nervous investors itch to get out regardless of the price and they sell using market orders to avoid further losses. They merely want the best available price.

Stop-loss

A *stop-loss order* (also referred to as a *stop order*) is a condition-related order that instructs the broker to sell a given stock in your portfolio only when the stock declines to your specified price. That price is based on a dollar or percentage amount below the stock's market price as you designate. If the stock's price is $50, for example and you want to limit the downside movement to $45, you can designate a limit of $5 or 10% (in either case, the resulting sale would be at your chosen stop price) to limit further losses. This order acts like a trigger so that when the stock price does reach it, the order is immediately converted to a market order to sell the stock as soon as possible.

In a relatively tranquil or stable market, the stock ends up selling at the stop-loss order's designated price. If it's at $20 per share, then you likely sell at $20 per share.

But what if it's a volatile market and prices move quickly? If that stock goes down to, say, $20 per share, it definitely triggers the order, but perhaps the ultimate price that it fills at could be at $19.50, for example, or possibly lower.

The purpose of the stop-loss order isn't (or shouldn't be) to protect you from the relatively small fluctuations of the day-in and day-out stock price movements. Its primary role is to protect 85–95 percent of your position (depending on how close you place the stop-loss order to the prevailing stock price). The stop-loss order is there in the event or threat of a major downward move of that given stock.

Your stock Yumping Yiminy Inc. (YYI) goes to $25 per share and you want to protect it against a decline in the near future. A stop-loss order at $22.50 (10 percent below the market price of $25) means you protect 90 percent of your investment in YYI. (10 percent is only used as an example; choose the position that's best for you — whether that's 10, 7, 3, or right away.)

The main benefit of a stop-loss order is that it prevents a major loss in a stock that you own. It's a form of discipline that's important in investing to minimize potential losses. Investors can find it agonizing to sell a stock that has fallen. If they don't sell, however, the stock often continues to plummet as investors continue to hold on while hoping for a rebound in the price.

So the stop-loss is great when the market is crashing and you look like a genius for limiting your loss when the rest of the market looked like it went over Niagara Falls. But the next thing you know, the market has a sharp rebound and you missed some gains. The stop-loss is an important loss-limiting tool and you should always be ready to use it but that doesn't mean you should use it in every instance.

If one of your favorite stocks was in danger of falling, you may not want to put it on a stop-loss order. Why? If you acquired it for dividend income and intended to hold it long term, a stop-loss order doesn't make sense. If you think the stock is still a solid investment that belongs in your portfolio, instead of selling it, you may find that a sharp pullback in its price offers a good buying opportunity.

What happens if your stock makes a significant (and very welcome) move upward? What if instead of triggering the stop-loss order, your stock prices increase?

Say that Yumping Yiminy Inc that you bought at $25 goes up to $40 (nice yump!). At this point, you still have that stop-loss order at $22.50. Well, if you do nothing and YYI reverses and gives back all its gains, it could go to $22.50 and then be sold — not what you want! You would do the old "coulda, shoulda, woulda" self-talk that would be torment. (See the upcoming section on how to set up time-related orders.)

If YYI goes to $40, you immediately cancel the old stop-loss order of $22.50 and replace it with a new stop-loss order at, say, $36 (which is $4 or 10 percent below this new stock price high at $40).

If YYI does indeed go down and then hits the new stop-loss order of $36, it triggers and you're sold out at $36. The great thing is that you had protected the old price of $25 and you also locked in a nice profit of $11 per share. Life is good.

REMEMBER

One of the drawbacks of the stop-loss order is that you need to constantly monitor where the stock's price is in relation to the stop-loss price. If the stock's price does rise, it's prudent to raise the stop-loss level too so you can keep protecting more and more of your position's value — both the original principal amount and the gain or appreciation portion.

Trailing stop

The trailing stop order allows you to minimize losses and maximize gains. It takes the lowly stop-loss order and turns it into a dynamic tactic for investing success. A trailing stop is an upgrade to the stop-loss order in that it makes the stop-loss order automated so that when the stock rises, the stop-loss is automatically adjusted upward (given your designated dollar or percentage amount), but the moment that the stock ceases to rise and subsequently declines, the trailing stop automatically becomes a stop-loss order to limit the downside potential.

When you set up a trailing stop order, you have two choices to make: 1) whether to set it up with a percentage or certain dollar amount and 2) as a day order or good-til-canceled (GTC) order. You make those same choices for time-related orders, which we cover in the next section.

WHEN TO SELL A STOCK

There are only two primary reasons you would sell a stock:

1. If the underlying company involved ceased to be worth holding (company is losing money, or the company's fundamentals are deteriorating, for example).

2. You need the money.

Time-related orders

A time-related order is just what it sounds like. The order is predicated on time. There are two basic types: day and good-til-canceled (GTC).

Day

A day order is a brokerage order to buy or sell a particular stock (or ETF or other marketable security) and that order expires at the end of that particular trading day (typically 4 p.m. Eastern time when stock market trading ends).

If you tell the brokerage firm "Buy DOA, Inc. at $43.00 and make it a day order," then you mean that you want to purchase that stock at $43 (or better) before the close of trading that day.

REMEMBER

If you enter an order and do not designate the time, most brokerage firms will designate it a day order by default.

When would a day order made sense for you? It depends on what you want to accomplish that day and the circumstances regarding your preferences. Day orders aren't used frequently because they're so fleeting and it benefits you to watch the stock's movement over a greater timeframe, such as a week or more.

Good-til-canceled orders (GTC)

GTC orders are used frequently in day-to-day trading. It's like a "set-it-and-forget-it" order.

A *good-til-canceled order* is just what it sounds like. You enter a timeframe for the order and choose when that timeframe ends (an expiration date). Keep in mind that GTC orders are very flexible. You can change or cancel them as long as they're not triggered. You can let them expire and you can re-issue them again as needed. The point is to seriously consider using them especially during uncertain or difficult market periods (for example, 2022).

Although the GTC can make you infer that there is not a timeframe involved, most brokerage firms do have a finite timeframe such as 60, 90, or 120 days. Some firms have it run longer or shorter. Inquire with your specific brokerage firm how long can a GTC last.

How the broker handles the GTC order can also vary. Some will tell you at the time you place the order when it expires. Some may send you an email or a text notice right before the order expires. Find out with your broker.

Of course the GTC order is always coupled with condition-related orders. After all, what type of order will ultimately be executed in that timeframe or may expire?

Say, for example, that you are eyeing the stock XYZ corp as an addition to your portfolio. You did the homework and you think based on valuation metrics (such as the price-earnings ratio) that you would be happy paying $40 per share and not a penny more. Meanwhile, the stock is trading at $45. In this case you can do a limit order at $40 or better as a GTC order (say for 90 days).

Using Margin

Used properly, margin can be a great brokerage tool in your wealth-building pursuits. *Margin* means buying securities (such as stocks, bonds, and ETFs) with borrowed funds from your stock brokerage firm using your stock or other portfolio securities as collateral.

Margin trading scenarios

Say that you think that the stock for the company Giga Byte Tech Inc (GBT), currently at $50 per share, will head upwards in the near future. You would like to buy 100 shares (for a total purchase of $5,000) but you only have $2,500. In this case, you're eyeing margin to make this trade. If you swing this deal, what are the possible scenarios?

GBT's stock price goes up

The price going up is the best scenario. If GBT goes to $65 per share, the investment is now worth $6,500 and the outstanding margin loan is $2,500. If you decide to sell, the proceeds from the sale amount would also pay off (liquidate) the $2,500 margin loan from the broker.

On paper, you banked a nice (taxable) capital gain of $1,500 ($6,500 sale amount less the original cost basis of $5,000). But your outlay for the initial stock purchase was only $2,500 (because you borrowed the other 50 percent or $2,500 with a margin loan directly from the broker) so your effective gain was 60 percent ($1,500 is 60 percent of your personal investment of $2,500). Oh yeah. . . you're a profit-generating beast!

REMEMBER

Using borrowed funds (leverage!) can be profitable. Just keep in mind that you have to ultimately pay back the debt with interest. Also, margin interest can be tax-deductible (more info in Chapter 20).

GBT's stock price trades sideways

If the stock is flatlining around the purchase price of $50 per share (give or take), the margin loan is still active and margin interest keeps adding up on a daily basis. Keep in mind that any dividends paid by GBT will certainly help pay down the margin debt and interest charged.

Stock that is generally not volatile (at least not relatively volatile versus aggressive growth stock) and that most certainly has a higher-than-average dividend is worth considering for margin. If your margin loan has a rate of 3 percent and your dividend-paying stock is yielding say 4.5 percent, then that is not a bad arrangement.

GBT's stock price goes down

Worst-case scenario is that GBT stock goes down sharply. It goes to $35 per share. Now what?

Those 100 shares of stock that you bought at $50 ($5,000) are now worth $3,500. Your equity shrinks to only $1,000 because you still have an outstanding margin loan of $2,500. Nothing worth jumping out the window about but at this moment your broker most likely contacts you (the "margin call") regarding the maintenance of your margin situation because the margin loan amount exceeds the 50 percent maintenance level.

You likely need to either add cash to the account or add marginable securities (such as common stock or ETFs) to raise the value of your portfolio to get back to a proper ratio of loan to stock values.

If you cannot come up with added securities or cash, then you must sell off other stock to pay off the margin debt.

Maintaining balance requirements

When you purchase stock (or any securities) on margin, you must (*must*) maintain a ratio of margin debt to equity of at least 50 percent. Some brokers may have a more restrictive balance (as low as 25 percent). In other words, if your margin loan balance is, say, $3,000, then you better have equity with a market value of at least $6,000 for those brokers requiring a 50 percent ration. If they require a 25 percent ratio, then you must have a market value of $12,000.

If you can't add cash or more securities to your account, then you need to sell some of your securities to reduce the outstanding margin debt. This can be all too common during market downturns and it may result in realized stock losses despite reducing your margin debt.

If the ratio exceeds the broker's limit, then you will either need to add more cash to the account (to reduce the margin loan balance) or add more marginable securities (to increase the market value of equity in the account).

Before you add a dollar's worth of margin debt to your account, it pays to read the margin requirements and guidelines at the broker's website. If they don't make it clear or you can't find or figure out their requirements, then contact customer support and get it clear so you don't find yourself with financial difficulties.

Different types of securities may have different margin requirements or may not be marginable:

>> **Listed (marginable) stock:** This stock is listed on a major exchange such as the New York Stock Exchange. This includes major stocks (large market capitalization) on Nasdaq. Typically the margin rate is 50 percent.

>> **Small-cap stock:** This also includes "over the counter" stock and penny stock. These securities are not usually marginable.

>> **Treasury securities:** This includes treasury bonds, notes, and bills (meaning short-term securities such as Treasury bills). These securities are typically marginable up to 90 percent.

>> **Municipal bonds:** These debt securities are issued by state, county, and city governments and their agencies. These securities tend to be marginable up to 80 percent.

>> **ETFs:** Typically marginable at 50 percent.

>> **Options:** Typically are not marginable.

Margin requirements for brokers are set by the Federal Reserve (www.federalreserve.gov) with Regulation T. Ask your broker about these requirements and guidelines before you decide to proceed with margin loans so you don't get surprised by market gyrations and how they affect your margin maintenance requirements.

Striving for success on margin

In early 2022, the general stock market has experienced corrections and bear market conditions. Many famous stocks have declined 30 to 40 percent and more. Any investor that held those positions exposed to margin requirements had a financially painful experience (ugh!) resulting in further losses and probably consumed too much antacid and adult beverages.

If you're going to buy stock or other securities on margin, be informed in advance and act with diligence and discipline. Here are some important points to keep in mind:

>> Keep your margin loan balance low. Ideally, keep it to a ratio of 40 percent or lower. In other words, if you have $10,000 in marginable securities, don't borrow any more than 40 percent or $4,000. Of course the lower, the better. Always avoid margin debt.

>> If you're going to do margin, consider large-cap stocks that are stable and pay good dividends.

>> Monitor your stocks.

>> Have a plan to pay back your margin debt.

>> Use stop-loss orders or trailing stop orders in conjunction with margin usage. (See the earlier sections for how to use these orders.)

Factor investing and margin

Obviously, margin should only be used if it can optimize your factor-based investing approach. If you're making your choices using growth-related factors, then margin investing can help you make some great profits (if you are correct). However, growth investing is a double-edged sword. In a down market, growth stocks get hammered and if you're using margin, then your pain can be magnified.

Timing is everything. In the beginning of a bull market, using margin can enhance your potential gains. But margin can bite you if you use it at the top of the market. Being a disciplined contrarian will serve you well. Buying on margin is popular during a market rally but when the market reverses it will do you harm.

It may seem counterintuitive, but using margin (if you are going to use it) after a major stock market decline is likely less risky than during an ebullient bull market or rally. Also, using margin with value stocks (using value factors) is less risky than using margin with growth factor approaches.

Lastly, it doesn't hurt to discuss your margin strategies with an experienced investment professional to gain more knowledge and confidence before you risk large amounts in your portfolio.

Chapter **11**

Using Macro Factors

t's said that "a rising tide lifts all boats" (at least the ones that can float). The point is that when the overall economy is doing well, then those investments that do well with the economy will do well in your portfolio.

In prior chapters, we covered factors that could be considered *microeconomic* factors — those primarily focused on the enterprise itself and its particular economic health (the "fundamentals" for example).

Macro in the context of factors refers to the general environment that your investments (such as public companies whose stock you own) operate within and what influential determinants are necessary for success or contribute to failure. A macroeconomic factor is a very influential event that has a systemic or sweeping effect on economic activities of a given region, sector, or an entire economy. For example, if you were a farmer in the Midwest, then the weather would be a macroeconomic factor. Also, price and availability of fertilizer and diesel fuels are also factors.

You might say that "micro" is about the fish and "macro" is about the fish pond. If the pond is doing well, then the fish will also do well. Of course, if the pond is in bad shape, then maybe switch to chickens.

Exploring the Main Macro Factors

The great thing is that for factor investing, you have plenty of economic data and indicators. But the bad thing is that you have plenty of economic data and indicators. The following sections cover a few of the major ones.

Gross Domestic Product (GDP)

Gross Domestic Product (GDP) is one the most closely watched indicators of the economy's general health so this macro factor is an obvious one. If the GDP is consistently in the positive — quarter-in and quarter-out — then stocks — especially growth-oriented stocks — perform well.

GDP is a comprehensive measure and widely tracked view of the U.S. economic activity. The GDP measures the value of the final goods and services produced in the United States without counting all the components that go into the final products. A positive (increasing) GDP is good for the overall stock market.

If the GDP contracts, it's a bad harbinger for the stock market (as well as the economy, overall). Stocks are a way to participate in the success of the underlying company. The stock market is, after all, the performance of thousands of companies that make up the productive capacity of the general economy. So stock market observers see the GDP as a vital barometer of public companies' overall success and in turn how well the stock market is performing.

If the economy is growing, then sales of goods and services are growing. If goods and services are growing, then the profits of public (and private) companies tend to grow as well. This, in turn, excites investors and they buy up more and more stock; that, in turn, means rising demand for stock, which results in higher stock prices.

Figure 11-1 shows a GDP chart.

For 2021, the GDP rose 5.7 percent and the stock market had a good year. The S&P 500 started 2021 at about 3,765 and ended the year at 4,778. This represents a strong gain of about 27 percent, making investors very happy.

But fast forward to early 2022. Not a great start to the new year. The GDP contracted about 1.5% during the first quarter of 2022 and the S&P 500 was down about 5 percent.

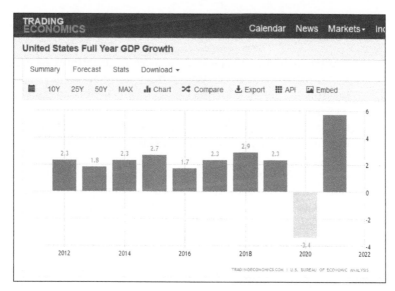

United States Full Year GDP Growth

FIGURE 11-1:
GDP chart for the
United States.

In mid-2022, the S&P 500 is at about 3.909, which is down 869 points from the year's opening of 4,778. It's definitely a bad first half for 2022 with the S&P 500 down 18 percent.

REMEMBER

GDP is considered a coincident economic indicator (see the "Coincident economic indicators" section, later in this chapter), so it can be difficult timing the start of an economic growth factor. Fortunately, GDP growth tends to last for years so you won't miss the boat on stock investing growth opportunities using this factor.

TRACKING GDP

Here are the top places to keep track (and find analysis of) GDP:

- The Bureau of Economic Analysis (www.bea.gov)
- National Bureau of Economic Research (www.nber.org)
- St. Louis Federal Reserve (www.stlouisfed.org)

The Bureau of Economic Analysis comes out with monthly and quarterly press releases about GDP (and other economic news). Bookmark it and check in regularly if you're serious about your factor-based investing approach.

Inflation

If anything in this chapter is a macroeconomic factor to be prepared for, inflation is it. Inflation affects everything from your day-to-day expenses to your stock investment choices. Inflation can erode prosperity and inflict great pain if you're on a fixed budget. The more you understand inflation, the more you can minimize the pain of paying rising costs while simultaneously being able to position your investment portfolio to maximize gains.

TIP

Don't forget the "do-it-yourself" factor, which is human need. Focusing on stocks and ETFs that, in turn, focus on human need is a prime consideration, especially in times of inflation and economic difficulty.

What is inflation?

Inflation (more accurately called *monetary inflation*) is the overproduction of a given currency (what you call money) by the issuer of that currency (usually the nation's central bank).

Because the currency is typically used in bartering ("I give you money and in exchange you give me a product or service"), the overproduction of the currency can then lead to price inflation.

As more units of a currency are chasing the same basket of goods and services, ultimately it takes more units of the currency to gain that same product or service.

Price inflation

When folks talk about inflation, they're referring to the price of consumer goods and services. Figure 11-2 shows a chart of inflation rates for the past few decades.

The economy and the financial markets can find a price inflation rate of 1–4 percent tolerable and the stock market can still perform well. But as you can see, the inflation rate started to rise in 2021. By the first half of 2022, the inflation rate exceeded 8 percent. Then what?

The first half of 2022 was the worst start of the stock market in decades. Take a look at this table for January–June 2022:

Market	Open	End	% Down
	January 1, 2022	June 30, 2022	
Dow Jones (DJIA)	36585	30741	15.97%
S&P 500	4778	3781	20.87%
Nasdaq	15732	11007	30.03%

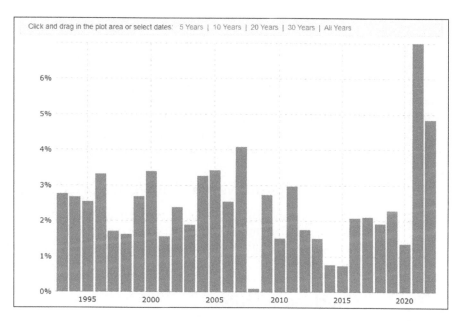

Click and drag in the plot area or select dates: 5 Years | 10 Years | 20 Years | 30 Years | All Years

FIGURE 11-2:
Historical
inflation.

As you can see from the table, stock markets got hit hard from macro events, such as rising inflation and interest rates. Toward the end of 2022, the markets have rebounded somewhat but are still down for the year and many analysts expect more downside to come.

Monetary inflation versus price inflation

Now you see that monetary inflation is the *problem*, price inflation is the *symptom*. Everyone (or most folks) experiences and talks about price inflation.

They talk about inflation as being the problem but forget that it's actually price inflation that is the symptom. There is a distinction, because if you don't know what the problem is and what the symptom is, then you will not solve the problem.

Inflation versus supply, demand, and flow

Keep in mind that monetary inflation is indeed the core of the problem, but there is still another part of this: supply, demand, and money flow. What does that mean?

If a central bank, for example, were to print a trillion dollars and gave it to you, and you, in turn, put 100 percent of that trillion dollars in your sock drawer, there would be little or no price inflation. Why? Because those dollars are not chasing anything so there is no pressure on prices to increase.

But what if those trillion dollars were to chase, say, toys or men's pants? Then the prices of toys and/or men's pants would increase significantly.

When you put that trillion dollars into the general economy, then those dollars through the dynamics of supply and demand would flow to products or services or other offerings in the market (such as assets or common stocks). Wherever that money flowed, the object of those dollars would force upward the prices of that given entity.

Asset inflation versus consumer price inflation

In recent years, trillions of dollars were produced by America's central bank (the Federal Reserve) but the American public did not experience inflation with consumer prices. Why? Because much of the money flowed to financial markets and other assets.

Tracking inflation

Inflation is certainly quantifiable and publicly provided by agencies such as the Bureau of Labor Statistics (www.bls.gov) and the Bureau of Economic Analysis (www.bea.gov). The following sections outline a few other places you can track inflation.

TIP

All too often, the "official" reported inflation numbers tend to underreport inflation. Because many things are tied to the official inflation rate (such as the cost-of-living increases done annually by Social Security), the inclination is to not report the full impact of inflationary prices. This is why serious investors check a diversity of information sources to get a more complete picture of inflation data.

CONSUMER PRICE INDEX (CPI)

The Consumer Price Index (CPI), computed by the Bureau of Labor Statistics, is the most widely reported measure of inflation. You can view complete info on the CPI at (www.bls.gov/cpi/.

As the BLS states at its website:

"The Consumer Price Index (CPI) is a measure of the average change over time in the prices paid by urban consumers for a market basket of consumer goods and services. Indexes are available for the U.S. and various geographic areas. Average price data for select utility, automotive fuel, and food items are also available."

As of May 2022, the CPI hit a record 8.6 percent. Therefore, your inflation macro factor should be firing on all cylinders!

SHADOW STATS INFLATION INDICATION

A good alternate to the government gauges of inflation is the one maintained by the economist Walter John Williams at Shadow Stats (www.shadowstats.com). Figure 11-3 shows a recent inflation comparison chart.

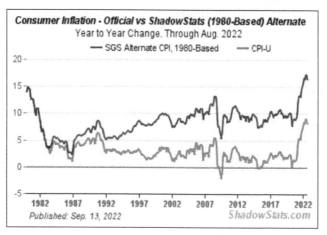

Source: Courtesy of ShadowStats.com

FIGURE 11-3: Shadow stats chart.

As you can see, the actual inflation measured the way it was formerly done before politicians modified it to underplay inflation.

PURCHASING MANAGERS INDEX (PMI) REPORT

The Purchasing Managers Index (PMI) report is published by the Institute for Supply Management (ISM). For investors, this may very well be the most important fore-warning of inflation. The ISM surveys its membership regarding purchasing at the wholesale level. When businesses end up paying more for things such as raw materials and so forth, ultimately these costs show up at the consumer level.

Another valuable aspect of this report is that it can gauge business activity that can frequently indicate business growth or a potential slowdown (such as a recession or worse). A point score of 50 or higher on the PMI report is considered positive or indicates good or improving business conditions. A score under 50 is typically considered a negative.

Asset inflation can create asset bubbles

From time to time, excessive money creation (monetary inflation) finds its way to assets in a major way and causes asset bubbles. *Asset bubbles* are when an asset's price is pushed to levels higher and more unsustainable than the asset's true intrinsic value.

This is where the value factor comes in handy (see Chapter 6). During 1999–2001, an asset bubble formed (and collapsed) with Internet stocks. During 2003–2007, an asset bubble formed in housing that collapsed, which in turned triggered the 2008 stock market collapse and recession.

The stock market bubble of 2020–2022 is unravelling and the historic bond bubble of 2010–2022 will likely deflate. Investors love inflation if it can boost their portfolios but hate the after effects when bubbles deflate and collapse (ouch). So yes, the inflation factor is very important to plan for in up and down markets.

Interest rates

For decades now, the U.S. economy has been to an overwhelming extent a credit-based one. Much of the economy runs on credit, whether it's credit cards, personal loans, or mortgages to buy homes and other real estate. The economy runs on credit and credit runs on interest rates.

Low interest rates make credit more affordable and doable. This in turn helps to make large purchases possible. When more large purchases are made, more people are employed. When you really think about it, interest rates are a powerful determinant of economic growth. But what if interest rates go up?

Rising interest rates make large consumer and business purchases much more expensive. Sometimes, higher interest rates can kill a deal or prevent a business from growing. You cannot avoid it. Interest rates are a major factor.

Figure 11-4 shows a chart of interest rates going back to the late 1960s.

As you can see, interest rates hit a mind-boggling 20+ percent by the early 1980s. This was done to combat the rising inflation that started during the mid-1970s and was heading much higher during the late 1970s and wreaking havoc on both the economy and the stock market.

The stock market experienced a severe bear market (a period of declining asset prices; in this case, stocks) during 1973–1975, where it went down about 50 percent.

The rising inflation rates plus the subsequent rising interest rates (used to fight inflation) was a double-whammy for both the economy and the stock market. Fortunately, this painful period did indeed ultimately bring long-term stability to price inflation and interest rates entered a long period of decline that resulted in both a stock and bond bull market. Any investor who followed these particular factors was successful.

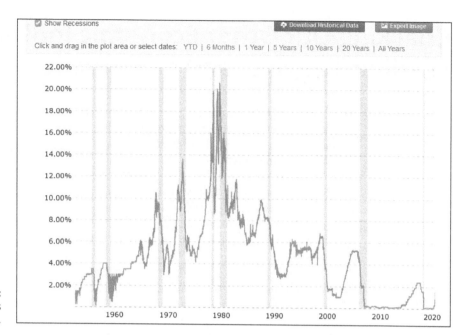

FIGURE 11-4:
Interest rates
history.

Fortunately, most financial media such as Marketwatch (www.marketwatch.com), CNBC (www.cnbc.com), and Bloomberg (www.bloomberg.com) report interest rate changes and anything the Fed is doing.

But if you want the source for interest rates, then keep an eye on the Fed either directly at www.federalreserve.org or through its various regional branches, such as the St. Louis Fed (www.stlouisfed.org).

TIP

When tracking interest rates, remember that

>> Low or decreasing interest rates tend to be positive for the economy and, by extension, the general stock market. A low interest rate environment (coupled with low inflation) is bullish (the upward movement of a given asset) for stocks. Look into bullish factors.

>> High or increasing interest ratess tend to be negative for the economy and, by extension, the general stock market. Go for stocks using factors for negative conditions or great safety.

Checking Out Other Economic Indicators: Leading, Lagging, and Coincident

Obviously, using the economic growth factor is important and generally easy to implement when the economy is growing right in front of you. But what if you wanted to get a jump-start on macro factors? Leading, lagging, and coincident indicators are your answer.

A way to remember what leading, coincident, and lagging economic indicators are is if you're driving your car. The leading economic indicators are about what you see through your car's windshield. Coincident indicators are what you see driving next to you in the adjacent lanes. Lagging indicators are what you see in the rearview mirror.

All three indicators are important and useful but because investors want to see the future possible events or what's coming, leading economic indicators tend to be the most watched. They help you see a pattern emerging and whether that pattern can become a profitable opportunity in your stock investing portfolio.

TIP

For more information on these economic indicators, go to the Conference Board's site at www.conference-board.org.

Leading economic indicators

An investor puts their money into a particular stock because of expectations they have for that stock. An investor feels or expects that a particular stock (or bond, ETF, or mutual fund) will perform well. Whether that is true remains to be seen, but expectation sums it up. If you ask the investor why, they may tell you that they believe certain economic conditions or events make conditions ripe for a given investment's potential success.

Push them further to inquire why economic conditions and events are favorable for their expected success, they may invoke the public data, which may be (directly or indirectly) leading economic indicators.

REMEMBER

Consider leading economic indicators as the precursors or the preliminary factors. Favorable leading economic indicators tend to come right before positive GDP numbers. It's a good strategy to incorporate leading economic indicators into your factor-based approach.

A good example of a leading economic indicator is housing permits. If you notice that housing permits just hit a record high, what would your investment logic tell you?

Home builders have to be approved (permitted) before they can start building. If housing permits are higher than normal, there will be plenty of housing being built in the near future. This means that more housing materials will be purchased. A housing-minded investor would definitely see record levels of housing permits to be a positive harbinger of growth in the world of home building and invest accordingly.

REMEMBER

Leading economic indicators point toward or warn about pending events or trends coming or unfolding. A pattern emerges that investors can seize as investment opportunities. Some examples of leading indicators are:

» The Purchasing Managers Index

» Initial jobless claims

» Average hours worked

Lagging economic indicators

Lagging economic indicators sound like you closed the barn door after the horses have left. What value do they have? Plenty.

The greatest bull markets have started in the depths of bad times. The most painful bear markets were born at the height of optimism and giddy tops of asset bubbles. The point is that yesterday's lagging economic indicators may have very well preceded tomorrow's leading economic indicators.

Examples of lagging economic indicators are:

» The Consumer Price Index

» Job openings rate

» Unemployment rate

Coincident economic indicators

Coincident economic indicators show economic activity as it currently is happening. Coincident economic indicators are frequently used with leading and lagging indicators to get a fuller picture of the business expansion and contraction cycle.

Some examples of coincident indicators (besides the GDP) are

>> Personal income

>> Industrial production

>> Manufacturing and trade sales

Watching Macro Factors and Trends

This chapter has been primarily concerned with big trends. Although focused on quantifiable, major economic events, it's helpful for you to look at an even wider picture. Including politics and culture is helpful to get more accurate clarity on where society is heading so you can have a better chance at positioning your portfolio for success.

Given that, a variety of political and cultural views tend to be precursors of economic trends (and macro factors!). Read the major news and views from across the political and philosophical landscape. What people think and discuss about today tends to materialize tomorrow and whether it's left wing, right wing, or chicken wing, read it all. For more on political/governmental factors to be aware of, check out Chapter 19.

TIP

Gerald Celente's Trends Research Journal (www.trendsresearch.com) gives an in-depth view of what is currently unfolding with politics, international events, economics, and more.

Chapter **12**

Combining Multiple Factors for a Powerhouse Portfolio

The factors worth adding to your portfolio are powerful, persistent, and add extra growth. The downside is that individually, they sometimes need long periods of time to pay off.

Some factors tend to outperform other factors at times (and vice versa), and which will perform well and which won't is hard to predict. Switching factors too many times is also costly to their performance, and could undermine your investment efforts. Combining factors is the key to investing.

In this chapter, we cover how, when you combine factors, you really harness their power, which allows you to settle in for that long-term growth.

Creating a Combination of the Right Factors

There are hundreds of so-called factors, but only a select few have proven to be persistent, robust, and not just a sub-feature of another factor.

According to Eugene Fama and Kenneth French, five factors (size, value, quality, low volatility, and momentum) can explain up to 93 percent of the difference in performance between diversified portfolios. (See Chapter 2 where we discuss the Asset Pricing Model.)

Exposure to these factors leads to a higher expected return over long periods of time. Additional factors have shown value as well, especially in combination with other factors.

Here are some key things we know that we'll need to try to optimize when adding factor strategy to our personal portfolios. These attributes interact in complex ways that are not always obvious to a new investor. We will never reach perfection, but our goal is to seek the optimal combination.

>> Size small caps tend to perform better than large caps (especially if you screen out small-cap growth).

>> Value tends to perform better than growth over time.

>> Consistently profitable stocks (low earnings volatility) tend to perform better than stocks with weaker and inconsistent profitability,

>> Companies with high margins, low operating leverage (strong balance sheet) and low financial leverage tend to grow better than companies without these attributes

>> Leadership of factors will rotate. One or another factor will always lead at any given time.

>> Timing which factor will lead (outperform in the short run) next is very difficult to predict. Getting this timing wrong can cost you more than the factor premium is adding.

>> Some factor strategies potentially have higher turnover and therefore may incur more trading costs and be less tax efficient than others.

>> Consider holding less tax efficient factor strategies in IRAs and other tax favored accounts.

- >> Rebalancing (selling a portion of each top performing holding and using the proceeds to buy more of your underperforming holdings to maintain your original allocation) in a portfolio at least once (ideally no more than twice) a year can further control risk and help you maintain a balanced portfolio, as well as help you to automatically buy low and sell high different factors.

WARNING

Some investors time individual factors to their advantage but this is harder than you may think and one mistake could wipe out any advantage you might gain. If you must time, consider timing just a portion of your investment capital (perhaps in a separate account), while holding the rest in a core portfolio that you rebalance yearly.

- >> Dollar cost averaging is a great way to add a prudent element of timing. See the later section in this chapter for more on dollar cost averaging.

- >> Factor investing isn't a get rich quick scheme, although compounding a few additional percentage points annually can really pile up over time.

- >> The value factor, especially, can stay out of favor longer than you may have patience for. Be sure to combine this one with other factors.

REMEMBER

These attributes interact in complex ways that may not always be obvious to you. Your goal is find a combination that's optimal for your portfolio.

Taking an Optimal Approach with ETFs and Funds

Multifactor exchange-traded funds (ETF) and funds enjoy efficiency advantages over individual factor funds, or clusters of funds. There are good reasons for this:

- >> Applying or replicating any factor involves transaction costs because the portfolio composition changes as new stocks are included and others drop out or are disqualified.

- >> Research and real-world experience shows that combining factors in a portfolio is the way to go and has a clear advantage of less drag from transaction costs (think higher gains!)

REMEMBER

- >> Lower costs mean higher gains (all things equal). It's not what your portfolio makes but what's left for you to pocket after expenses (and taxes) that matters.

HOW CAN FACTORS BE COMBINED?

Investors are showing increasing interest in combining factors according to recent financial industry data. A recent survey from FTSE Russell Smart Beta showed that over 70 percent of investors who are currently using factor or smart beta strategies (index-based factor methods that exclude shorting) are using two or more factor strategies in combination.

Forty-seven percent of respondents are also using or interested in using multifactor combinations and strategies, and the average number of factors they use is four.

One big reason to combine factors is because of overlap. A stock or holding may screen out of one factor but may be introduced into another factor at the same time. This may sound like a contradiction, but factor investing is about manufacturing odds in your favor, using historical attributes (factors) that have demonstrated clear outperformance over time.

These factors don't always coincide, and to question one over the other factor is to take on a massively complex set of market forces that, to be honest, even academia doesn't fully understand.

In a multifactor portfolio, when a stock drops out of qualifying for one factor but makes the grade for another one, the portfolio manager can avoid transactions costs completely by netting these two trades out. The more factors in a portfolio, the more likely such transactions are possible, reducing drag and increasing performance.

WARNING

One exception to these efficiencies might be a small portfolio where each factor has a lower allocation. If a lower allocation results in trade amounts being too small, transactions might actually become more expensive. It depends on the trading arrangement of the platform used by the portfolio or fund. This means you may want to avoid a just launched factor or smart-beta fund until their assets under management have grown to a healthy level. Just be aware and look up the current asset size of each fund you're researching.

Using the Optimal Approaches for Factor Investing

Traditionally, there are two approaches most traditional investors take when investing:

>> **Composite index:** You average the stock weights across a number of single factor indexes.

>> **Composite factor:** You use a composite of the target factors to create a factor index.

REMEMBER

While these approaches likely leave you with market-like returns, they also leave you with lower diversification and and higher risk. Factor investing leads to a diversified portfolio with lower risk exposure and better returns.

In the following sections, we talk about two better approaches to take for factor investing.

Creating diversification

A *holistic approach* is the most effective and powerful way to combine factors. This approach incorporates, coordinates, and optimizes the removal and addition of holdings that make the factor grade in one big portfolio.

Figure 12-1 demonstrates that using an averaging or composite approach isn't as effective as running a single portfolio with multiple factors cointegrated. A composite approach may actually result in less exposure to all target factors, which over time would dilute the results you're seeking.

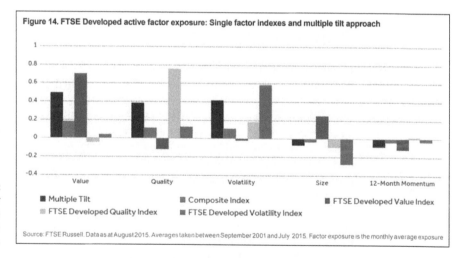

Figure 14. FTSE Developed active factor exposure: Single factor indexes and multiple tilt approach

■ Multiple Tilt ■ Composite Index ■ FTSE Developed Value Index
▨ FTSE Developed Quality Index ■ FTSE Developed Volatility Index

Source: FTSE Russell. Data as at August 2015. Averages taken between September 2001 and July 2015. Factor exposure is the monthly average exposure

FIGURE 12-1:
A multifactor approach is a good long-term strategy.

One fundamental motivation for combining factors is to enjoy the benefits of diversification.

Just like different asset classes have their own risk and return attributes, the sequence of returns or lumpiness of the various factors can also be viewed as distinct sources of additional diversification through various market conditions and economic cycles.

Here's one example of how this works. The value factor is usually thought to be a *pro-cyclical* performer, one that does especially well during times of robust economic growth and expansion.

In contrast with value, the quality factor is usually a *counter cyclical* performer, meaning it shines best in tough times and periods of economic stagnation when lesser companies have a tough time.

You can easily see how combining these two factors provides the potential benefit of additional diversification in a portfolio. Combining additional factors provides additional synergies that only help your portfolio.

REMEMBER

The whole idea of diversification is really to help you reach your investment goals as steadily and dependably as possibly, and with optimal growth. It means having great non-correlated holdings that move at different times, smoothing out the ride as well as eliminating as much as possible the potential for the failure of one bad stock, sector, or market to derail your investment portfolio and wealth building goals. It's not about collecting hundreds of holdings, but about holding a carefully selected mix of the best ones. Factors are guard rails that keep you safely on the track to optimal investment success.

Dollar cost averaging

If you contribute to your portfolio regularly (say, $200 each paycheck or monthly), you have the opportunity to harness an advantage called dollar cost averaging (DCA).

DCA is actually an underappreciated and hidden form of prudent market timing. By investing every month, you're automatically buying more shares in months when prices low and less when they are high, lowering your average cost. This approach is prudent because the advantage of lowering your average cost occurs over time, and isn't dependent on any one large reallocation of investing capital, which could be risky.

DCA can be an extremely powerful tool to use over the long term because it harnesses both market forces and takes the guesswork out of trying to time the market. It's powerful because it helps you automatically buy low and add regularly to your investments by treating them as you would any other bill.

REMEMBER

DCA automatically lowers your average price per share over time if you stick with it. There's no guarantee but DCA is about as close as it gets.

Figure 12-2 shows how if you invest $300/month in a stock or ETF for five months in a volatile period where the average share price is $20 a share ($30+$10+$20+$15+ $25 = $100 divided by 5 = $20). However, because your $300 bought more shares at the lower share prices, your average purchase price is $17.24 ($300 x 5 months = $1,500 invested divided by 87 shares purchased = $17.24). By simply using DCA and automating your purchases, you are able to buy low.

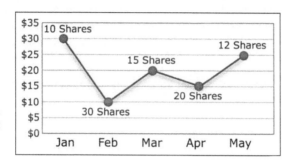

FIGURE 12-2: Dollar cost averaging in action.

Following the DCA method might not be the most exciting way to invest, but you can achieve the bulk of your investment wealth through your automatic contributions. Decades of $500 monthly contributions could turn into millions. Think of those automatically monthly payments as paying yourself in the future.

TIP

If you want to get started with DCA, set a budget for how much you want to invest as well as the interval to set the frequency.

Taking Advantage of the Professionals

While constructing your own portfolio is a worthwhile endeavor (not to mention a fantastic learning experience), the reality is that it's easier to work with a financial professional for a portion of your portfolio.

Working with portfolio managers

That could mean a financial advisor, but you could also look at professionals who manage and run ETFs and funds.

The proliferation of factor and smart-beta investment products in just the last few years has fueled not just aggressive competition for the best factor exposure but also put downward pressure on fees and expenses that portfolio managers charge. Which means, of course, that you get to keep more and make better returns!

In addition, select multifactor fund providers have worked out the details and learned how to minimize internal trading fees by transferring stocks inside the fund without having to actually trade and incur the associated costs and bid/ask spread. Another advantage for you.

TIP

The bid/ask spread is another hidden cost of investing caused by the difference in price between the buying and selling the same stock at any moment. It's the market maker's take (whether traditional human trader or electronic marketplace) and can range from a fraction of a penny for heavily traded, liquid stocks, and as high as a dollar or two for thinly traded, small-cap, or foreign stocks.

Taking a core and explore approach

Instead of having a financial advisor or manager manage your entire portfolio, consider a core and explore approach, which allows you to use both professionally managed funds and still take a do-it-yourself approach.

The core of your portfolio — for example, 70–80 percent — is professionally run by using multifactor funds or ETFs.

The explore portion (20–30 percent of your portfolio) is where you'd apply judicious selection of single factor funds and if you desire, some individual stocks that have ranked highly for most, if not all, your factors.

A refinement of this approach involves holding the multifactor funds in your taxable (brokerage) account and the higher turnover/higher potential tax components in an individual retirement account (IRA).

Depending on your savings goals, and desired degree of involvement, you might hold single factor ETFs and your carefully factor-selected individual stocks in your IRA.

TIP

The reason to consider holding factor selected individual stocks in your IRA is the assumption that factor investing will lead to capital gains. The downside is that losses cannot be taken in an IRA (though they can help offset taxable gains in a regular brokerage account), so if you find you have frequent losers, either improve your selection, pivot to focusing on single factor funds rather than stocks, or consider holding your individual stocks out of the IRA so you can take advantage of capital losses.

WARNING

This is not tax advice. Be sure to discuss your unique tax situation, tax bracket, and any tax concerns with your CPA or tax pro. Mid-November is usually a great time to assess the impact of capital gains and losses, and what if any, action it might be helpful to take tax-wise before year end.

Chapter **13**

Going Global with Factor Investing

Y ou might want to just focus on investing in your home country, and also invest in international stocks.

Today's world is a dynamic place undergoing change and disruption at a pace that continually surprises even the most experienced investors. The markets in the United States dominated for most of the last century, and investors worldwide still frequently refer to the U.S.-based S&P 500 as *the market.* But new markets are opening and creating new export industries and supply lines, while other countries appear to be increasingly walling themselves off from global trade and commerce.

So, in this chapter, we take a look at why you should consider globally investing, the global markets, and where we think you should take your factor-based approach in a global direction.

The one constant is change. Increasingly, if you ignore global investing, you're missing out on the action.

REMEMBER

Exploring Why You Should Invest Globally

Figure 13-1 shows a reputable estimate of how the global stock market may look (in terms of market cap by country) by 2030. You'll want to make sure that you profit from it. The following sections give you reasons why.

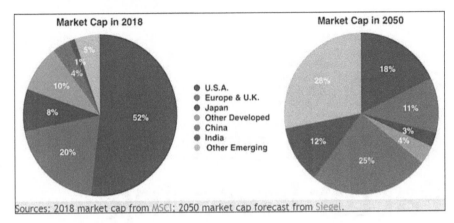

Sources: 2018 market cap from MSCI; 2050 market cap forecast from Siegel.

FIGURE 13-1:
2030 forecast composition of global stock market by country.

Global economies are always shifting

By 1890, the United States overtook the British Empire as the world's most productive economy, and within a few decades the markets followed, with the dominant trading floors moving from London to New York. For the following 130 years, the United States had been the world's largest economy.

Generations of investors have operated with this reality, but change is once again happening. The world economy continues to grow and is expected to pass the 100 trillion dollar mark by the end of 2022. By 2035 the world's Gross Domestic Product (GDP) is expected to double. Although China's growth has been held back a few years by its zero COVID-19 policies, its economy is expected to eclipse that of the United States by 2030.

India, another rapidly expanding economy, is expected to be the third-highest global economy (by GDP) by the same time.

If history is any guide, the stock markets (which are linked to, but aren't the same as the economy) of both China and India will also expand rapidly as a percentage of global equity markets, further changing the investment landscape.

For Americans, domestic stocks in 2022 represent a whopping 54 percent of the global stock markets. For investors in other countries' their stocks comprise at most 2 or 3 percent of global stocks, making diversifying globally beyond their home country even more important!

New technologies lead to new asset classes

Long-ignored countries are increasingly putting themselves back on the global financial map with investments in brand new industries and even entirely new asset classes such as crypto. Digital mining operations are revitalizing towns in South America and villages in Iceland where they're developing local energy projects to provide the huge amounts of electricity a crypto blockchain requires. This world-changing technology didn't even exist a few years back and now employs millions!

Obscure rare earth minerals are suddenly in high demand at seemingly any price for car batteries and defense systems, turning backwaters into boomtowns. Billions are pouring into Africa from China's Belt and Road Initiative (an infrastructure project that stretches from East Asia to Europe) as nations jockey for economic dominance to fill emerging power vacuums and secure access to the raw materials their economies depend on.

In addition, world events increasingly cause currency dislocations that have to be accounted for when assessing the risk/reward of any investment out of your country and currency. The U.S. dollar is currently soaring versus nearly all currencies globally, and non-U.S-based investors in American stocks benefit from the tailwind of having their investments rise in value versus their home currency, in addition to any gains the markets make. Of course, the current conditions can reverse, and have in the past (making non-dollar stocks in other ountries more attractive again), and will inevitably cycle in the future.

Good ideas are everywhere

No matter where you live, there are long-term diversification benefits from owning strong global stocks. In effect, not just holding your investment eggs in many investment baskets, but making sure some of those baskets are spread across different continents and currencies around the globe.

Sir John Templeton (who started the Templeton Growth Fund) believed that you could look at the investment world as an ocean and you should buy what brings you the most value for your money. His globally informed view of investing had his fund beating the market with a rate of growth averaging over 15 percent per year for an unbelievable 38 years while under his management. That's close to doubling your money every 4 1/2 years for almost four decades.

Templeton taught that overseas markets offered as much opportunity as U.S. markets and analysis of his methods reveals a fascination with value, quality, and other factors, long before academia took notice of these market anomalies and premiums.

Diversity is the key to investing

We as humans tend to like what's comfortable and prefer the familiar, including what we invest in. In an age where most data is right at your fingertips, it's a flimsy excuse for ignoring innovation and growth happening beyond your home borders.

History shows that, in the long run, no one country is destined or entitled to outperform and investing with that assumption is naive. U.S.stocks were the stars of the last decade (2010–2020), but many individual Asian and Chinese stocks outperformed by a wide margin. There were many other market highlights as well:

» In 2020, South Korea, Taiwan, and Vietnam had banner years.

» In 2017, stock markets in Turkey, Argentina, and Nigeria were stars, and in 2018 Macedonia and Ukraine excelled.

» In 2019, Greece was the top performer, not just in Europe but globally!

» China and most European indexes outperformed the United States from 2000–2010 due to its dot-com crash.

The Credit Suisse Global Investment Returns 2020 Yearbook highlighted the fascinating data summarized in Figure 13-2. Remember, these numbers are real returns meaning they're adjusted to account for inflation. These numbers represent entire stock markets from which it would have been possible to apply factor investing principles to further screen for likely winners, and screen out (or select for short-selling) likely losers. Odds are you could have beaten these gains by a wide portfolio-enlarging margin!

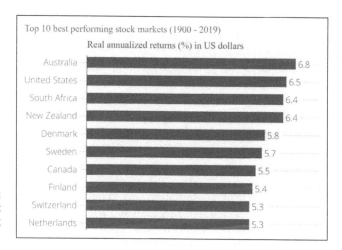

FIGURE 13-2:
The ten best
performing
markets.

You may want to look at global stock markets as different sandboxes, where amazing castles are being built. No matter what anyone says, you don't have to stay in yours! With today's trading platforms and low expenses, you can play in many different sandboxes at once, using factors to select only the most promising stocks with the highest potential for appreciation.

We talk throughout this book about diversifcation. The more diverse your portfolio, the more succesful you'll be long term. Diversification includes thinking globally. In addition to diversifying across factors, assets, strategies and sectors, you can find tremendous value in further diversifying your portfolio globally across geographies and countries.

TIP

Even if you've never felt comfortable investing outside your home country, consider starting with a solid stock or ETF that ranks well for the factors covered in this book.

Investing in Environment, Social, and Governance

In recent years many institutional investors have been incorporating environmental, social, and governance (ESG) considerations into their stock picking and portfolios, with some institutions (for example, BlackRock) going so far as to make this a mandatory part of its portfolio manager's investing processes.

The public has responded largely positively to this development towards integrating an element of social and environmental responsibility into investing, spawning many new funds and other investment products.

Though some investors are willing to sacrifice returns in pursuit of these values, other investors have been concerned about the negative impact ESG might have on their wealth building and retirement accumulation goals, especially when seeking enhanced returns through factor investing.

Early indications are that they need not worry too much. Several studies indicate that properly overlaid ESG screens only minimally impact factor strategies. In some cases, research seems to show that adding an ESG factor may actually enhance the potential of a factor.

REMEMBER

Traditionally, the role of a corporation was to maximize profits for the benefit of its shareholders (stockholders). ESG is an approach where a corporation works on behalf of its stakeholders, which include environmental, social and governance goals in addition to those of its stockholders.

ESG will certainly impact you at some point in your investing career. The percentage of investment funds managed with an ESG or sustainable component is growing rapidly as Figure 13-3 shows, and is expected to make up 50 percent of all professionally managed assets worldwide as soon as 2024.

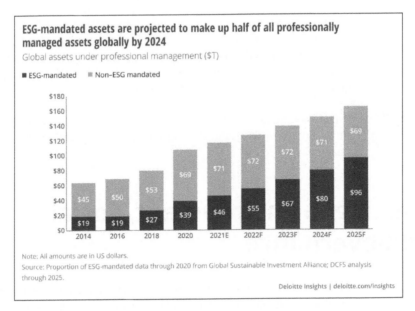

ESG-mandated assets are projected to make up half of all professionally managed assets globally by 2024

Global assets under professional management ($T)

■ ESG-mandated   ■ Non–ESG mandated

	2014	2016	2018	2020	2021E	2022F	2023F	2024F	2025F
Non–ESG	$45	$50	$53	$69	$71	$72	$72	$71	$69
ESG-mandated	$19	$19	$27	$39	$46	$55	$67	$80	$96

Note: All amounts are in US dollars.
Source: Proportion of ESG-mandated data through 2020 from Global Sustainable Investment Alliance; DCFS analysis through 2025.

Deloitte Insights | deloitte.com/insights

FIGURE 13-3:
ESG asset growth.

The widely read paper "Factor Investing and ESG Integration" by Dimitris Melas, Zoltan Nagy, and Padmakar Kulkarni explored the impact of incorporating ESG into factor strategies including quality, value, momentum, size, and minimum volatility. They wanted to see whether factors remain significant sources of investment return after integrating ESG in real-world situations. You can read it for yourself at `https://www.unpri.org/Uploads/a/a/h/Factor-Investing-and-ESG-Integration.pdf`.

Specifically they were looking to answer:

>> What is the impact of ESG on portfolio performance and characteristics?

>> How does ESG alter the risk profile and the factor exposures of portfolios?

>> How does it affect investors' ability to pursue their investment strategy?

Here's a quick summary of some of their findings. The research paper, which is well worth taking some time to read (and much less boring than a prospectus), concluded that ESG scores had "positive correlations with size, quality and low volatility." Regarding how much optimizing ESG might alter ideal factor exposure, they found

>> They were able to significantly improve the ESG score while still keeping most of the desired factor exposure.

>> Some factor strategies were more negatively affected than others. Value factor suffered the most while optimizing for the ESG score.

>> Quality factor, on the other hand, actually improved slightly when ESG was applied, likely because companies with high quality characteristics tend to have higher than average ESG ratings relative to their peers.

>> Value, momentum, and size factors proved slightly more difficult or costly to integrate ESG scores.

They concluded that

..*"significant improvements in the ESG profile of these strategies, of the order of 30%, were achieved with relatively modest impacts on target factor exposure, ranging between 7% and 22%. When we seek to achieve more substantial ESG improvement, the reduction in target factor exposure becomes greater. For 50% ESG enhancement, the impact on target factor exposure ranged from 23% to 54%."*

WARNING

Factor-based strategies need to be able to maintain high exposure to their target factors and investors who wish to integrate ESG considerations into a factor portfolio need to be aware of how doing so could affect performance, and make an informed decision.

If you use ESG as part of your screening process on top of your factor-based approach, consider taking a balanced approach among quality, value, momentum, and small size factors. While enhancing ESG scores by up to 30 percent, the impact for most factors isn't that significant, but when fine-screening to raise ESG scores by 50 percent, much more factor exposure is eliminated as an unfortunate side effect.

REMEMBER

If you screen too zealously for ESG, be prepared to give up some degree of outperformance over the long term, because of reduced exposure to the factor premium.

The degree to which you apply ESG rules (or buy funds that do so) is strictly a personal decision. Many investors who care deeply about the planet and humanity prefer that corporations keep their time-honored focus on making solid, honest profits for their shareholders and let those shareholders in turn decide how to make the world better with the profits they earn. These investors simply prefer to keep their investment strategy simple — invest in well run companies that focus on profiting shareholders, and shareholders having the freedom to decide the best use for their earnings.

Chapter **14**

Performing Technical Analysis for Factor Investing

Technical analysis attempts to discern where a stock's price is going based on very recent market behavior that is present in its trading data, such as price and trading volume data. The stock's recent price and market movement gives you what you need to know to make short-term trades. You look at data through visuals, such as charts or indicators. Technical analysis also doesn't look at the intrinsic value of a given investment. It believes that the price and its movement can help you see the potential trend (bullish, bearish, or neutral).

Because a factor-based investing approach is typically intended for long-term or intermediate timeframes, technical analysis isn't something most investors concern themselves with. So, why do we include it here in a book about factor investing?

REMEMBER

Timing is key to success. The greatest value of technical analysis in the world of factor investing is about entry and exit points in your positions. If you can get in at a favorable price (as low as possible) and/or get out at the most favorable price (as high as possible), you enhance your wealth-building success.

In this chapter, we take a look at some of the tools used for technical analysis, such as the relative strength index, trend channels, and moving averages, and how you can use them in a factor-based approach.

Tracking a Stock's Relative Strength Index (RSI)

It's a real bummer that, after much consideration and using the appropriate factors, you choose a stock (or ETF) that you know would please the gods of factordom only to see it drop within days of you buying it (ugh). That shouldn't bother you (really) because you didn't buy it for short-term considerations. You bought it for a much longer period (say 3–5 years or longer).

REMEMBER

One of the great lessons of buying (or selling) stocks is that the short term can be irrational and the stock's price movement can seem counter-intuitive. The stocks of good (strong) companies will zig-zag upward over time, while the stocks of weak or troubled companies will zig-zag down over time. This is generally true most of the time, but it doesn't take the sting out of buying 500 shares of a $30 stock on Monday just to see it at $26 a few days later. You'd kick yourself and say "I coulda, shoulda, woulda bought it a few days later and saved the difference."

Perhaps technical analysis coulda, shoulda, woulda helped — and it often can. One thing to look at is the relative strength index (RSI).

The RSI is an indicator alerting you when a stock's price momentum is overbought or oversold based on recent volume of buy and sell sales data. RSI is especially useful when you use it in conjunction with the momentum factor (Chapter 7).

The RSI is typically listed as "RSI(14)" at major sites such as Investing.com and other investing sites. The "14" is a reference to number of trading days (or periods) used to calculate the RSI.

The RSI parameters

The RSI was developed by J.Welles Wilder in 1978 when he introduced the concept in *New Concepts in Technical Trading Systems*. The RSI is a technical momentum indicator and it's also referred to as an "oscillator."

Oscillators are technical indicators of momentum showing fluctuations in the stock's price that are range-bound and provide signals of overbought and oversold conditions. Oscillators are often used in tandem with moving averages to help indicate when a stock's price may experience a price change such as a breakout or a reversal.

The RSI has a maximum range of 0–100. Here are the important levels of this range:

>> A stock with an RSI over 70 is overbought and is in danger of reversing price movement and could decline.

>> A stock with an RSI under 30 is oversold and may experience a reversal and potentially head upwards.

>> A stock with an RSI of 50 may signal a bullish move.

>> If a stock was higher than 50 and it goes down past 50 it could be a bearish signal.

REMEMBER

The RSI is not merely a point in time. Watch its movement or momentum:

>> When a stock's price is rising and you notice the rising RSI, it could signal a good bullish entry point (buying some shares).

>> If the RSI is plateauing after a rise, it may signal that the price is stalling. You may opt to put on a stop-loss order or a trailing stop. (See Chapter 10 to employ those tools.)

If you're income-oriented, the RSI may signal a good entry point to do a passive-income strategy such as a covered call option (more info on these in Chapter 18).

>> If the stock's RSI is heading downward, it could be a short-term bearish signal. Or if it is a stock that you're considering acquiring, this dropping RSI (heading toward oversold conditions) may signal a buying opportunity.

>> If you're income-oriented, this potentially oversold condition may signal a good entry point for writing a put option (also covered in Chapter 18).

RSI drawbacks

The RSI can be a useful short-term indicator and a great technical tool in your overall wealth-building arsenal of strategies and tactics. But it's not perfect.

Yes, a stock can be overbought or oversold, but this condition may last a while. If a stock passes 70 (overbought level), it doesn't mean that the stock's price will collapse tomorrow. In strong bullish conditions (growing economy), that stock could stay overbought for weeks or months. Therefore, like other technical indicators, it isn't an infallible or perfect indicator.

TIP

Use the RSI with the other indicators we cover in this chapter and data on the stock's fundamentals to get a clearer picture before you act.

REMEMBER

The RSI doesn't tell you a stock is intrinsically or fundamentally good or bad. It just tells you whether a particular stock's movement is over-extended over a relatively brief period of time. What if a really great stock was oversold (RSI below 30), does that mean it's a bad stock? Not necessarily.

If the stock is tied to a profitable company with strong fundamentals, then you may be looking at a great buying opportunity. In 2009 (in the wake of the 2008 crash and great recession), many sharp investors bought oversold stocks of fundamentally strong companies and rode onto spectacular gains.

If a stock's RSI is north of 70 (overbought) and it's a strong company, than there is nothing to do. But what if the company is unprofitable and has weak or bad fundamentals? Then it presents a great selling opportunity.

Checking a Stock's Technical Charts

Technical charts, as a topic, could easily be a book and a course all by itself. Whenever you are considering a new stock to add to your portfolio (factor-based or not), it makes sense to get a look at its recent price action.

Figure 14-1 shows the chart of a typical stock making its move in recent months.

The squiggly lines in the middle of the channel are the stock's daily price moves. The trend lines (both top and bottom) are plotting the highs and lows of the stock's best (and worst) moves during that journey in that given timeframe.

The chart's value is to either affirm the general direction of the stock or warn you about moving out of the channel, and may alert you to either a selling or buying opportunity in the near term.

What you need to watch for is if the stock breaks through one of the trend lines. If it moves above the higher trend line, it's bullish and may signal that the stock may achieve higher price levels in the near future.

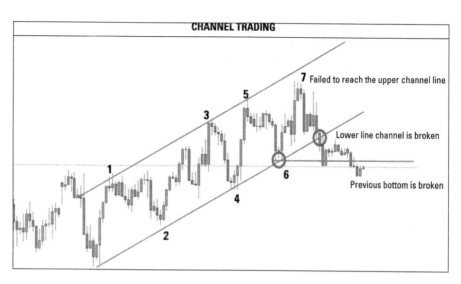

FIGURE 14-1:
A trend channel.

If the stock's price declines and moves below the lower trend line, that may be bearish for the stock.

The trend lines also illustrate a very important dynamic in the world of technical analysis:

- >> *Support* is when a stock's price tends to have a strong floor (deduced from recent trading data). It's illustrated by the chart's lower trend line. If a stock keeps falling to, say, $30 per share and then rallies upward, the support is $30. A stock that breaks support is considered bad news and the potential is for further declines in the stock price.

- >> *Resistance* is the ceiling of the stock's price rise (again, according to recent trading data). If a stock keeps hitting, say, $50 per share, and relents and it continues to do this, then the resistance is $50. A stock that breaks through resistance and achieves a higher price leve is considered bullish.

If a stock continues upward, then the trading data will likely exhibit new price levels for both support and resistance. Support and resistance are also key concepts with moving averages (a topic we discuss in the next section).

Head and shoulders charts

Technical analysts look for key formations and patterns that may provide potential warnings of where a stock's price may move. The stock's price can move in ways that can be either be good or bad omens given the structure of the price movement.

Figure 14-2 shows a typical chart formation that would typically tell analysts that the stock looks bad for the near term (bearish potential).

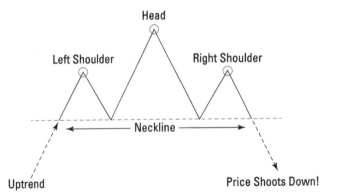

FIGURE 14-2:
A head and shoulders pattern for a stock.

As you can see, the stock made the first move upwards (the left "shoulder"), then succeeded to a new high (the "head"), but retraced its steps and made a new attempt to rally (the right "shoulder") but that failed.

For analysts, this is typically a very bearish chart pattern.

TIP

For your factor-based strategy, this technical chart suggests to wait until the stock has ceased its bearish move and stabilized.

Besides waiting for a good entry point, you could also check out the stock's RSI to see confirmation of the negative decline. (See the earlier section for how to track the RSI.) You could be looking at a great stock with a great price that has bottomed and ready for a pending rally (sweet!).

Reverse head and shoulders

Figure 14-3 shows the reverse situation from Figure 14-2.

The reverse (or "inverse") head-and-shoulders chart pattern is considered very bullish. The bullish short-term traders and speculators would definitely sit up and take notice.

For your factor-based strategy, the bullish position in a quality stock or ETF is ready for a near-term rally. It could mean a good entry point for writing a put option (see Chapter 18 for details).

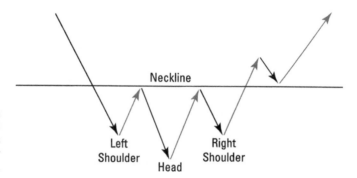

Neckline

Left Shoulder

Head

Right Shoulder

FIGURE 14-3:
A reverse head
and shoulders
pattern for
a stock.

With technical analysis, timing is everything.

REMEMBER

Adding Up Moving Averages

One of the most watched technical indicators is the moving average (MA). This can be represented as a graphic on a chart or as a calculated number (which is what we use in this section).

The MA is a numerical tool derived from an accumulation of a recent range of trading days. It's used to provide stock price averages that act as support and resistance.

For example, you may see XYZ stock at $40 per share and with a 20-day MA at $38. XYZ trading above its 20 MA is a good thing. That $38 acts as the "support" or the stock price's floor. If it falls below it, that is bearish and the MA will then change to include this new trading data and show a lower support.

The most used price periods of moving averages are 5 days, 10 days, 20 days, 50 days, and 200 days. Short-term traders look at the 5, 10, and 20 MA ranges the most.

TIP

As a factor-based investor, the 200-day MA is most useful. Because investing is a long-term pursuit, the 200-day MA is a sturdy support level for long-term stock price trends and therefore better timeframes. Some investors use the 200-day moving average to help them calculate a stop-loss order or a trailing stop amount in their brokerage account to minimize potential losses. (See Chapter 10 regarding brokerage orders.)

Moving averages can help you have a better grasp of stock price movements in the short term and give you the best clues when the time comes to make your trades more optimal. They help you know when to buy and when to sell and at what prices you should set stop-loss orders and trailing stops and optimal times to place call and put options (if you were speculating).

WARNING

Moving averages aren't inherently predictive because they're lagging indicators (they use historical data). If you see Apple's six-month MA, it won't tell you where Apple's price will be in the next six months.

Simple moving averages (SMA)

Simple moving averages (SMA) are a common type of moving average and are easy enough that you most likely can use a calculator or a spreadsheet. Say that you are doing a 5-day simple moving average. Here is how it would go:

Day 1 = $20

Day 2 = $21

Day 3 = $22

Day 4 = $21

Day 5 = $22

You add it (20+21+22+21+22) for a total of 106. You then take that total (106) and divide it by 5 (number of trading sessions or trading days) to get $21.20. That is your 5-day SMA.

Of course, the moment a new trading day is added to the calculation and the oldest trading day is dropped, you have a new 5-day SMA. This changes everyday (we said *moving!*), which is useful to see how the stock price is trending and as more data is used, the support and resistance prices emerge.

Exponential moving average (EMA)

Another commonly used moving averages is exponential moving averages (EMAs).

Technical analysts prefer exponential moving average (EMA) over the SMA because the EMA tries to be more accurate by giving more weight to more recent trading sessions. It's a more complicated calculation but the financial websites can do it for you (such as www.investing.com).

THE WORLD OF TECHNICAL ANALYSIS

This chapter is barely a teaspoon's worth of guidance on technical analysis. It covers a few simple strategies that you can easily use to augment your factor-based investing approach.

Buf if you want to try some advanced technical analysis, here are a few more:

- Stochastics
- Elliott Wave
- Bollinger Band
- Williams %R
- Moving averages conversion/diversion (MACD)
- ADX
- Ultimate Oscillator
- Pivot points
- Candlestick patterns

Here are some resources to look into if you want to keep your toes into the technical analysis waters:

- Investing.com (www.investing.com) has excellent resources and provides extensive technical analysis on stocks, commodities, and currencies.
- Big Charts (www.bigcharts.marketwatch.com) includes a flexible and powerful tool for creating charts for technical analysis.
- Incredible Charts (www.incrediblecharts.com) offers both free and paid charting services for investors and specializes in technical analysis charts.
- StockCharts (www.stockcharts.com) offers both the ability to do charts and also has a database of common popular charts and indexes.
- *Stocks & Commodities* magazine (www.traders.com) has news, views, and resources for technical analysis for both stocks and commodities.
- TraderPlanet (www.traderplanet.com) is another active resource for traders using technical analysis strategies.
- *Technical Analysis For Dummies,* 4th Edition, by Barbara Rockefeller (John Wiley & Sons) is an excellent resource on technical analysis for beginners.

(continued)

(continued)

- *Stock Charts For Dummies* by Greg Schnell and Lita Epstein (John Wiley & Sons) offers great guidance and information on the topic of stock charts.

- *Candlestick Charting For Dummies,* 2nd Edition, by Russell Rhoads (John Wiley & Sons) is a great primer for beginners on this very popular sub-section in the world of technical analysis.

Chapter **15**

Using Stock-Screening Tools in Your Factor Investing

S creening tools can be an invaluable (or valuable) part of your factor investing strategy. You know the factors you want to invest in — see Chapter 1 to find out what kind of factors there are, such as quality and size — but you don't know where to go from there.

This chapter gives you the answer. A screening tools allows you to enter the factors you want and it gives you choices that all conform to those factors. You can find screening tools for stocks and exchange-traded funds (ETFs) — everything that you could want to include in your factor-based strategy.

REMEMBER

The best screening tools tend to be paid ones but there are also some great free ones. You can also take advantage of the screening tools that your brokerage site offers you, if you're a customer of one. They can be just as advanced and useful as a paid screening tool.

Finding Investments with a Screening Tool

When you use a search engine, you tend to enter specific information such as a person or company's name or "how to boil water" or "make myself invisible to aliens" — the more specific, the better. But when using a screening tool, you want to stay as broad as possible so you don't accidentally screen out possibilities.

You enter qualities and parameters (such as factors!) to discover what securities fit your chosen qualities and parameters. This set of qualities provides a profile so you can see what stocks or ETFs are suitable candidates for your investment consideration.

The Yahoo Finance basic screening tools (`https://finance.yahoo.com/screener/new`) are a great example of free and easy screening tools you can use. See Figure 15-1.

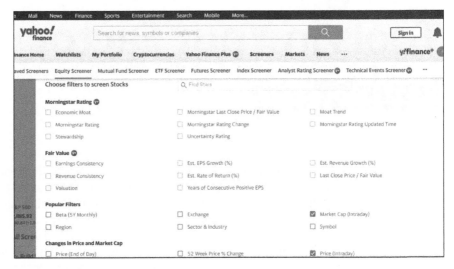

FIGURE 15-1:
The Yahoo stock
screener.

Yahoo provides a suite of screeners:

>> **Equity screener:** This option is for finding and analyzing stocks, which is what we cover in this chapter.

>> **Mutual fund and ETF screeners:** When you're looking for the right mutual fund or ETF, use these screeners. (More about choosing ETFs and mutual funds in Chapter 16.)

>> **Futures screener:** Futures are tied to commodities so this screener is useful if you're using inflation factors. (See Chapters 11 and 17.)

>> **Index screeners:** Many indexes are used in financial markets but we don't address them in depth in this book.

For some great sites that have stock-screening tools (especially for factor-based investing), check out the following:

>> Yahoo! Finance (http://finance.yahoo.com)

>> FinViz (www.finviz.com)

>> Investing.com (www.investing.com)

>> MarketWatch (www.marketwatch.com)

>> Nasdaq (www.nasdaq.com)

All these have free basic stock-screening tools with the ability to upgrade to a premium version. Some have tutorials on using the tools. Start by choosing a sector and and then choosing your value factors.

REMEMBER

Every online stock-screening tool is different in same way. Some even treat the same term or concept differently. Fortunately most of the stock specific terms are generally similar.

The following sections cover terms, categories, and filters that most screening tools typically have.

Choosing a category

What category is your potential stock in? That's a trick question. There are a batch of categories to check out. Here are some categories for your consideration.

Market capitalization (market cap)

For the size factor, the market capitalization category is obviously important. It's the market size of a company, which is calculated as the total shares outstanding times the price per share. A company that has 10 million shares and the price per share is $30 has a market cap of $300 million (10 million shares times $30/share).

Most screeners tend to have three market cap categories (large, mid, and small) but you might find a few that have five categories (ultra cap, large, medium, small, and micro cap). The ultra cap category only includes companies with market caps exceeding approximately $170 billion. The micro cap category only includes companies with market caps in the $0 to $1.5 million range.

Sector and industry

Sector and industry is an important criteria. A stock in a winning or growing sector has a better chance of success in your portfolio than one in a struggling sector. Whatever stock you seek or the factors you use in your selection process, take this criteria seriously. Additionally, sectors matter if you're using factor ETFs or mutual funds. (See Chapter 16 for details.)

Stock price

Do you want stocks that are priced under $1 per share because you're looking for micro caps or penny stocks? How about stocks over $50 per share? This criteria is for you if the stock price per share matters to your selection process.

Other business facts

Is the stock optionable? This could be a desirable category for you if you are looking to speculate or seeking greater income through writing options (see Chapter 18 for details). Does the company have high revenue or no revenue? Some also give you criteria such as what exchange or index the company is on or how large the company is in terms of total employees.

Choosing screening filters

The filters and parameters involved are subcategorized so you can hone in on what specifically are your priorities. Here are the subcategories and some common filters in them.

Company profile

In this category of filters you may be able to screen with criteria such as market size, total number of employees, years in business, its ESG (environmental, social, governmental) score, and so on. You can also find out whether the company's stock is optionable (such as with call and put options that are covered in Chapter 18).

Dividends

For the income-minded, this category of criteria helps you screen for dividend amounts, dividend yields (%), dividend growth rates, and so on. These screening filters will come in handy for Chapter 9.

Profit (or earnings)

This is an important category because profitability may be the single most important aspect of a company's success. Some key criteria to check is earnings per share (EPS), earnings growth percent over 3–5 years, and its price-earnings (P/E) ratio.

Valuation

Valuation is an important criteria. You don't want to overpay for more than the company is worth. Some key criteria is the price-to-book (P/B) ratio, price-to-sales (P/S) ratio, and the price-earnings (P/E) ratio. More on valuation in Chapter 6.

This category is worth paying attention to during bad econmonic times.

Growth

This subcategory focuses on criteria for growth such as sales, earnings, and net worth. Typical criteria includes sales growth over 3–5 years, equity growth, book value growth, and so on. More on growth in Chapter 5.

Management efficiency

This subcategory provides measurable insights into how efficient or resourceful management is. Criteria includes gross profit margin (GPM), return on equity (ROE), and return on assets (ROA).

Stock performance

This subcategory focuses on how the stock itself has performed. Criteria includes the 52-week high and low for the stock's price, percentage and nominal gains over the past year, 5-year track record, and so on.

Volatility

This criteria looks into various measurements of volatility such as the beta of the stock and the stock price's behavior in recent periods and various other stocks in the same sector/industry.

Technical analysis

This subcategory views the stock through the window of technical analysis. Criteria includes moving averages such as the 10-day, 20-day, 50-day, 200-day, and through the most prominent oscillators and indicators. Technical analysis is covered in Chapter 14.

Analyst ratings/opinions

This subcategory covers the views and ratings from prominent market analysts. If you have done your homework as a diligent investor, you can seek affirmation (or not) for your stock choice here.

Entering search settings

The search you do would either be a word search (such as a keyword for an industry or sector) or a numerical to find a stock or ETF with a suitable factor-oriented profile. If the criteria you seek is numerical, you need to set these financial parameters:

>> **Set numerical criteria,** such as "greater than" and "lesser than" or minimum (min) and maximum (max).

>> **Set numerical values,** such as the highest dividends available, in which case you enter "999" as a default maximum.

REMEMBER

The more criteria and parameters you enter, the fewer companies will be found and that is likely what you want to limit your choices to those stocks or ETFs that strictly meet your criteria. There are thousands of choices, and filtering out 99 percent of them is a good thing. You may not find the perfect stock (and if you do, let us know!), but perhaps what is more important is troubled or impaired companies. Companies with losses or that have too much debt are particularly vulnerable in difficult times (such as may be the case during 2022–2023).

Using a Screening Tool to Find Factor Stocks

Screening strategies can help you optimize your approach in stock selection. Choosing a factor criteria is of course important, but a better approach may be a multifactor screening approach (see, here is where we justify the price of your purchase of this book) where you combine a macro factor element with your style or micro factor criteria. In the following sections, we present some useful scenarios for you to experiment with.

Growth stock approach

Say that the economy (via the GDP growth factor) is looking good and the outlook for growth stocks is positive. Then consider the following criteria:

>> **Growth sector:** Choose a sector (or industry) that is considered cyclical (such as technology or industrial goods).

>> **Size factor:** Choose a small-cap filter because smaller companies have a greater potential for growth versus more established, large-cap companies.

For more guidance on growth factor strategies, go to Chapter 5.

Value stock approach

Say that the economy is struggling. Cyclical, growth stocks aren't a prime choice; the better choice for now is to be defensive. Consider the following criteria:

>> **Defensive sector:** Choose a sector (or industry) that is considered defensive such as consumer staples or utilities.

>> **Valuation:** Use filters for value criteria such as price-earnings (PE) ratio and the price-to-book (PB) ratio.

>> **Dividends:** Dividend-paying stocks tend to be safer than growth-oriented stocks during slow economic periods.

For more details on value–based factors, check out Chapter 6. For some insights on the general economy, you can check out Chapters 11 and 19.

Dividend income stock approach

Looking for dividend income? Here are some screening criteria for you:

>> **Sectors with income potential:** Some sectors are better known for dividends than others. Real estate, telecommunications, and utilities have more potential for steady dividend payers.

>> **Dividend yield criteria:** Use a criteria for dividend yield and set it for "greater than" and enter a number such as 2.5 percent or 3 percent.

Speculating with a bearish screening approach

If you're looking for *bad stock* (stocks that are in danger of declining or crashing) and seeking profits by shorting stocks or buying put options, this criteria is for you.

You can also use this approach to avoid these stocks and ensure they're removed from your portfolio before your losses add up.

Finding ETFs with Screening Tools

If stocks are unappealing to you, then consider ETFs, which are an excellent way to unleash your factor-based investing wealth-building plan. But of course with literally hundreds of choices, how do you narrow them down? There are a few well-known sites specifically for ETFs:

>> ETF.com (www.etf.com): This is one of the central hubs of information on the world of ETFs and it includes a great screener too.

>> ETF Database (www.etfdb.com): ETFDB is a comprehensive ETF site that provides extensive information on virtually any publicly traded ETF. Figure 15-2 shows this tool.

>> ETF Trends (www.etftrends.com): Provides news, ETF trends, and profiles of successful and popular ETFs.

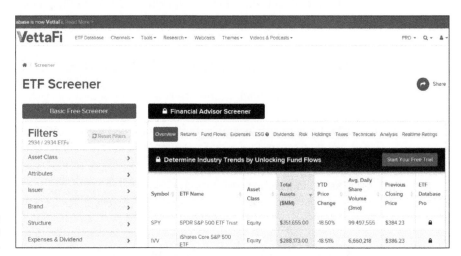

FIGURE 15-2:
The ETF database screening tool.

The great thing about ETFs is that you're not worried about trying to find a single stock; you're basically seeking either the right sector, industry, or type of ETF.

PAID SCREENING TOOLS

While free stock and ETF screening tools may suffice, you could also check out premium (paid) screening and analytical tools. Many come with a free trial period.

- Benzinga Pro (www.benzinga.com)
- Stock Rover (www.stockrover.com)
- Trading View (www.tradingview.com)
- TC2000 (www.tc2000.com)
- Seeking Alpha (www.seekingalpha.com)
- Hammerstone Markets (www.hammerstonemarkets.com)

Remember: Your broker may have suitable stock and fund screening tools at its site. Call or email customer service. Some even have tutorials too.

You may easily find more than one ETF that matches the criteria that is important to you. If so, a comparison tool can help you. ETF has one at https://www.etf.com/etfanalytics/etf-finder, where you can weigh the pros and cons of multiple ETFs. It's shown in Figure 15-3.

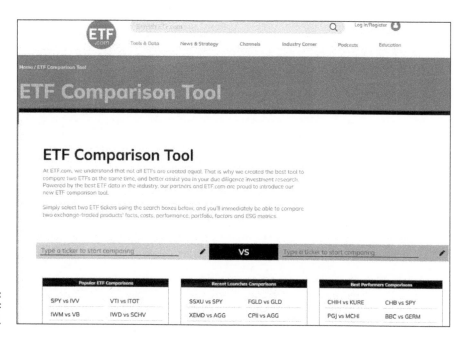

FIGURE 15-3:
An ETF
comparison tool.

4

Applying More Complex Investment Tactics

IN THIS CHAPTER

» **Trying out other exchange-traded products**

» **Investing in sectors**

» **Using mutual funds in your factor investing**

Chapter 16

Outsourcing with ETFs and Mutual Funds

You shouldn't over-complicate or over-think your factor-based investing. You can easily leave the heaving lifting to the folks who oversee exchange-traded funds (ETFs) and mutual funds and can do the advanced stuff and the heavy lifting. Your job is to choose the ETF or mutual fund that serves your factor-based approach and get back to your favorite program. ETFs are appropriate for virtually any portfolio — whether conservative, aggressive, speculative, or even semi-comatose.

In this chapter, we go through the world of ETFs (and other types of funds) with a *bullish slant* (a view that the stocks in this area are expected to go up for an extended period of time) on either the entire market or a very specific industry or niche.

REMEMBER

No investment vehicle is perfect but ETFs come close, especially when you carefully pick and match it to your needs and goals.

Comparing ETFs to Other Investments

In a financial galaxy long, long ago and not-too-far away, there were stocks, bonds, and mutual funds. That was about it for retail investors. At the time you bought stocks (and/or bonds) through a brokerage account and you typically dealt directly with the financial firm that managed mutual funds. Now you have an alternative to mutual funds: the ETF.

A mutual fund is a pool of money (which comes from a group of investors such as you and other folks) that is managed by an investment firm (such as Vanguard, Fidelity, or BlackRock) and this pool of money is used to invest in a broad, diversified portfolio of stocks and/or bonds or other types of investments. This pool of money is actively managed where the money manager buys, sells, and holds securities that meet the criteria of the investment manager.

ETFs versus mutual funds

An exchange-traded fund (ETF) is similar to mutual funds in that it's a pool of money that is invested in a diversified portfolio of securities but there are two crucial differences:

>> Mutual funds have an actively managed portfolio of securities (typically stocks and bonds) while ETFs have a static portfolio. In other words, mutual funds oversee a portfolio where securities are regularly bought, sold, and held. The typical ETF held, say, the top 50 or so stocks in a given sector or that represented an index (such as the Nasdaq 100).

>> You invest in mutual funds either directly or through an intermediary (such as a brokerage account) on a cash basis. ETFs are bought and sold as shares in the same way that stocks are bought and sold. As the name indicates, the fund's shares are traded on an exchange (hence "exchange traded"). While you may invest $500 or $1,000 to a mutual fund, you buy shares (50, 100, or whatever) of an ETF.

And then there are minor (yet significant) differences to also consider:

>> **Transparency:** ETFs tend to have a small edge against mutual funds when it comes to transparency. Most of the major financial and ETF-focused sites show you the top ten or more holdings of a given ETF. Because most ETFs have a static portfolio, the holdings from several months ago will look very similar to their holdings today. Because mutual funds are actively managed, the composition of their holdings from several months or a calendar quarter

may look significantly different today. This means that although a mutual fund can be transparent, the view can be quickly dated and not as useful.

>> **Fees:** Mutual funds typically tend to have larger fees than ETFs for the simple reason that an actively managed portfolio has more transaction costs than an ETF's static portfolio. While many ETFs seemingly have a set-it-and-forget-it portfolio, mutual funds must pay a team of active managers overseeing the constantly changing portfolio.

>> **Taxes:** Because ETFs usually have a static or fixed portfolio, they're considered tax efficient in regards to capital gains and losses. Mutual funds, given their greater activity, result in greater taxable gains in many cases. In terms of dividends, both are similar tax-wise. For more details regarding taxes and your investments, head over to Chapter 20.

In terms of tax-advantaged accounts, such as 401(k) plans and IRAs, both types of funds are suitable and exceptional vehicles.

TIP

Before you infer that ETFs are automatically superior to mutual funds, think again. For some investors (including retirees), an actively managed portfolio may be appropriate as the portfolio managers can modify a portfolio as the economic and financial conditions change.

ETFs and stocks

ETFs can be bought in shares, making them as easy to purchase as stocks. Whether you're buying 1, 50, 100, or more shares, the process is the same.

But as a further beneficial point, ETFs have some of the same features and/or advantages of stocks such as

>> You can buy or sell ETFs through market orders, limit orders, stop-loss orders, trailing stops, and so on. (These are covered in Chapter 10.)

>> ETFs can be marginable (also covered in Chapter 10).

>> You can short-sell ETFs. Short-selling is a risky activity and generally not a good consideration with your factor-based approach.

>> ETFs may be optionable so that you can implement call and put option strategies with them. (Chapter 18 cover some basic option strategies.)

Given all these features, ETFs are hard to ignore and easy to implement in your overall wealth-building action plan.

ETFs and other investments

Although stocks are highlighted as underlying assets of ETFs throughout this chapter (and stocks are covered through much of the book), don't forget the alternatives that ETFs bring to the table for you, especially in a factor-based approach.

The same way that a single ETF purchased through your brokerage account is similar to buying a "stock that invests in a basket of stocks," it can do the same for bonds, commodities, and other securities and/or assets. ETFs can cover bonds, too. (See Chapter 17 for bonds.)

Virtually any major security or asset that is investable and has a broad market will likely have some accompanying ETF for your consideration.

Diving into the Broad Market of Exchange-Traded Products

ETFs are the most popular and most prominent segment of exchange-traded products (ETP). Those terms are sometimes considered interchangeable but ETP is the "universe" while ETFs is the "largest galaxy."

But ETFs are not the only "galaxy." There are two others to take note of — especially because they can play a role in the world of factor investing.

Exchange-traded notes (ETNs)

Exchange-traded notes (ETNs) are traded similarly to ETFs in that they trade like stocks but there are some crucial differences:

>> ETNs are debt-based securities. They don't hold assets such as stocks or commodities. The security is unsecured debt that is linked to a market index or some other standard.

>> The ETN has a finite life like a bond. At maturity, it pays the holder an amount equivalent to the value of that market index at the time of maturity (less management fees).

As a factor-based investor, you shouldn't consider this type of security due to the risks involved. Debt factors are tied to quality and ETNs are better off for speculators.

Exchange-traded commodities (ETCs)

In days gone by, if you mentioned the word "commodities," it instantly conjured the image of aggressive speculation that drove you to the poor house due to the risks and potential losses associated with them. But ETFs have changed this situation and have made commodities more doable even in a regular account or a retirement account.

Exchange-traded commodities (ETCs) are essentially ETFs that focus on underlying assets tied to commodities (such as futures contracts) instead of stocks or bonds. You won't be off-base if you refer to them as commodity ETFs.

If you focus on the inflation factor, these vehicles become a good consideration. During 2020–2021, when oil was skyrocketing from $20 a barrel to above $100, oil ETFs soared. During that same time, agricultural commodities such as wheat, corn, and soybeans also soared and those ETCs that focused on them outperformed the general market.

Factor-specific ETFs

ETFs (and other types of ETPs) can get specific or specialized — very specific in fact. If you only want dividend-paying stocks that have raised their dividends every year for ten years or more, you can find an ETF. If you want to invest or speculate in gasoline, uranium, or investment-grade municipal bonds, there's an ETF for you.

But the great thing for you is the rise of factor-based ETFs.

Factor-based ETFs as a category has over 280 ETFs (most of them listed in Appendix B). What better way for busy investors to succeed?

These factor-based ETFs cover the following asset categories:

>> Asset allocation

>> Equity

>> Commodities

>> Bond

>> Alternatives

>> Currency

The great thing is that factor ETFs are growing and popular sites such as etf.com (https://www.etf.com/channels/multi-factor-etf) provide major coverage for them, as shown in Figure 16-1.

Combining Sectors with Macro Factors

Using sector ETFs — groups of inter-related industries — with your macro factors (covered in Chapter 11) can be a great way to invest with the big picture in mind and without worrying about investing in a single stock or bond. Which sector you invest in depends on how the economy is doing.

The economy is expanding

When the economy is expanding (as evidenced by the Gross Domestic Product factor), consider investing in sectors that do well when the overall economy is doing well such as technology, consumer discretionary, and other sectors that perform above average during periods of economic growth. Size factors would also do well (such as small-cap stocks covered in Chapter 8).

The economy is contracting or flat

In this scenario, the sectors that are best considered are utilities, consumer staples, and other defensive sectors. When the economy is struggling or contracting (such as in a recession), folks don't spend as much on luxuries or on fancy restaurants and vacations. However, they do spend on necessities (food and water), being able to turn on the lights (utilities), and paying for other necessities.

Categories of sector ETFs

At a given time in the ebb and flow of the economic cycle, sectors correspondingly take turns growing and contracting. There will always be sectors that are doing well, which means opportunities to move your money from one sector to another as times change.

TIP

One way to look at the economy is to see the difference in spending between "needs" and "wants." When the economy is in good shape and everyone is generally doing well, people are more apt to spend on "wants." In that case, a sector such as consumer discretionary would do well. However, when the economy is not doing well, folks will dial back spending on "wants" but will, of course, keep spending on "needs."

These are the basic sectors:

>> **Basic materials:** This sector is best when the economy is growing. It covers base metals and related building materials.

>> **Communications:** Communications can be neutral because as a sector it generally performs equally during good and bad times.

>> **Consumer discretionary:** This sector covers restaurants and leisure industries, such as travel. It performs best when the economy is doing well because that's when people tend to spend their money on these luxuries.

>> **Consumer staples:** This sector covers necessities such as food and beverage and considered defensive meaning. It performs best when the economy is in recession or struggling.

>> **Energy:** This is one of the most important sectors and includes oil, gasoline, natural gas, and other fuels. When the economy is growing or there is inflation, this sector outperforms other sectors.

>> **Financial:** This covers banks and other financial and credit institutions. It generally does best when the economy is growing and more people and businesses need to finance large purchases or business expansion.

>> **Healthcare:** Healthcare is a complex sector in that it has both cyclical industries and defensive industries. When the economy is doing well, cyclicals such as heavy equipment and medical technology do well. When the economy

is in recession or struggling, defensive industries such as drug retailing do well.

>> **Industrial goods:** This sector covers manufacturing and related industries and performs best during growing economic times.

>> **Services:** Services cover contracting and professional/consulting services and can be mostly cyclical as people tend to spend more for services when the economy is doing well.

>> **Technology:** The technology sector tends to perform best during growing economic times.

>> **Transportation:** This sector includes trucking and air transport and this typically does best during good economic times.

>> **Utilities:** This sector covers gas, electric, and water utilities and is best during recessions and contracting periods because this sector is defensive.

Exploring Factor Mutual Funds

Thousands of mutual funds are available to you today in a variety of major categories (growth, income, and so on) and sub-categories (such as industries and sectors). Yet there aren't as many factor-oriented mutual funds as there are ETFs. While there are hundreds of factor-based ETFs, there are far fewer mutual funds with this specialty.

BlackRock Total Factor Fund, Invesco World Bond Factor Fund, and Dodge and Cox Stock Fund are 3 of about 20 financial firms that have factor-based funds among their many mutual fund choices.

REMEMBER

Just because a firm doesn't make it obvious that it uses factors, many mutual fund portfolio managers do employ factors to make their portfolio decisions in their day-to-day management.

As more and more mutual fund managers employ factors, you have more choices as well. To locate them, check out these mutual fund resources

>> Mutual Funds (www.mutualfunds.com)

>> SEC mutual fund search page (https://www.sec.gov/edgar/searchedgar/mutualsearch.html)

>> ETF & Mutual fund directory (https://minafi.com/funds)

ETF RESOURCES

For more info, news, and views on the ETF world, check out these sites:

- ETFDB (www.etfdb.com).

- ETF.com (www.etf.com)

- ETF Daily News (www.etfdailynews.com)

- ETF Trends (www.etftrends.com)

Appendix B also has an extensive list of factor-based ETFs. The appendix is broken down by category so you should easily find one or two ETFs that meet your personal preference and criteria.

Chapter **17**

Bonds and Factor Investing

N
o matter what the economy and financial markets look like, carefully selecting investment vehicles for your portfolio is always important. But when the economy and markets are not at their best (such as 2022), it's even more difficult. How do you proceed?

We have decades of experience on dealing with the market in turbulent times (fortunately or unfortunately). Using factors is vital to your success.

Bonds are income alternatives to stocks that can diversify your portfolio and be as easily acquired in your brokerage account as stocks. In this chapter, you find out all you need to know about bonds, which are loans to a public company or government entity (municipal, federal, and so on) that then uses the loan for its operations. You, as the investor, receive interest on your investment. Chapter 19 covers a different alternative (commodities).

Defining Bonds

The main reason for considering bonds as a diversification from (or with) stocks is that bonds as an investment are considered safer than stocks and typically act differently than stocks in the same economic environment. Historically, investors shift more of their portfolio to bonds during recessionary times and away from stocks. In times of economic growth and expansion, investors typically shift money away from bonds and to stocks. Bonds provide income and usually hold their value during recessions when stocks typically decline.

Bonds operate differently from stocks. While a stock is considered "ownership" in a given public company, bonds are a form of debt — you're essentially lending money to an entity. That entity (a public company or governmental entity) periodically pays you interest (usually semi-annually) and at the time of maturity, your investment (the principal) is returned to the you (typically 20, 25, or 30 years).

These bonds are publicly traded just as stocks are. Just because you bought a 30-year bond doesn't mean you must hold it the full term. You could buy a bond this week and sell it at any time before maturity.

At the time of the bond's issuance, you usually pay the face amount of the bond (referred to as *par value*), which is usually $1,000, $5,000, or $10,000 depending on the type of bond and what type of entity issues them.

WARNING

Traditionally, bonds and stocks offered counter-vailing advantages and disadvantages to provide diversification in your portfolio with a mixed blend of income (from bonds) and growth (from stocks). In periods of economic growth, stocks excel. In recessionary periods, bonds are superior. The problem in today's world is that the traditional dynamic between stocks and bonds have changed. During 2021–2022, both stocks and bonds generally declined. The issue is that during that period, both stocks and bonds entered *bubble territory* (a condition of being overpriced compared to their value and susceptible to sharp declines) and faced multiple adverse conditions including inflation, rising interest rates, and general economic weakness (more on these issues in Chapters 11 and 19).

TIP

Make sure the bonds you choose are high quality and that the interest rate is (preferably) adjustable.

Using Factors with Bonds

There are factors to take into consideration with bonds, just as there are with stocks. The following sections cover a few.

Duration

The duration factor is a reference to the time remaining of the bond you're holding. If you just acquired the bond and the bond matures in 30 years, the duration is the same — 30 years. However, if the bond you acquired was issued 25 years ago, then your duration would only be 5 years.

Duration is a safety concern. The longer the duration, the greater the potential risk. A bond maturing next year or within a few years will most likely not default. Short duration is a plus.

Momentum

The momentum factor may be fine for short-term stock moves (see Chapter 7), but what about bonds that are more long term? Momentum takes into effect the trailing 6 to 12 months of price movement and assumes that trajectory can continue going forward.

During 2020–2023, stocks and bonds have reversed course on many occasions and bonds currently have many head winds (such as inflation and rising interest rates). Be sure to take a look at the later section "Looking at Savings Bonds" for more about bonds.

Quality

High-quality bonds don't pay a higher rate than low-quality bonds but in an age of defaults, the quality bonds keep their market value while low-quality bonds (junk bonds) lose market value and/or will be in danger of default. We tell you how to find out a bond's rating (which is an indicator of its quality), in the later section, "Bond ratings."

WARNING

In times of economic difficulty (including inflation and rising interest rates), quality will outlast low-quality bonds that may offer higher interest rates. Sometimes, a return on your money isn't as important as a return of your money.

Value

The value factor is different from quality. Value refers to whether you're getting your money's worth in terms of yield. Say that you must choose between two similar bonds and that both are high-quality (AAA rating), but one bond is getting a ¼ percent higher interest rate. That is the better bond from a value factor point of view.

TIP

Don't worry if you may find it difficult to find, compare, and distinguish bonds of varying value. An exchange-traded fund (ETF) that specializes in multifactor bond portfolios (with value being one of the top factors in the selection process) can help take the worry out of the process. See the last section in this chapter about bond ETFs.

Taking into Account the Key Issues with Bonds

Bonds certainly have a place in most portfolios and at many times and conditions. An extensive study spanning 220 years (1800–2020) showed that quality bonds held up well during much of that period except for the occasional economic crisis.

The first thing to keep in mind is that bonds are a diverse vehicle, similar to stocks, commodities, or currencies. There are different categories, varieties, and risk levels. Following a factor strategy can help you choose the right ones.

Quality factor

The overriding issue of quality is paramount in times of economic and financial difficulties. During 2022–2024, many analysts expect defaults on low-quality bonds and various bankruptcies among struggling financial entities.

When we mention quality and or the accompanying quality factor, we're really referring to the financial strength of the underlying payer (debtor) of the debt in question. When you buy a Treasury bond, for example, you're counting on the credit worthiness of the U.S. federal government.

The U.S. government is considered the safest entity on the planet in terms of credit worthiness. It's automatically considered the highest rated debt on the global market. As a matter of fact, the United States has never defaulted on a single bond in its history (going back to the Civil War when federal debt came into prominence as an investing vehicle).

TIP

Regardless of what bonds (debt) that you buy and from who, the easiest way to judge quality is the bond rating. For more info, see the section, "Bond ratings," later in this chapter.

Adjustability

While most bonds are fixed interest or fixed income securities, some bonds have adjustable rates, which can be an advantage in periods of rising interest rates. Rates that adjust according to the market provide greater safety. Typically, interest rates rise during periods of inflation so adjustability is an important feature.

Duration factor and bond terms

All things being equal, a bond maturing in one year is considered a safer investment bet than a bond maturing in 25 years. The *term* is how long the bond is still active until maturity. Short-term bonds are generally safer than long-term or intermediate-term bonds.

Understanding the Elements of Bonds

When folks are looking at bond factors, it's good to look under the hood so you know what the factors are gauging. These are the elements and features of bonds so you get a better handle on the value of factors.

Principal and interest

A bond is an investment in debt. You are the creditor, loaning your money. The person or entity that is borrowing your money is the debtor. Credit and debt are essentially two sides of the same money. You as the bond investor play the role of creditor and the money you're lending is the principal and in the form of a bond. You're doing this to be compensated through interest income.

The debtor, in this case of a bond, is typically either a public company (*corporate bonds*) or a governmental entity such as the federal government (*Treasury bonds*) or a state or local government (*municipal bonds*). These bonds are referred to as *domestic debt* (entities within the United States), but bonds can also be issued from international sources such as corporations and/or governments internationally from Europe, Asia, and so on.

The debtor must pay the creditor (you, the investor) interest and the full principal is typically due at maturity. Bonds are usually long term such as 25 years or 30 years although some may have a shorter duration (and there have also been 40-year bonds, although these aren't as common).

The bond market

You can buy bonds when they're issued (in the primary or *first* market) and you can also buy bonds in the bond market (the *secondary* market) through your brokerage account. Thousands of various corporate and governmental bonds are bought and/or sold every business day throughout the world on the secondary bond market. Dollar-wise, the bond market is much larger than the stock market.

Once a bond is in the secondary market, its price is subject to supply and demand through buyers and sellers much in the same way that stocks are.

You can choose amongst the bonds covered in the following sections.

Treasury obligations

Issued by the federal government, Treasury obligations (Treasury bonds, notes, bills, and savings bonds) are considered the safest category. The interest is taxable (for federal income tax purposes) but it's free from state and local taxes. This category meets the criteria for the quality and/or safety factor.

Treasury bonds have a maturity of up to 30 years while Treasury notes have a 10-year maturity and Treasury bills (T-bills) are under a year and typically six months or less.

Agency obligations

Agency obligations are typically bonds of individual federal government agencies or government-sponsored enterprises (GSE) such as the Federal National Mortgage Association (FNMA) or Fannie Mae. These are generally assumed to be high quality because of the federal government's implied backing.

Municipal obligations

Municipal obligations (municipal bonds) are debt issued by state, county, and/or cities and towns and their agencies. Interest paid is generally free from federal taxes and the interest may be free from state and local taxes or if you live in that particular state. However, keep in mind that municipal bond interest may be free of taxes in a given state, but states do tax other states' interest.

WARNING

Be very selective when it comes to municipal bonds because quality can vary among issuers. Check the bond ratings. The higher the ratings (AAA or AA), the safer the bond. Some municipal bonds have a low rating (B or lower). They may offer a higher interest rate that can be enticing but the safety (low quality) makes them risky.

Corporate

Corporate bonds are offered by public companies. These tend to offer a higher interest rate than Treasury or municipal bonds but, as a category, tends to be riskier. Given that, pay close attention to the bond rating.

REMEMBER

Some bond and financial sites may break out low-rated (high-yielding) bonds in a separate category but these riskier bonds are present in both the municipal and corporate categories. Just be aware of the bond rating, which we cover in a later section, "Bond ratings."

Savings

We include these even though many bond information sites may ignore them because they're not marketable securities as the prior categories. However, the U.S. Treasury issues them and they have excellent advantages that investors should be aware of. (See the "Looking at Savings Bonds" section later in this chapter.)

Bond yields

In most cases, yields on a given bond vary and you should understand why.

Nominal yield

Nominal yield is also called *face rate* or *nominal interest rate*. If a bond states that it pays 3 percent, then the nominal yield is 3 percent.

Current yield

Current yield is the annual income (interest or dividends) that you receive from a bond divided by the current price of the bond.

Say you bought the bond at face value and the nominal interest rate is 3 percent, then the current yield is the same as the nominal yield. But what if you bought the bond at a discount? Say you bought a 3 percent bond on the market at 90. This means that you bought a $10,000 bond for $9,000 (90 percent of the face value). If that bond pays you a nominal rate of 3 percent ($300), your current yield would be 3.333 percent ($300 interest is 3.333 percent of $9,000).

If you bought a 3 percent bond at 105, then you paid 105 percent of the nominal yield. In that case, that $10,000 bond was purchased for $10,500 (105 percent of $10,000). The bond pays $300 in interest (3 percent of the face amount), but the current yield would be 2.857 percent ($300 interest is 2.857 percent of $10,500).

You might pay more than the nominal amount for the bond if market interest rates are lower than the bond's nominal interest rate.

Yield to maturity (YTM)

Yield to maturity (YTM) is a slightly different calculation than the current yield because it's calculated as if you held the bond to maturity. It's essentially the percentage rate of return for a bond that you hold onto until its maturity date.

If you bought that bond at a discount (see the next section), then your YTM tends to be higher than both the nominal yield and the current yield. If you bought the bond at a premium, you likely have a YTM that is slightly lower than the nominal or current yield.

Discount or premium?

When you buy a bond at issuance, all things being equal, you get the nominal yield. For example, you bought $10,000 of face value (or *par value*) corporate bonds of the public company Lotsa Debt Inc. (LDI) and it has a nominal interest rate of 5 percent. The bond then pays you $500 in interest annually ($500 is 5 percent of $10,000).

If you held that LDI bond until maturity, it continues to pay you $500 per year; at maturity, you get $10,000 (the principal). So far, so good. But say that during the life of the bond, interest rates in the marketplace rise to 10 percent. Now what? The market value of the bond falls below the face amount and it's now a *discount* bond, meaning that you could purchase it in the bond market at discount.

What if interest rates fall below 5 percent? The bond's market value would likely rise and anyone that bought that bond would be buying it at a premium, meaning you paid more than the face amount.

Bond pricing versus market interest rates

One long-time observation that you need to remember is:

When interest rates rise, bond prices fall.

When interest rates fall, bond prices rise.

Imagine that you're holding a 3 percent, 30-year Treasury bond. The issuer (the federal government through the Treasury department) is considered the safest issuer on the planet, and U.S. Treasury obligations are automatically considered the highest rating (AAA). So safety and quality are not issues here.

Say you bought it at issuance at the full nominal yield value of $10,000. At 3 percent, the bond gives you an annual interest of $300 ($300 is 3 percent of the face amount of $10,000). So far, so good! But what if market rates rise to 6 percent?

If your plan is to hold that bond to maturity, then no problem. Your principal (the $10,000 invested) is safe and the interest being paid annually is expected to be safe as well. But say that you're thinking about selling your 3 percent bond and using the proceeds to buy bonds with the now higher rate in the marketplace of 6 percent. What will happen?

As you look at the market, you now find that the market value of your bond has plummeted to only $5,000 (yikes!). Why at that level? Because for you to gain the equivalent rate of the new market interest rate of 6 percent, the bond's market value needs to fall. In this case, the bond would continue to pay 3 percent. The $300 of interest is 6 percent of $5,000.

WARNING

Although a bond may have financial safety (no risk of default by the issuer), it may have market risk because bond prices do move inversely to interest rates. This is why you should not only employ style (or microeconomic) factors but also macro factors such as with interest rates.

TIP

If you are going to invest in bonds, especially long-term bonds, consider bonds that have an adjustable rate (instead of a fixed rate) when market rates (using the credit or interest factor) are rising. Fixed interest rate bonds are best when market interest rates have peaked or are leveling off. Once you are there, you may be able to take advantage of the opposite market dynamic — you have a high interest rate when market interest rates are dropping.

If you have a long-term bond earning, say, 6 percent and general market interest rates are dropping, then this can boost the value of your bond and give you the potential for a nice capital gain (on top of the interest income).

Bond ratings

Bond ratings are one of the most important elements of a publicly traded bond. Bonds are rated by independent bond rating agencies such as Standard and Poors, Moody's, and Fitch. For any bond you're considering, you should definitely check the bond rating as part of your factor-based analysis.

Here are the major categories of bond ratings:

>> **Investment:** Ratings of AAA, AA, and A are considered the highest quality (in terms of financial safety).

>> **Medium:** Ratings of BBB, BB.

>> **Low (junk ratings):** Ratings of B and lower are considered very speculative.

TIP

All the rating agencies have slight differences in how they grade, how they rate quality, and so on. Check at least two or more bond rating agencies before you make a determination.

Looking at Savings Bonds

Savings bonds aren't bought through your broker. You buy them directly from the U.S. Treasury at www.treasurydirect.gov.

EE bonds

Double E or EE bonds are very affordable and can be bought for as little as $25 and they have the same quality and tax advantages as other Treasury securities. One of their great features is that the rate is adjustable, which is a great during a rising interest rate period. The interest rates on EE bonds are pegged 100 percent to the average 5-year Treasury note rate.

I bonds

In an inflationary environment, an I bond can be excellent to include in your portfolio. They can be bought for as little as $50 and have the same safety and tax advantages as other Treasury securities. The interest rates are pegged to the Consumer Price Index (CPI) and can be a great holding during periods of rising inflation. The maximum you can buy is up to $15,000 per person per calendar year through TreasuryDirect.gov. The maximum is a little tricky in that $10,000 is the limit for electronic I bond purchases with the additional $5,000 in paper I bonds purchased through your federal income tax refund (see its site for more details).

Investing in Multifactor Bond Exchange-Traded Funds

If you or your advisor believe that an optimal mix of bonds using the key factors of value, quality, and momentum are a good diversification with your other assets (such as stocks), than one of the best ways of accomplishing this in your personal financial situation is through a multifactor bond exchange-traded fund (EFT). (Some are listed in Appendix B.)

TIP

Investing in a single bond or several bonds can be pricey and not as practical and as versatile as buying a multifactor bond ETF. It provides income and a good diversification to your asset mix but also offers the advantages that ETFs offer.

To buy (or sell) a portfolio of bonds with a few clicks just as you can with any stock is very convenient. However, with the ETF format, you get more:

>> You can do stop-loss orders or trailing stops to limit downside risk. (See Chapter 10.)

>> Many ETFs are optionable so you could boost the income from this bond ETF through covered call writing. (Chapter 18 covers options.)

>> You can easily buy 1, 10, 50, 100, or more shares with a few clicks.

>> Bond ETFs are marginable (also in Chapter 10) if you want to add this aggressive tactic.

REMEMBER

Any bond ETF has the same inherent issues as the underlying bonds themselves because an ETF is a "conduit" or a vehicle that, in turn, holds the bonds directly. If an ETF has bonds that are declining in value or can default, that risk is present with the ETF as well. The ETF's risks can be mitigated by using safety tactics such as stop-loss orders or trailing stops (covered in Chapter 10).

Chapter **18**

Using Options with Factor Investing

Make no mistake about it — call and put options are about speculating. No matter how you describe it, you're essentially making a bet. However, there are different options strategies for different goals and different levels of speculating. Buying call and put options is aggressive speculating, but selling (or writing) call and put options can be relatively safe.

Your chosen factors, in fact, can identify option opportunities that could safely boost the income potential from your stock and exchange-traded fund (ETF) portfolio by an additional 3, 5, or even double-digit percentage and do so with near-zero risk as long as you understand how selling (writing) options work *before* you implement them.

In this chapter, we focus on two income strategies that can comfortably augment your factor-based approach: calls and puts.

REMEMBER

We don't mean for this chapter to be a comprehensive source of information on general option strategies. Option strategies that seek aggressive gains aren't complementary with factor-based investing. Other option strategies have a more modest goal to enhance the income potential of an investment portfolio.

Writing Call Options

A call option is a contract that gives the option buyer the right, but not the obligation, to buy a specific security (such as a stock) at a specific price (the *strike* price) between now and when the option expires. The call option buyer is speculating that the underlying stock or ETF will go higher and pay a fee for the option (called the *premium*).

A call option is not an investment; they are marketable contracts.

The option is a binary transaction. For every buyer, there must be a seller (the *writer* of the option). The option buyer and the option writer have differing expectations for the underlying security. The best way to illustrate the pros and cons for both the call option buyer and the call option writer is through the eyes of each in an example. There are other scenarios, but we're keeping these simple.

The call option buyer

A person buys a call option because they believe that the price of a chosen security (again, stock or ETF) will rise in the near future and wants to profit from this up move.

Imagine that Bob is a speculator and he believes that Beast Company Inc. (BCI)'s stock will do very well in the near future. BCI is a $50 stock and Bob thinks that BCI stock will soar to $60 and beyond. So he buys a call option (contract) for $200 (the premium) giving him the right, but not the obligation, to buy 100 shares of BCI stock (the underlying asset) at $55 per share ($55 is the strike price or the agreed price in the option) and this call option expires June 2023.

Here are the possible scenarios that may happen to Bob with BCI stock:

>> The worst case scenario is that the option expires worthless because BCI's stock doesn't rise anywhere near $60. Bob would lose the full $200 (but he knows the risk up front).

>> Bob may exercise the option and buy BCI for $55 per share (100 shares/contract at the $55 strike price). This was Bob's right (but not obligation).

>> If Bob is losing money on his option, he could close out the option, take a loss, and recoup some money without losing the entire amount. Say, for example, that BCI does not go anywhere near $55 and the option will expire in a few months and Bob sees that the option is only worth $90. He can then decide to

sell (or close out the option) for $90 and take a loss of $110 ($200 original amount paid less market value of only $90). He would do this to avoid a total loss of $200 at expiration time.

» If BCI goes to the strike price and beyond, Bob stands a chance for making a great profit as the value of his option rises significantly. Say that BCI goes to $60 (yay!). This means that the option goes up in value. Because the option gives Bob the right to buy the stock at $55 (a total of $5,500 because the option contract is tied to 100 shares), that option could be worth at least $500 because the new market value for BCI stock is $6,000 (100 shares times $60 per stock). In this example, the call option gives Bob the right (but not the obligation) to buy $6,000 worth of stock for only $5,500; the option's new market value would be worth at least the difference ($500). If he bought the call option at $200 and he decided to sell that call option for $500, he would realize a gain of $300 or a percentage gain of 150 percent (the $300 gain is 150 percent of $200).

The call option writer

The flip side of the call option is the option seller (or writer) Mary. Mary has 100 shares of BCI and she would like to generate additional income from this stock holding. So she decides to write a *covered call option*. Covered call options are selling the call option on a stock that you already own. By owning the stock, you're protected if the stock rises and the call option expires.

Here are the possible scenarios that may happen to Mary with BCI stock:

» The option may expire worthless. For Mary, that's great! She keeps her stock and she keeps the $200 from the premium (cool!).

» The option may be exercised, thereby compelling Mary to sell her stock at the strike price. She keeps the $200 cash from the option's premium and sells her stock at the higher price (the option's strike price). She still comes out ahead in this scenario.

» If BCI goes higher than the strike price (no matter how high), Mary is limited to only selling the stock at the strike price. When she entered the option contract, part of the tradeoff (when receiving the premium income) is that she would forego any stock gains greater than the option's strike price of $55 (that's the breaks!).

Benefits and pitfalls of covered call writing

The primary benefit of a covered call option is that you can generate income from stocks in your portfolio, whether the stocks themselves pay you dividends or not. It's a strategy that you can actually do over and over again as long as you have optionable stocks that are in round lots (for example, 100 or 200 shares) because a single option contract is based on 100 shares of stock. If you have 200 shares, you can cover two contracts.

The main pitfall is that, done right, the worst that happens is that you may be obligated to sell your stock at the higher, designated strike price. If your stock is at $50 and the option's strike price is at $55, then you will be obligated to sell your stock when it hits $55. If your stock goes higher than $55, you're still obligated to sell the stock at the agreed-upon price of $55 (the strike price).

WARNING

A second, and potentially more dangerous, issue is if you change your mind in the middle of the call option period. Say that you have stock at $50 and the covered call is at $55. What happens if the stock shoots up to $60 but you suddenly change your mind (meaning that you don't want to see your stock at $55 according to the option terms)? If the stock is now at $60, that option may now be worth $500 (or more). That means to get out of your obligation, you would have to buy back your option (to remove your obligation). However, that means paying $500 and taking a loss of at least $300 ($500 minus the initial $200 premium).

For optimal timing in your covered call option writing strategies, see the "Being Strategic with Your Options" section, later in this chapter.

Selling the Put Options

A put option is a contract that gives the option buyer the right, but not the obligation, to sell a specific security (such as a stock) at a specific price between now and when the option expires. The put option buyer is speculating that the underlying stock or ETF will go lower and pays the premium for the option.

The put option is also a binary transaction. For every buyer, there must be a seller (the writer of the option). The option buyer and the option writer also have differing expectations for the underlying security. The best way to illustrate the pros and cons for both the put option buyer and the put option writer is through an example. Again, we're keeping the scenarios simple; other scenarios are possible.

The put buyer

A person buys a put option because they believe that a chosen security (again, stock or ETF) will decline in the near future and wants to profit from this decline.

Imagine that Xavier is a speculator and he believes that the stock price of Downtrodden Inc. (DI) will fall in the near future. DI is a $80 stock and Xavier thinks that DI stock will fall to $70 or lower. So he buys a put option (contract) for $250 (the premium) giving him the right, but not the obligation, to sell 100 shares of DI stock (the underlying asset) at $70 per share ($70 is the strike price) and this put option expires August 2023.

Here are the possible scenarios that may happen in this put option with DI stock:

>> The worst case scenario is that the option expires or is worthless if DI's stock doesn't fall anywhere near $70. Xavier would lose the full $250 (but he knows the risk up front).

>> The option may be exercised thereby compelling the put writer to buy DI stock at the strike price. This essentially obligates the put writer to buy stock at the market price and relinquish it at the strike price giving the option buyer the difference as a profit.

>> If Xavier is losing money on his put option, he could close out the option, take a loss, and recoup some money without losing the entire amount. Say that DI stock stayed in the range of $75–$80 per share and doesn't approach $70 during the life of the option. With a few months to go until the expiration date, Xavier sees that the market price for his put option is only $75. He decides to cash in (close out his put option) and take a loss of $175 ($250 less $75). Not a good outcome but certainly better than waiting until expiration and losing 100 percent of the premium.

>> If DI falls to the strike price and lower, Xavier stands a chance for making a great profit as the value of his option rises significantly. Say that DI stock falls to $60 per share. The put option would be worth at least $1,000 (because 100 shares of a $60 is lower than the value of 100 shares of a $70 stock by $1,000). Xavier can then sell the put option for $1,000 and make a $750 profit ($1,000 sale price less the original put option cost of $250). That's a neat profit of 300 percent (cool!).

The put writer

When a put option comes into being (when an option order is entered through your brokerage account and the marketplace matches a put writer or seller with a put buyer), the put writer is seeking income (from the put option premium) and is willing to, in exchange, undergo the legal obligation to buy the underlying security should it hit the strike price during the life of the put option.

The put writer (we'll call her Jane) should only write puts on stock that she would love to own at that given strike price. This is really the only risk so you must be sure that it is a stock worthy of your portfolio.

Here are the possible scenarios that may happen to Jane with DI stock:

>> The option may expire worthless. For Jane, that's great! She keeps her $250 from the premium (cool!) and she could decide to do it again to generate more premium income if she chooses to.

>> The option may be exercised, thereby compelling Jane to buy the stock at the strike price. This scenario is a good outcome too, because she keeps the $250 cash from the option's premium and still buys a desirable stock at a lower price (the option's strike price).

>> If DI goes past the lower strike price (no matter how low), Jane is obligated to buy the stock at the strike price. When she entered the option contract, part of the tradeoff (when receiving the premium income) is that she is obligated to buy at $70 (the option's strike price), even if the price is much lower.

Benefits and pitfalls of writing puts

The most obvious benefit of writing puts is the added income you can generate in your portfolio.

The most obvious pitfall is that you may be obligated to buy the underlying stock (100 shares per contract) at the option's designated strike price. The obligation shouldn't be a bad outcome because you should only write puts on stocks or ETFs that you would be pleased to buy at the lower, designated strike price.

WARNING

A second, and potentially more dangerous, issue is if you change your mind in the middle of the put option period. Say that you wrote a put option and received $225 and the put option's obligation was that you must buy the stock at $30 per share and the stock is currently at $35. What happens if that stock falls and it goes below the strike price and is at $25 (or lower)?

If you do nothing, you end up buying the stock at $30, even if it's at $25 or lower. But if the stock goes to $25 and you change your mind and decide to get out of this obligation, you would need to buy back the put option to relieve yourself of that stock purchase obligation. But if the stock is at $25, that put option would be worth at least $500. Paying $500 to get out of the option means that you would legalize a net loss of $275 ($500 minus the $225 premium).

For optimal timing in your put option writing strategies, see the next section.

Being Strategic with Your Options

Selling (writing) options can be a reliable way to boost income even with a small portfolio. You can earn thousands in added income annually from a portfolio of 10 to 15 or more optionable stocks.

Figure 18-1 shows a generic stock chart with optimum times to sell options to generate income.

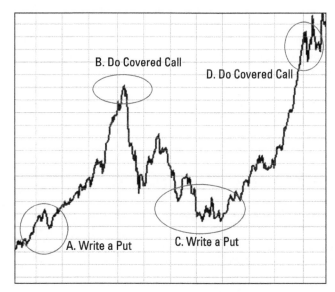

FIGURE 18-1:
Stock chart for
selling options.

The same stock can offer multiple opportunities to sell options even within a single year. The four optimal times become income opportunities that, when you add up all the premiums, translate easily to an added yield on your single stock position of 5–10 percent or more.

REMEMBER

If you own the stock, the income from selling options is in addition to any dividends you would be receiving. When you add up all the potential income you can easily generate a double-digit yield.

The following sections go into specific details on call and put strategies.

Covered call option strategy

There are two optimal periods of time to write a covered call (B and D); refer to Figure 18-1. Because the stock's price went sharply upwards, it means that the call options on this given stock have gained much value (option buyers are paying a lot for the call options). This provides a great selling (writing) opportunity that translates into great premium income for the covered call writer.

When both the macro factors and the style/micro factors, it's a good time to write a call option.

Put option writing strategy

There are two optimal periods of time to write a put option (A and C); refer to Figure 18-1. Because the stock's price went sharply downwards, it means that the put options on this given stock have gained much value (option buyers are paying a lot for the put options). This provides a great selling (writing) opportunity that translates into great premium income for the put option writer.

When both the macro factors and the style/micro factors, it's a good time to write a put option.

MORE OPTIONS RESOURCES

If you want to learn more about options, here are resources:

- The Options Disclosure Document (ODD) from the Options Clearing Corporation: Free for download at https://www.optionseducation.org/news/new-investor-resource-odd-quick-guide.

- Chicago Board Options Exchange (www.cboe.com): For options on stocks, stock indexes, and ETFs, this is the place to go. The CBOE provides news and market data for options and you can get price quotes on options as well as extensive information and tutorials about options in general.

- Options Industry Council (OIC) (www.888options.com): All the exchanges that provide a market for options are members of the OIC. The OIC also offers extensive information and education on options as well as news, views, and market data for the world of options.

- OIC's Options Education (www.optionseducation.org): This is OIC's education site and offers excellent and free courses on both the basics of call and put options as well as more sophisticated options trades and strategies.

- *High-Level Investing For Dummies*, by Paul Mladjenovic (John Wiley & Sons): Covers stocks, ETFs, and basic and advanced options.

- *Trading Options For Dummies,* 4th Edition by Joe Duarte (John Wiley & Sons)

- Ultra-Investing with Options online course by Paul Mladjenovic at www.RavingCapitalist.com

Chapter **19**

Watching the Factors that Lead to Major Market Moves

The bulk of the factors covered in the previous chapters ran the gamut from style (*microeconomic*) factors to macro (*macroeconomic*) factors. Syle or micro factors are the fish, while macro factors comprise the pond the fish live in. But how about the more dominant factors that can affect (and supersede) both the fish and the fish pond?

Understanding what wider events are happening in the world from a cause and effect perspective can greatly enhance your factor-based approach. And it can definitely have a magnified effect on your investing and financial pursuits.

In this chapter, we discuss what these larger factors are that you should watch out for, and then discuss *commodities* (basic goods used in commerce, such as grains, base metals, and energy) that are always good to invest in no matter what is happening in the world because commodities are the stuff we need every day in our lives.

Tracking the Early Warning Signals

The factors we discuss in the following sections are early warning indicators or red flags — they precede any macro or micro factors. When you track what policies and legislation are happening, you can position your portfolio accordingly.

Tax factor

In any discussion about the Great Depression, significant factors are usually left out of the narrative.

REMEMBER

Taxes are always a major cause of bad (or good) general economic activity. Increased taxes are a sign (or a catalyst or cause) of an impending bear market, while lower taxes typically ignite economic growth and can be a catalyst for a bull market.

Increased taxes under Hoover (up to 60 percent) did indeed have a detrimental effect on the economy, which in turn had a detrimental effect on the fundamentals of public companies. Once the Great Depression was underway, tax rates were radically raised again during the Roosevelt years to 90+ percent!

Income taxes affect production or the output from entrepreneurs, employers, and employees. Higher income tax rates have a negative impact on productivity. Lack of productivity is why the Gross Domestic Product (GDP), and subsequently the stock market, always gain when tax rates are decreased. Increases in general income tax rates tend to depress or diminish productive output. The GDP, in turn, tends to hurt the fundamentals (net income, for example) of public companies that, in turn, tends to diminish the performance of their stocks.

For more information on taxes and the economy, head over to the Tax Foundation (www.taxfoundation.com) and check out the resources at the end of this chapter.

Another example of how taxes affect the economy is the Economic Recovery Tax Act of 1981 (ERTA; H.R. 4242 passed Congress in 1981). ERTA lowered tax rates from a top rate of 70 percent to 50 percent. Tax rates were again cut in 1986 (establishing a top tax rate of 18 percent).

After a severe recession in 1981, the tax cuts helped in creating economic expansion. The end result was that the 1980s were a time of economic expansion (growing GDP). Using the growth factor (see Chapter 5) right after ERTA was passed would have been a profitable choice.

In 1981, the Dow Jones Industrial Average (DJIA), which is a widely followed gauge of large-cap stocks, was under 900. But by the end of the decade, the DJIA was above 2,700 — a gain of over 200 percent. Many individual stocks and sectors (and Nasdaq stocks) did even better.

Regulation factor

When the federal government passes laws, rules, and regulations, there will be winners and losers among the economy's consumers and businesses. When these major regulatory events occur, it's prudent to ask:

» What sectors and industries will benefit? How can I invest to gain?

» What sectors and industries will suffer? How do I avoid losses?

For an example of the regulation factor in action, look at the Telecom Act of 1996 (`https://www.fcc.gov/general/telecommunications-act-1996`). It was passed without fanfare in the mid 1990s but it unleashed the power of competition, technology, and innovation among the industry's big and small companies, along with entrepreneurs and startup newcomers. The end result was that growth was a thousand-fold and long-term investors were rewarded with outsized gains.

The Telecom Act was one of the few times that a massive piece of government legislation actually fulfilled its singular, deregulatory goal as stated in the congressional statement:

"To promote competition and reduce regulation in order to secure lower prices and higher quality services for American telecommunications consumers and encourage the rapid deployment of new telecommunications technologies."

Wow! Politicians doing what they set out to do (a major piece of legislation that actually accomplishes what it was intended to do).

Government spending factor

The government spends. As of 2021, the spending portion (expenditures) of the federal government's annual budget exceeded $6 trillion. Given a deficit of approximately $2.8 trillion, the federal government took in tax revenue of approximately $3.2 trillion.

When the federal government spends $X billions (or trillions) in a given sector, those public companies in that particular sector flourish financially. The companies show great earnings and sales, which in turn means higher stock prices. This, in turn, means a fatter stock portfolio for the investor (you!).

What would happen if the federal government were to spend billions on vaccines? In 2021, it did just that and pharmaceutical stocks soared and their profits hit record highs. You get the picture.

TIP

A great site that tracks government spending so you can see where the trillions go is at https://www.usgovernmentspending.com/. You can also find out what new laws are coming so you can be a step ahead with your portfolio moves by checking the Congress legislation website at www.congress.gov.

The Fed factor

The Federal Reserve (Fed) is America's central bank and it's considered the most influential central bank in the global economy. Its primary role is to manage the U.S. money supply. It's also the leading participant in the nation's financial and credit markets such as setting interest rates and lending practices. In addition, the Fed is the lender of last resort for both the financial sector and for the U.S. government.

The Fed can have a systemic effect on the general economy and financial markets and has caused many events both good and bad and the rule for investors is simple: Don't ignore the Fed!

WARNING

Due to its oversized impact, the Fed has, since its inception in 1913, created many conditions that have lead to booms, busts, recessions, and bubbles. This is generally acknowledged by both advocates and critics. Given this, you can understand that its macro effect in the economy, currency, and credit markets have led to major trends (both bullish and bearish) and issues with stock and bond markets.

You're most likely familiar with the Wall Street crash of 1929, which lead to the Great Depression. But you also need to remember the stock market crash (like most stock market crashes) is an effect; it's a response to the cause that is typically a bubble. What preceded the 1929 crash was the "Roarin' 20s" and the Federal Reserve had pursued policies that resulted in an unsustainable stock market bubble. A *bubble* (or *asset bubble*) is when an asset's price (in this case, stock prices) rises to a level much higher than the actual economic value of the asset itself.

Bubbles keep expanding until they pop and prices tumble. This happened with the stock market in 1929 but it has happened very frequently in modern times such as the Internet Stock Bubble that crashed during 2001–02, the housing bubble (2005–07) where real-estate prices crashed, and the stock market again in 2008.

TIP

Watch what the Federal Reserve is doing and act accordingly where possible. During 2022–23, the Federal Reserve has created high inflation and rising interest rates.

Chapter 11 touches on these macro factors. This is a good example of a how a factor (the government central bank) precedes or is the catalyst for macro factors (such as inflation and interest rates).

When you see both of those coming, you can position accordingly. Add positions that benefit from inflation (such as food and beverage stocks/ETFs, commodities, and so on) and you'll do well. When interest rates rise, reduce your exposure to long-term, fixed-interest rate securities (such as regular government and corporate bonds) and either switch to short-term debt (such as with money market funds) or to adjustable rate Treasury debt (such as EE & I savings bonds).

Chapter 17 covers bonds in greater detail. For more information on the Fed and its policies, head over to www.federalreserve.gov.

Navigating Volatile Periods

Addressing political factors in your factor-based investing approach is important. The economy and financial markets always have volatile periods. When they are, you face

>> Rising inflation

>> Rising interest rates

>> Food and supply shortages

>> Regional conflicts that could escalate

>> Record federal government deficits ($1 trillion+)

>> Record levels of debt (federal government, corporate, and so on)

>> Societal health issues stemming from pandemic and lockdown fallout

REMEMBER

This is a short list. Prosperity is not a destination but an ongoing process.

Given these issues, here are some factors that you should consider going forward:

>> **Value:**

- *Stocks:* Make sure that your stocks and exchange-traded funds (ETFs) have strong fundamentals (see Chapter 6).

- *Bonds:* Make sure any debt you invest in is quality (investment grade bond ratings) and won't be hurt by rising interest rates such as adjustable rate bonds and/or having a short-duration (less than two years). For more information on bonds, check out Chapter 17.

>> **Inflation:** Commodities tend to be great performers during inflationary times and there are many quality commodity-related ETFs. Find out more about ETFs in Chapter 16 (and commodities-related ETFs for factor investing can be found in Appendix B.)

Investing in Commodities

During 2020–2023, *commodities* (basic goods) have caught the attention of investors and for good reason. Due to inflation and related factors (shortages and supply/demand issues), grains, energy, and related necessities have experienced significant price increases. These price increases have become a major global and political concern.

When the economy is in a major bull market, worldwide demand outpaces the global supply. Rising demand with flat or shrinking supply results in rising prices. Given that, you can position yourself by using the inflation factor and supply and demand data.

Figure 19-1 shows a commodities chart from the St. Louis Federal Reserve (https://fred.stlouisfed.org/) that indicates the price movement of an index reflects the general price movement of a basket of commodities on the global market during 2020-2022.

Commodities in general are rising, but individual commodities (such as gasoline, corn, wheat, and others) have performed much better.

The problem of rising inflation was one of the major catalysts for a brutal decline in the general stock market during the first half of 2022 and will still be a challenge for investors during late 2022 and for 2023. Many commodities analysts see the supply and demand fundamentals as being bullish for commodities in general and some commodities in particular (such as goods and energy).

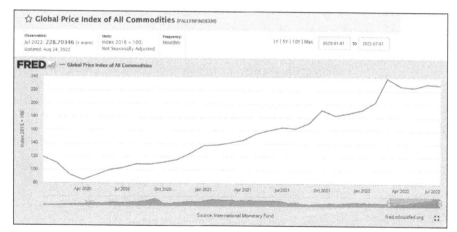

FIGURE 19-1:
A commodities
chart.

Source: Courtesy of the St Louis Regional branch of the Federal Reserve

TIP

The best way to boost your portfolio is by adding commodities-related stocks and preferably ETFs. Information and resources on commodity-related ETFs can be found in Chapter 16 and you can find factor-based commodities-related ETFs listed in Appendix B.

Because commodities are an important macro-consideration during this period (the 2020s) due to protracted conditions in food and energy such as rising prices and supply and demand issues, it's an important area of both challenges and opportunities. Given that, check out these commodities-related resources:

» *Investing in Commodities For Dummies* by Amine Bouchentouf (published by John Wiley & Sons)

» Feedspot's directory of the top 40 commodities blogs and websites (https://blog.feedspot.com/commodity_blogs/)

» Commodities ETF Channel (https://www.etf.com/channels/commodity-etfs)

» Commodities Investing (online course) by Paul Mladjenovic (https://www.ravingcapitalist.com/commodities-investing/)

» ETFDB's list of commodities ETFs (https://etfdb.com/etfs/asset-class/commodity/)

RESOURCES

Obviously, the more you know what political events, government policies, and macro-economic and geopolitical events are coming down the pike, the more you can act accordingly and proactively with your investment portfolio. That means reading sources you agree with along with those you may not agree with. *The point is to be informed.* Here are resources for your consideration:

- Zero Hedge (www.zerohedge.com): This popular site looks "under the hood" on the major political and economic events, issues, and news of the day.

- Trends Research Journal (www.trendsresearch.com): Gerald Celente's site gives you the early news and views on upcoming major social, political, and economic mega-trends.

- Mises Institute (www.mises.org): This leading economics site covers major issues of the day and the economic consequences from a free market perspective.

- Market Sanity (www.marketsanity.com): This site regularly features top economic and financial market analysts and leading researchers giving their insights on unfolding events.

- Market Watch (www.marketwatch.com): This financial site providwa news and views on the stock market and related topics.

- CNN business (www.cnn.com/business): A popular news source that reports on news that impacts the economy and financial markets.

- Real Clear Politics (www.realclearpolitics.com): A digest of news and views that span across the diverse political and public policy landscape.

- Real Clear Markets (www.realclearmarkets.com): This news sources specializes in the world of business, markets, and finance.

Chapter **20**

Considering Taxes

O kay — you've done well with your factor investing approach. The gains are good, but the government wants its share. Now it is time to address the downside of successful investing — taxes!

Taxes can be complicated, infuriating, and feel like legalized theft. Of course, they have their downside too. Regardless, tackling this issue before the year is done (and not during tax season) can pay off. More planning and preparation means more bucks left in your account.

As you know, the topic of investment taxes can easily fill its own book (which we're grateful we're not writing) so don't assume that this chapter is all encompassing and answers all your concerns.

REMEMBER

Throughout this chapter we refer to the IRS, tax laws, and IRS publications. The site you'll most likely visit or refer to is www.irs.gov. That site has every tax form and tax publication available for easy download.

In the event you need some questions answered by a live IRS customer service person, you can give them a shout at 800-TAX-1040 (800-829-1040). If you need hard copies of forms and publications (for the current tax year or a prior year), you can call the IRS publications department at 800-TAX-FORM (800-829-3676).

All that aside, we focus on the main points as related to factor investing, which is primarily tax treatment of capital gains and losses and income from dividends and interest.

TIP

An easy place to go to see the tax reform changes is at the IRS's site www. taxchanges.us. Currently it shows the tax changes from the most recent major tax legislation (circa 2018), but expect updates in the near future as more tax changes (both big and small) become reality.

Understanding the Tax Treatment of Different Investments

The following sections include a breakdown of the most common types of income you come across in your factor investing approach.

Understanding capital gains and investment income

Profit you make from your stock investments can be taxed in one of two ways, depending on the type of profit:

» **Ordinary income:** Your profit can be taxed at the same rate as wages or interest — at your full, regular tax rate. If your tax bracket is 28 percent, for example, that's the rate at which your ordinary income investment profit is taxed. Two types of investment profits get taxed as ordinary income (check out IRS Publication 550, "Investment Income and Expenses," for more information).

» **Dividends:** When you receive dividends (either in cash or stock), they're taxed as ordinary income. This is true even if those dividends are used to reinvest in stock through dividend reinvestment plan (whether through the stock brokerage account or through a formal dividend reinvestment plan).

If, however, the dividends occur in a tax-sheltered retirement account, such as an individual retirement account (IRA) or 401(k), then they're exempt from taxes for as long as they stay inside the retirement account. (See the later section, "Investing in a Retirement Account" for more information on retirement accounts.)

REMEMBER

» **Ordinary dividends versus qualified dividends:** Keep in mind that dividends can be either ordinary or qualified and both are taxed differently. Ordinary dividends are taxed as ordinary income, which is the highest tax rate. Qualified dividends are taxed at a greatly reduced tax rate and fortunately the dividends of most stocks and exchange-traded funds (ETF) are qualified (whew!).

» **Interest:** Most interest income, such as interest paid by corporate bonds, Treasury bonds, and regular bank accounts, is considered ordinary income and taxed at the higher ordinary income tax rate. Keep in mind that interest from municipal bonds can be tax-free but check with your tax advisor about this.

» **Short-term capital gains:** If you sell stock for a gain and you've owned the stock for one year or less, the gain is considered ordinary income, which is the highest tax rate for individuals. To calculate the time, you use the *trade date* (or *date of execution* as reported on the trade advice from your brokerage firm). This is the date on which you executed the order, not the settlement date. Keep in mind that if these gains occur inside a tax-sheltered plan, such as a 401(k) or an IRA, no capital gains tax is triggered.

» **Long-term capital gains:** These are usually taxed at a much better (lower!) rate for you than ordinary income or short-term gains. Yes — the tax laws reward patient investors. When you wait at least a year and a day (after the year since the purchase). you get to keep a bigger chunk of your gain.

IRS publication 550 covers capital gains and losses in great detail.

REMEMBER

A capital gains tax may be a coercive event (so much for "voluntary" taxation) but the good news is that you control the timing and circumstance of the tax. You can delay the sale so that you can lower your capital gains tax (from short term to long term). You can even time it to take advantage of different tax calendar years.

TIP

Everyone meets with their tax person during the tax season to prepare and submit the tax return for the prior tax year but consider also meeting with your tax person in November or so to discuss which stocks should be sold before year end and which stocks should be delayed to the subsequent year (or decide to not sell a stock at all).

A common strategy is to sell losing stocks in a given year to help minimize or remove potential capital gains taxes. And if a stock with large unrealized gains needs to be sold then sometimes it makes sense to defer the stock sale until the new year to postpone that potential gain to a future tax year.

When you buy stock, record the date of purchase and the *cost basis* (the purchase price of the stock plus any ancillary charges, such as commissions). This information is very important come tax time should you decide to sell your stock. The date of purchase (also known as the *date of execution*) helps establish the *holding period* (how long you own the stocks) that determines whether your gains are considered short term or long term.

Fortunately most stock brokerage websites let you easily download a spreadsheet of your positions and you can easily separate and view those positions with realized gains/losses and those with unrealized gains/losses so that you can optimize net gains and losses with both your financial advisor and your tax person.

Commissions are not deductible per se; they're added to the transaction as part of the basis (in both buying and selling). If you bought some stock for $1,000, for example, and paid a $5 commission, then your purchase amount (for calculating capital gains/losses) would be $1,005 (($1,000 plus $5). If you sold stock, for example, for a total of $2,000 and you paid a $6 commission, then the total sales amount would be $1,994 ($2,000 less $6).

Capital gains example

The following table shows you the difference financially between the short-term capital gains tax (ordinary income tax) and the long-term capital gains tax (more favorable):

Simple scenario example	Short-term capital gains scenario	Long-term capital gains scenario
Gain	Short-term gain of $10,000	Long-term gain of $10,000
Tax Category	Ordinary income	Long-term capital gains
Tax Rate	28%	15%
Tax Amount	$2,800	$1,500
Tax Savings	Nothing. . .ugh!	Save $1,300 on taxes ($2,800 less $1,500)

This simple example shows how you can save. Your tax scenario is most likely more complex and you should discuss it with your tax professional but this example should help you understand the concept.

Say, for example, you bought 100 shares of Lotsa Dough Inc. (LDI) at $10 per share and you pay a stock brokerage commission of $5. Your cost basis would be $1,005 (100 shares x $10 plus $5 commission). If you sold that LDI stock at

$35 per share and pay a $6 commission, then the total sale amount would be $3,494 (or 100 shares x $35 per share less $6 commission). The realized capital gain would be $2,489 (sale proceeds of $3,494 less the original cost basis of $1,005).

If this sale occurs a year or less after the purchase date, then it's a short-term capital gain.

If this sale occurs a year and a day or more after the purchase date, then it's a long-term capital gain.

WARNING

Those sneaky folks in Washington DC are always looking for new ways to get a growing piece of your money so don't be passive about it. In early 2022, there were rumblings among the politicians about finding a way to tax unrealized gains, which is shocking. Imagine paying taxes on a gain that you didn't realize. . .ugh! It hasn't become a formal piece of legislation at the time this book is being written but keep watching. The point here is to keep yourself informed (some tax resources are listed at the end of this chapter) and to communicate to your representatives how you feel about tax increases (don't be shy!).

Minimizing capital gains taxes

Long-term capital gains are taxed at a more favorable rate than ordinary income. To qualify for long-term capital gains treatment, you must hold the investment for at least a year and a day (yes, that specific).

Building on a prior example, assume you have stock in Lotsa Dough Inc. (LDI). As a short-term transaction at the 28 percent tax rate, the tax would be $697 (28% of $2,489).

However, if that gain was long term, what would the tax be? That gain of $2,489 would be taxed at the more favorable long-term capital gains tax rate of 15% or a tax of $373 (a tax savings amount of $324).

REMEMBER

Capital gains taxes *can* be lower than the tax on ordinary income, but they aren't higher. If, for example, you're in the 15 percent tax bracket for ordinary income and you have a long-term capital gain that would normally bump you up to the 28 percent tax bracket, the gain is taxed at your lower rate of 15 percent instead of a higher capital gains rate. Check with your tax advisor on a regular basis because this rule could change due to new tax laws.

Don't let the "tax tail wag the investment dog." Don't sell a particular stock or ETF just because it qualifies for long-term capital gains treatment, even if the sale eases your tax burden. If the investment is doing well and meets your investing criteria, hold on to it.

Plus if it's a dividend-paying stock, then it may be serving your passive income needs. Lastly, that dividend may very well be a qualified dividend, which means lower taxes on it.

Cutting taxes with capital losses

It's always good to have stock investing gains, but losses do have a consolation prize: lowering your taxes.

A capital loss means that you realized a loss on a given investment. The loss amount is generally deductible on your tax return, and you can claim a loss on either long-term or short-term stock holdings. This loss can go against your other income and lower your overall tax.

Say you bought Total Freakin Loser Co (TFL) common stock for a total purchase of $5,000 and you sold it later for $700. This means you realized a capital loss of $4,300 ($5,000 purchase price less the $700 sale price). Your tax-deductible loss would be the same: $4,300.

WARNING

The one string attached to deducting investment losses on your tax return is that the most you can report in a single year is a net loss of $3,000. On the bright side, though, any excess loss isn't really lost — you can carry it forward to the next year.

If TFL is your only loss ($4,300), then you can deduct $3,000 of it in the first year and carry over the remaining $1,300 to a subsequent year.

And remember that any loss you realize can go against any gains that you realize because that $3,000 loss limit is a net amount after you calculate all your gains and losses.

Before you can deduct losses, you must first use them to offset any capital gains. If, for example, you realize long-term capital gains of $7,500 in Stock A and long-term capital losses of $6,000 in Stock B, then you have a net long-term capital gain of $1,500 ($7,500 gain less the offset of $6,000 loss). Whenever possible, see whether losses in your portfolio can be realized to offset any capital gains to reduce potential tax. IRS Publication 550 includes information on capital gains and losses.

TIP

Here's your optimum strategy: Where possible, keep losses on a short-term basis and push your gains into long-term capital gains status. If a transaction can't be tax-free, at the very least try to defer the tax to keep your money working for you.

Evaluating gain and loss scenarios

Of course, any investor can come up with hundreds of possible gain and loss scenarios. For example, you may wonder what happens if you sell part of your holdings now as a short-term capital loss and the remainder later as a long-term capital gain. You must look at each sale of stock (or potential sale) methodically to calculate the gain or loss you would realize from it.

Fortunately tracking sales and expenses is easier than ever before because every brokerage site gives you the ability to download transactions to either a spreadsheet or a data format that you can easily import and use in financial and/or tax software.

Figuring out your gains or losses isn't that complicated. Here are some general rules to help you wade through the morass. If you add up all your gains and losses and

» **The net result is a short-term gain.** It's taxed at your highest tax bracket (as ordinary income).

» **The net result is a long-term gain.** It's taxed at 15 percent if you're in the 28 percent tax bracket or higher. Check with your tax advisor on changes here that may affect your taxes.

» **The net result is a loss of $3,000 or less.** It's fully deductible against other income. If you're married filing separately, your deduction limit is $1,500.

» **The net result is a loss that exceeds $3,000.** You can only deduct up to $3,000 in that year; the remainder goes forward to future years.

Sharing with the IRS

Of course, you don't want to pay more taxes than you have to, but as the old cliché goes, "Don't let the tax tail wag the investment dog." You should buy or sell a stock because it makes economic sense first and consider the tax implications as secondary issues. After all, taxes consume a relatively small portion of your gain. As long as you experience a *net gain* (gain after all transaction costs, including taxes, brokerage fees, and other related fees), consider yourself a successful investor — even if you have to give away some of your gain to taxes.

TIP

Try to make tax planning second nature in your day-to-day activities. You don't have to immerse yourself with a dumpster full of forms and paperwork, but keep receipts and maintain good records for all your taxable transactions. When you make a large purchase or sale, pause for a moment and ask yourself whether this transaction will have positive or negative tax consequences.

In the next sections, we describe the tax forms you need to fill out, as well as some important rules to follow.

Tax forms

You report your investment-related activities on your individual tax returns (Form 1040). Here are the reports that you'll likely receive from brokers and other investment sources:

- **Brokerage and bank statements:** Monthly statements that you receive
- **Trade confirmations:** Documents to confirm that you bought or sold stock
- **1099-DIV:** Reporting dividends paid to you
- **1099-INT:** Reporting interest paid to you
- **1099-B:** Reporting gross proceeds submitted to you from the sale of investments, such as stocks and mutual funds
- **K-1**: If you invested in ETFs you likely receive this form for any distributions

REMEMBER

The IRS schedules and forms you need to be aware of and/or attach to your Form 1040 include the following:

- **Schedule A:** To report investment interest and investment-related expenses
- **Schedule B:** To report interest and dividends
- **Form 8949 and Schedule D:** To report capital gains and losses
- **Form 4952:** Investment Interest Expense Deduction

You can download these forms from the IRS website. For more information on what records and documentation you should hang on to, check out IRS Publication 552, "Recordkeeping for Individuals."

The wash-sale rule

WARNING

This is for those of you who are thinking of getting imaginative with your stock buying and selling tax strategies. You may think "Hmmm. Maybe I should sell those stocks that have unrealized losses in December and gain those capital losses and then buy the stock again in January." Would that work?

Not really. The IRS zapped that crafty idea with the *wash-sale rule*. This rule states that if you sell a stock for a loss and buy it back within 30 days, the loss isn't valid because you didn't make any substantial investment change. The wash-sale rule applies only to losses. The way around the rule is simple: Wait at least 31 days before you buy that identical stock back again.

Some people try to get around the wash-sale rule by doubling up on their stock position with the intention of selling half. Therefore, the IRS makes the 30-day rule cover both sides of the sale date. That way, an investor can't buy the identical stock within 30 days just before the sale and then realize a short-term loss for tax purposes.

Taking Advantage of Tax Deductions

As you oversee and manage your portfolio, you may incur expenses along the way. Some expenses can be tax-deductible and some won't be — even some that you would think would logically be deductible. Keep in mind that logic and tax law are not always in sync.

The most common place where you would take investment-related expenses legitimately would be on Schedule A, which is an attachment to Form 1040 (which is frequently referred to as the *long form*).

For 2022 and forward, the standard deduction for individuals increased so you may not need to (or be able to) itemize. Here are the standard deductions for 2022:

Type of 1040 filer	Your 2022 standard deduction is
Married Filing Jointly or Qualifying widow(er)	$25,900
Head of Household	$19,400
Single or Married Filing Separately	$12,950

TIP

The standard deductions come from Form 1040-ES, which is used for estimating taxes and related data for anyone who plans their taxes (always a good thing to do!) by checking the upcoming year (in this case 2022), but you should make it a habit to always check out and estimate your potential tax liability for a subsequent year.

If you are reading this in early 2023), then you should check out the 1040-ES for 2023 so that you can stay a step ahead of your tax liability and be able to strategize with your tax person about how to lower it.

REMEMBER

You report most investment-related expenses on Schedule A as itemized expenses along with other qualified, deductible personal expenses (such as state and local taxes and charities). However, the total deductible expenses on Schedule A are only valuable to you to the extent that they exceed (in total) the amount for your standard deduction. If, for example, you're filing married and filing jointly and you have Schedule A total deductions of $30,000, then you could use this more beneficial amount instead of the lesser standard deduction amount of $25,900. But if your Schedule A itemized deductions only tally up to a total of, say, $23,000, then the standard deduction (of $25,900) would be more advantageous for you tax-wise.

Investment interest

If you pay interest such as *margin interest* (the interest charged by your broker) in your stock brokerage due to borrowing to acquire a taxable investment (such as common stock or ETFs), then that interest is categorized as investment interest and can be fully tax-deductible in the interest category of Schedule A.

WARNING

Be careful because not all interest is deductible. *Consumer interest* (such as what you may pay on balances on your credit card) are not deductible. Also, the use of funds matter regarding the deductibility of the interest.

For example, if you borrow money from your broker (via a margin loan that is secured by your securities portfolio) and use those funds for investment purposes (such as acquiring other taxable stock), then the interest is deductible as investment interest. However, if these borrowed funds are used to make a consumer purchase (such as furniture for your home or a vacation), then the use is characterized as a consumer loan, which means that the interest is considered consumer interest and therefore not deductible.

Again, tax rules can change from time to time so keep checking with IRS publications and other tax resources (see the end of this chapter) and check with your tax person.

Foreign taxes on investments

In recent years many U.S. investors have been able to purchase shares of foreign securities (such as European or Asian stocks) in their brokerage accounts. Typically there may be taxes charged by those governments (such as on dividends).

You deduct and report foreign taxes on Schedule A.

Miscellaneous expenses

For individual taxpayers, reporting and deducting investment-related expenses are usually done on Schedule A (an attachment to your Form 1040).

Even more specifically, they're reported as miscellaneous expenses on Schedule A:

>> Any tax-related expense such as tax software, tax preparation fees, tax courses, and so on.

>> Legal fees in investment-related issues such as stockholders lawsuits

>> Fees paid to investment advisors or investment managers (however, fees paid for advice or service on tax-exempt investments are not deductible)

>> Bank safe deposit box fees for holding taxable securities

>> Fees for investment advisory services

>> Travel expenses to advisors regarding investments

>> Service charges for collecting and distributing income from taxable dividends and interest

>> Expenses for accounting/bookkeeping

>> If you use a computer 50 percent or more to help you manage your expenses, you may be able to partially deduct this expense

REMEMBER

On Schedule A, you can deduct only that portion of your miscellaneous expenses that exceeds 2 percent of your adjusted gross income. For more information on deducting miscellaneous expenses, check out IRS Publication 529.

Donating securities

Many folks have a favored charity and many typically donate cash. Some who are feeling particularly generous may feel the impulse to cash out a stock (or other security such as a bond or ETF) and donate the proceeds. It's a noble idea but you may want to rethink how you do it.

Say you purchased stock for, say, $2,000 and it's now worth $10,000. If you sell the stock, receive the $10,000 in cash and give it to charity, you would feel good, but you would likely owe taxes on that $8,000 realized gain after all is said and done. Not a good way to do this.

You could also simply donate the $10,000 worth of stock directly without selling it. Simply transfer the stock to the charity of your choice. You get the full benefit of the $10,000 (at the time of transfer) as a tax deduction but without the tax pain. The charity can then either hold it or sell it and keep all the proceeds. It's good for you and for them.

For more details on this type of transaction so you can do it right, check out IRS Publication 526 on charitable contributions and discuss the pros and cons of this with your tax person.

Non-deductible items

In case you 're tempted to deduct some non-deductible items, here is what you can't deduct:

>> Financial planning events

>> Investment seminars

>> Any travel expenses to a stockholders' meeting

>> Home office expenses (as you manage your portfolio).

For more details on investment income and expenses, check out the IRS publications listed at the end of the chapter.

Investing in a Retirement Account

Long-term investing is best done in retirement accounts that offer tax benefits so you can maximize your long-term success. The following sections cover the most obvious tax-advantaged accounts.

IRAs

Individual retirement accounts (IRAs) are accounts you can open with a financial institution, such as a bank or a mutual fund company. An IRA is available to almost anyone who has earned income, and it allows you to set aside and invest money to help fund your retirement. Opening an IRA is easy, and virtually any bank or mutual fund can guide you through the process. Two basic types of IRAs are traditional and Roth.

Traditional IRA

The traditional individual retirement account (also called the *deductible IRA*) was first popularized in the early 1980s. In a traditional IRA, you can make a tax-deductible contribution of up to $6,000 in 2022 (some restrictions apply). Individuals age 50 and older can make additional catch-up investments of $1,000. For 2022 and beyond, the limits will be indexed to inflation.

The money can then grow in the IRA account without being encumbered by current taxes because the money isn't taxed until you take it out. Because IRAs are designed for retirement purposes, you can start taking money out of your IRA in the year you turn 59 1/2. (If you want your cash at age 58 7/8 then you are out of luck!?)

The withdrawals at that point are taxed as ordinary income. Fortunately (or hopefully!?), you may be in a lower tax bracket during your retirement years so the tax shouldn't be as burdensome.

REMEMBER

You are likely required to start taking required minimum distributions (RMDs) when you reach age 72 (a bummer for those of you that prefer a later time like 73 2/3).

WARNING

If you take out money from an IRA too early, the amount is included in your taxable income, and you may be zapped with a 10 percent penalty. You can avoid the penalty if you have a good reason. The IRS provides a list of reasons in Publication 590-B, "Distributions from Individual Retirement Arrangements (IRAs)."

Keep in mind that to contribute money into an IRA, it must be earned income (such as from a job or net business income) and that the amount you are contributing is equal or less than your earned income.

For more details, check out IRS Publication 590-A, "Contributions to Individual Retirement Arrangements (IRAs)."

Roth IRA

The Roth IRA is a great retirement plan. Here are some ways to distinguish a Roth IRA from the traditional IRA:

>> The Roth IRA provides no tax deduction for contributions.

>> Money in the Roth IRA grows tax-free and can be withdrawn tax-free in the year that you turn 59½.

>> The Roth IRA is subject to early distribution penalties (although there are exceptions). Distributions have to be qualified to be penalty- and tax-free; in other words, make sure that any distribution is within the guidelines set by the IRS (see Publication 590-B).

The maximum contribution per year for Roth IRAs is the same as for traditional IRAs. You can open a self-directed account with a broker as well. See IRS Publication 590-A for details on qualifying.

401(k) plans

For employees, the 401(k) plan is the holy grail of retirement accounts (or is that the 800-lb gorilla?). Generally this account is managed by financial institutions (utilizing a menu of mutual funds) but there are self-directed plans too (especially if you own and run a business).

Even if your particular 401(k) is conventional and you have no role in its management, you do have input ability in terms of mutual fund selection. Perhaps not today but in due course you may have greater latitude in choosing funds. As factor investing gains prominence, more and more 401(k) administrators will likely add these choices to the mix.

For 2022, employees can contribute up to $20,500. Those employees that are age 50 or over can be eligible for an additional catch-up contribution of $6,500.

At the time of this writing, the limits for 2023 have yet to be determined.

Keeping Up on Tax Resources

This chapter doesn't cover everything tax-related to factor investing. Here are more resources to keep your tax savings rolling.

IRS publications to get

Here are the main IRS publications you (and or your tax person) should be aware of and you can find at www.irs.gov:

>> Estimated taxes info for an upcoming year (Form 1040-ES)

>> Personal tax guide for 1040 filers (Publication 17)

>> Retirement plans tax info (Publication 560)

>> Investment income and expenses (Publication 550)

Tax sites

Here are some places to visit for help on keeping your tax bill as low as possible. (Most of them have free basic info.)

>> Tax Foundation (www.taxfoundation.org)

>> Tax Mama (www.taxmama.com)

>> CPA Journal (www.cpajournal.com)

>> National Taxpayers Union (www.ntu.org)

>> Americans for Tax reform (www.atr.org)

Tax software

Tax software can keep you from leaping off into the nearest ravine. Here are three major popular tax software sites to help you with your daunting tax preparation issues:

>> Turbo Tax (www.intuit.com)

>> TaxCut (www.hrblock.com)

>> Tax Act (www.taxact.com)

Financial sites with tax info

These investor resources also have some great tax information. Some of these have a dedicated section on taxes while with others you need to do a search for "tax information".

>> Kiplinger's www.kiplingers.com

>> Market Watch (www.marketwatch.com)

>> Seeking Alpha (www.seekingalpha.com)

>> Investopedia (www.investopedia.com)

WARNING

It's always best to double-check with your tax advisor because tax laws can (and do) frequently change or get modified. Usually the laws change annually but occasionally they can change mid-year if there are outstanding situations.

5

The Part of Tens

Chapter **21**

Ten Do-It-Yourself Factors

Who said that you had to follow some stuffy academic's chosen factors to be successful in the world of stock investing? After all, you have common sense and if you have books like this one, by golly, you have what it takes to successfully enact your own personalized factor investing approach.

As stock experts, we've seen, over and over again, those factors or indicators that are truly worth watching for. Some of these are factors treated in depth in the other chapters, but some are important indicators and early warning signs to watch out for and are worth turning into a factor.

The important reason they're in this top ten list is because they're things you should not ignore. They can become your "do-it-yourself" factors for stock (and ETF) investing success.

Profit

The net profit of the company is easily the most important element of a successful company. You could even say that profit is the single most important element of a successful economy.

Profit (net profit actually) is the difference between total sales and total expenses. It's what's left after all expenses have been paid for.

Profit keeps the company in business, provides capital for growth, and generally means that the company is well run. Profitable companies have a bright future; unprofitable companies will struggle or worse.

WARNING

Frequently, you see great press about glamorous companies with sexy new technology with financial pundits touting the company's future prospects. But when you look under the hood, the company is losing money. We can't dissuade you from putting your money in the stock of a losing company. but if you do so, you're not investing; you're speculating.

Speculating is akin to gambling. Maybe not exactly but pretty close. For every speculative company that climbed into financial strength, there are a hundred that declined into bankruptcy.

Sales

Sales is a reference to the total revenue (or total sales) of a company. It's typically viewed as a quarterly or annual number. Total sales tend to pay all the expenses with the remaining amount being the net profit.

In the same way that net profit is referred to as the bottom line, sales is referred to as the top line. Many analysts like the top line number because it tends to be a cleaner number than the net earnings. During the quarterly earnings season when many companies report their net earnings, a common complaint is that the earnings number is often skewed or fudged based on how the company reports it.

Fortunately, the top-line gross sales number tends to be straightforward and a reasonable barometer of overall company health. And it is easy to compare with prior years. Rising sales is indeed a good factor.

But ya know, there's only one thing better than a great year of sales, and that's multiple years of sales.

Consistency

The stocks of consistently well-performing companies tend to do much better over the long term than the stocks of companies that are not performing consistently well. The consistency factor is a simple point.

How well has that company performed over three years or longer in key metrics such as sales, net profit, and growth in net equity? Today's financial websites (such as investing.com, Nasdaq.com, and Marketwatch.com) make this information easily accessible in a few mouse clicks (or smartphone taps).

Having a solid net profit in a given year is good (or lucky?) but doing it year after year points to great management and the key to a well run company.

Debt

All things being equal, the stocks of companies that have too much debt do not perform well long term compared to companies that have lower (or manageable) debt. High debt leads to needing more money to maintain debt and greater interest expense. Debt that is too high and too unmanageable can lead to default, insolvency, and possible bankruptcy.

Even companies that have adequate cashflow to cover the terms to carry their debt may ultimately have less ability to accrue capital to take advantage of opportunities and put themselves on a growth track.

The bottom line is that you should watch the debt load for the companies you have in your portfolio.

TIP

Check out the debt-to-asset ratio of your given company. Go to a major financial site such as Investing.com (www.investing.com) or Market Watch (www.marketwatch.com) and see the company's balance sheet and see its total debt (total liabilities) and its total assets. If the company has $1 million in total debt/liabilities and $3 million in total assets, then its debt-to-asset ratio is .33 or 33 percent.

Debt that is only 33 percent of the total assets is good! The lower the better. A debt-to-asset ratio of more than 100 percent — the total liabilities is more than the total assets— is bad for the company and does not bode well for you as the investor.

Price-Earning Ratios

Imagine you're choosing between two companies. Both are similar in many ways: They are in the same industry, they both have made a similar net profit, they both have earnings per share of $2. But Company A has a share price of $30 while Company B has a share price of $400. Which one is a safer bet?

This is where the price-earnings (P/E) ratio comes in handy. The P/E ratio is one of the few ratios that ties the bottom line results of the company (the net profit quoted on a per-share basis) to the market value of the company's stock (also on a per-share basis).

Company A's P/E ratio is 15 ($30 per share divided by $2 net income per share). Meanwhile, Company B's P/E ratio is a whopping 200 ($400 per share divided by $2 net income per share). In Company B's case, you're paying a lot for the same earnings. Many veteran investors would say that Company B is overvalued, or overpriced. You're simply paying too much for the company's earnings.

If the economy is doing well and the stock market is bullishly chugging along, it may not be a huge concern.

But what if the economy is heading into difficult times? During bad times, all things being equal, stocks with low P/E ratios tend to perform better (or at least survive better) than high P/E stocks.

WARNING

Companies with high P/E ratios (say, more than 50 or in triple digits) are indeed riskier than companies with lower P/E ratios (again, all things being equal). In bad economic times or bearish conditions for the stock market, high P/E stocks usually decline and in volatile times can crash. But worse than a high P/E ratio stock is one with no P/E ratio at all (or a negative P/E ratio). In other words, imagine buying a stock at, say, $100 per share but there are no net earnings (the company is losing money).

Chapter 6 goes into more detail on price-earning ratios.

Dividend Income

Few things are as a good a sign (factor, baby!) as getting income from your investment. Companies that regularly pay dividends are one of the great constants of successful long-term investing. With companies that have regularly paid an increasing annual dividend for decades, you can certainly see that the performance of their share prices has equally and strongly trended upward over time along with their dividend payouts.

Investing in dividend-paying stock is a good consideration for any long-term conservative investor. For more on dividend income opportunities, check out Chapter 9.

Human Need

The economy isn't always strong. Inflation, food and energy shortages, geo-political conflicts, plummeting stock and bond prices, and so much more give many investors and consumers sleepless nights and shrinking wallets. What's a factor investor to do?

Think of two words that have acted as a long-time, reliable (although unofficial) factor: human need. You don't need to be a Wall Street analyst or financial pundit to figure this one out. Your common sense can guide you.

In tough economic times, those investments tied to human need tend to do better than those tied to human wants. What do investors and consumers keep buying no matter how good or bad the economy is?

People will continue to buy food, beverage, utilities, and so on. Therefore, those companies profitably benefit.

Optionable

If you seek to boost the income potential of stocks (and also some ETFs), then *covered call writing* is worth investigating. This option strategy is used by many money managers and experienced investors. It has the potential to increase your annual income from your portfolio by 5 percent, 8 percent, or possibly more.

You should find out whether your stock(s) are optionable, which means that you have the ability (when approved to do so) to write covered calls.

The details on this intriguing strategy can be found in Chapter 18.

Industry Top 20%

The only thing better than investing in a great industry (such as through an ETF or a sector mutual fund) is to invest in the stocks of the companies that are among the best in their specific industries. It doesn't have to be number one because that position can change frequently; consistently in the top 20 percent is a sign of success.

One way to find a top stock in a solid industry is to check out the recent portfolio of a top ETF or mutual fund in that given industry (or sector). If you know that many fund managers like a particular stock and they have chosen this stock through their rigorous standards, it can give you confidence in addition to your own homework as you check out the company's fundamentals and the appropriate factors (such as some of the ones highlighted in this chapter).

Political and Economic

Politics and economics (macro factors) play a *huge* role in the growth and well-being of your stock choices.

When the economy is stable and the political establishment is leaning through pro-growth policies (such as low taxes and sensible regulations), then the environment is conducive to economic growth, which means a better environment for stocks in general.

When the economy is down, focusing more of your portfolio toward companies that have greater flexibility to succeed in an inflationary environment (such as food/beverage and commodities-related companies) is always good. When you see the big picture and what is likely coming, then you can adjust your general portfolio strategy accordingly.

Chapter **22**

Ten Ways to Mess Up Your Investment Plan

E very successful investment plan comes with a dose of volatility. Dealing with market corrections and bear markets are a normal part of long-term investing.

Studies show that the average investor buys high and sells low — the exact opposite of what legendary investors such as Warren Buffett teach. What's worse, these investors repeat this same mistake cycle after market cycle. Some people even feel cursed by the market. It's not that they lack intelligence. Far from it! Many smart people such as doctors and lawyers, feel they just cannot win in the stock market.

TIP

If you feel this way, you might find value in outsourcing your investments to a competent professional team.

After decades of listening to frustrated do-it-yourselfers, several roadblocks to success keep emerging. Most of them have to do with either our amygdalas (flight or fight part of our caveman brains), or investment sayings that aren't actually true.

When you're doing your own investing, it's important to pay more attention to how your natural, instinctive behavior can sabotage your portfolio and wealth-building plan. So, in this chapter, we present ten ways you can screw up your investments. Avoid these mistakes.

Breakevenitis

One great way to mess up your investment plans is to succumb to breakevenitis, a term generally attributed to investor Ken Fisher. Market corrections are not bear markets (generally defined as market declines of over 20 percent), but any normal decline of over 10 percent from a previous high.

TIP

A great way to improve your investing behavior and outcomes is to pull up your investment statements (easily done online at most brokerages) for months after a correction to examine whether you sold positions as soon as they got back to the price you bought them at. If so, breakevenitis is affecting your wealth.

The average decline of the 28 market corrections that have occurred since WWII has been 13.7 percent. Corrections happen on average every 1.9 years and historically take around six months to find a bottom, allowing the bull market to resume. Trying to avoid these things is something no one's ever been able to do very well. As markets regain pre-correction levels, many investors feel the urge to sell, fearing a new drop in markets. *Breakevenitis* is the desire to get out where you got in, right as a correction is resolving so you can tell yourself you haven't lost anything. It's a sort of emotional relief that destroys wealth building.

It's very important that when you see a correction rebounding, you don't succumb to the need to settle for the comfort of breaking even as you will miss out on the rebound over the next 6–18 months.

REMEMBER

No investor ever bought stocks with the goal of going through an unpleasant downturn and then holding to break even. In times like these it's important to focus on long-term goals and objectives, and not on what the market has just done.

This Time It's Different

We live in a world dominated by a 24-hour news cycle, and every news organization is in a competition for your eyeballs and attention. This means big headline grabbing news stories that get you hooked and return for more. It means "shocking", 'unprecedented," or "world changing" events are constantly being presented to you.

The problem with this is that when it coincides with a downturn or correction in the market, it can have the effect of making you throw out everything you've painstakingly learned about markets and investing because this time, it's different.

The truth is, that it's almost never different, though masses of investors succumb to this thinking every time. As the wise bards of old said "there is nothing new under the sun" and "what has been will be again and what has been done will be done again." Although market history may not repeat exactly, the basic themes of fear, greed, and innovation repeat, and what will never change is your caveman brain kicking you into adrenaline fueled fight or flight mode, wanting to sell everything because this time it's different.

It's probably not.

Cutting Winners Short and Letting Losers Stay

This is a very common way investors shoot themselves in the foot, and many never realize they're actually doing it.

It's simple but powerfully destructive. Investors who have holdings that perform poorly, or even stocks that experience accounting fraud or massive revenue losses (such as Enron), tend to leave them in the portfolio, often for years, because they believe the stocks will bounce back. When pressed, the rationale given is often that the stock or fund is too far down to sell or they don't want to sell at a loss.

Those same investors often sell a winning stock as soon as it's up 5 or 10 percent. These are the investors who sold Amazon and Google 10,0000 percent ago, and likely every few years since, taking tiny gains because they've got to take a gain while they can.

Obviously, they're applying a double standard to their winners and losers that guarantees they will let losers accumulate in their portfolios while kicking out winners far too soon. This is not a recipe for success!

Letting Fear and Greed Lead

Fear and greed can be powerful allies, but only if you take a contrarian approach. One famous investor when asked when he knew it was a good time to buy answered "when I reach the puke point."

Most investors sell on fear and buy on greed and euphoria. This means they buy when markets are high and everyone they know is bragging about recent investment successes, and they sell when markets are low and everyone is depressed about their investments.

Train yourself, like a Pavlovian poodle, to salivate when fear and bad news abound, and to lighten up when the future looks permanently rosy and people who haven't invested for decades are opening new accounts and telling you that the market always goes up.

Here are a few pithy, time-honored adages worth tucking away:

"The time to buy is when there's blood in the streets, even if the blood is your own."

—Baron Von Rothschild

"I will tell you the secret to getting rich on Wall Street. You try to be greedy when others are fearful. And you try to be fearful when others are greedy."

—Warren Buffett

"Bull markets climb a wall of worry. Bear markets slide down a river of hope."

—anon

"When shoeshine boys are giving stocks tips and a summary of the days financial news, the market is too popular for its own good."

—Joseph P. Kennedy explaining how he knew to sell before the 1929 crash

Buying the Hype

Professional portfolio managers are almost religious about position sizing. This typically means that no matter how much they love a stock or asset class, they maintain discipline and allocate only a set percentage of a portfolio to a particular stock or sector. This means diversifying factors as well, and not blindly placing everything into the trendy factor, or the one that appears to be working the best right now.

Investors who know better often go wrong because they get swept up in the hype of whatever's moving right now, whether it's tech stocks, crypto stocks, pot stocks, or hot meme stocks. When an asset class jumps 20 percent or more, outpacing everything else, it's easy to become unmoored while visions of sugar-plums, instant wealth, and new vacation homes dance in your brain. While there will always be someone who bets everything and retires early, it's not the way to bet and almost always leads to disaster, or at least to sleepless nights and underperformance.

REMEMBER

With your investment portfolio, you want to have a plan, and then work the plan. It's okay to tilt your allocation a little one way or the other to suit your need for speed, but never buy the hype and don't over-concentrate all your eggs in a few baskets.

Even for aggressive investors, a slow-and-steady approach should be cultivated. The investment highway is strewn with the remains of hares that ran into brick walls with their one or two investment eggs, while the tortoises laden with egg baskets plod on past the finish line.

Using Leverage

Margin, the ability to borrow against your portfolio, is now offered in most non-IRA investment accounts. Once set up, it takes no approval and is effortless to use. The interest charged, which is far lower than most consumer loans, accrues in the portfolio and doesn't have a set monthly payoff schedule. You can even pull cash out to use for other purposes while leaving your portfolio positions to grow, and keeping all the gains that result.

Margin is a powerful tool, yet the process is deceptively simple and gets a lot of people into trouble. It's a form of leverage, and leverage magnifies both your gains and your losses. The serious problems start when you've bought using margin near a high, and then decline into a market low. What might have normally been a normal 13.5 percent correction results in a 27 percent drop for your portfolio (if you are 100 percent margined) or even a 40.5 percent loss if you are 200 percent margined as some brokerages will allow depending on your underlying holdings.

It gets worse. If this happens, you won't have the luxury of riding it out. You'll get a margin call from your broker and have a limited number of days to either sell a large part of your holdings to cover your margin loan, or add new funds to your losing portfolio (often a bad idea).

Bottom line? You could be forced to sell low after buying high. Not a great way to build wealth!

Leave margin use to the experts. Your odds of enhancing your gains long term (net of interest cost) are slim, and the downside can derail your investment plan. If you insist on using margin, practice for a few months by real-time *paper trading* (managing a portfolio based on real stock prices but with imaginary money). There are many online sites and brokerages that offer this feature.

Buying or Selling Everything at Once

This is a version of "I have to do something" behavior and it's really a false dilemma.

This mindset often applies to new investors entering the market, as well as to investors managing portfolios through corrections and bear markets.

A typical scenario is an investor who has saved, decided on a portfolio, and is now looking for the time to start investing and put all the money to work.

"Hurry up and wait" can be a good mantra here. Why not decide to get into the market over a few months instead? Your average cost will smooth out the volatility without you having to agonize about the best day to get in.

The same idea applies if you're looking to reduce exposure to a position in the portfolio or perhaps needing to raise a chunk of cash for say, a college tuition payment. Rather than worrying about selling it all at once, start a few months before you need the funds and leg out of the position.

Getting Impatient with Positions That Aren't Working

The desire to get rid of a stock or fund that's not doing anything is almost universal when sitting down for a monthly or quarterly portfolio review. The very definition of diversification (and why you should take a factor-based approach) is that not everything will move at the same time. In fact, if it does, that means all your portfolio holdings are correlated and that may be cause for concern.

A well-constructed portfolio is by definition going to include some holdings that seem to be lagging or stagnating at times. This does not mean they're not worth keeping. While it's always important to review holdings to make sure that your original premises and reasons for including them are still in place, temporary underperformance alone is no reason to kick a stock out of the portfolio.

In fact, as many have no doubt experienced, investments that seem to be stagnant always seem to catch a new tailwind the second they are sold. Mr. Market sure seems to have a diabolical sense of humor.

Borrowing or Going into Debt to Invest

Going into debt to invest is almost never a good idea. This is a related but separate issue from margin investing.

Borrowing to invest includes using home equity loans, cash out refis, credit card cash advances, and loans from family or friends in an attempt to take advantage of a bull market and get ahead.

It's almost without exception a bad idea. "We took out 100K from our house at 4 percent and invested it in the market. Oh, by the way, it's a variable rate." (What happens if rates go up to 13 percent like the 1980s and all your stocks are down at the same time you decide to pay off the home equity loan?)

Firstly, there is interest charged with all these options, which means that right from the start you have a hurdle rate of the interest plus taxes. In other words, to pay the 6 percent home equity loan interest you'd have to earn at least 8 percent before taxes, which means that your brilliant investment plan doesn't really start working until you've made the first 8 percent in gains. Actually, it's worse than that. You start out each new year owing 8 percent to someone else, whether or not your plan makes a gain.

With a credit card advance (at 15–18 percent interest rate or even more), the hurdle rate becomes almost insurmountable. Yes, there are investors who try this despite knowing better. Don't do it.

Micromanaging Your Portfolio

Believe it or not, there was a time when Al Gore hadn't yet "invented the Internet" and most investment accounts produced just one quarterly or even annual statement, and monthly statements were considered an extra.

Now, with instant, secure, online access, investors often check on their long-term portfolios daily or even hourly.

Unless you're a professional trader, trying to profit from short-term moves in stocks (a tough profession with a high burnout and heart attack rate incidentally), checking your portfolio this frequently serves little purpose other than entertainment.

REMEMBER

Even the best factor strategies don't unfold over hours and days. Focus on months and years.

It may sound counterintuitive, but there's a point at which meddling with your portfolio becomes counterproductive. If you've designed (hopefully using some of the great ideas in this book) a high performance portfolio, incorporating factor advantages and using funds that you don't need for several years at least, there comes a point at which less is more.

A great portfolio needs time to work its magic. Each component and factor will outperform at different times in the market cycle, and it's important to resist the temptation to tweak things every time you log in to view your accounts.

Chapter **23**

Ten Non-Factor Strategies and Considerations

M ost factor investing approaches are either intermediate or long term, which means that the approach is not a quick move. Investing means an investment of time as well.

The last thing you need is to see your factor investing approach get derailed — not seeing your approach bear fruit such as capital appreciation and income from dividends. It's a common event that investors abandon their approach or liqui-date too soon because of seen and unforeseen events.

Given that, here are some things to either watch for, plan for, or avoid during your factor investing.

Pay Off Debt

This is more than an issue with your personal debt; it's also about debt that's bearing down on you or could occur in the near future. 2022 is unfolding as a very hazardous year. Inflation is such a burdensome issue that the latest data shows that many people are using their credit cards to afford common everyday expenses such as groceries. . .yikes!

In the bigger macro picture, total debt across many categories (personal debt, mortgages, corporate debt, government debt) has crossed into unsustainable levels. Financial struggles with past-due debt and debt defaults are facing dangerous levels. These obligations ultimately force the sales of stocks and other securities, which mean declining markets (and declining portfolios).

This situation means taking great caution in managing debt so that it doesn't endanger or bankrupt you. Get ahead of any issues by discussing difficulties with your creditors and exploring debt management strategies.

WARNING

Because credit card debt can be expensive and burdensome if you're not careful, talk with your financial advisor about alternate strategies. Some folks have found success with paying off their unsecured consumer debt by borrowing on margin from their brokerage account. The portfolio acts like collateral and the dividends and interest income generated by the portfolio can help pay off this debt. For more on using margin, check out Chapter 10.

Save an Emergency Fund

It's been reported for years that a significant portion of working adults in the United States are only one or two paychecks away from a financially painful event (such as a health issue, major auto repair, or job loss).

Given that, it's imperative to get ahead of such as issue. Everyone (to varying extents) should have an emergency fund or "rainy day" fund in a safe venue such as a bank savings account or money market fund. How much should you have?

When times are good and you're doing well (job is secure, investments are growing), you should have a minimum of three month's worth of gross living expenses stashed away in your savings account. If your monthly gross expenses are typically $3,000, then you should have at least $9,000 (3x$3,000) in a savings account. This serves as a financial cushion so that you don't have to prematurely liquidate any positions in your portfolio.

However, if times are looking bad, you should have more in your savings account. Preferably at least six month's worth of gross living expenses.

TIP

When you feel the economy and financials are entering a rough period, caution and safety should be in your action plans. Discuss defensive strategies with your financial advisor.

Plan for Taxes

Part of the cost of being productive and hard-working and of building your net worth with growing investment accounts and assets is addressing taxes. For many, taxes paid (both directly and indirectly) can be the single greatest expense in your personal financial picture. Of course, every dollar that goes to taxes is one less dollar going elsewhere (such as your investments or your pocket). For most folks, this means thousands of dollars year in and year out.

Given that, tax planning with an experienced tax pro is worth it for you and your loved ones.

The first place to start with your taxes is Chapter 20.

Consider Insurance

Insurance is meant to cover those life-changing events but also as stop-gaps in your picture. Life insurance is there because if the primary bread winner dies, insurance can make a significant payment to the family. Health insurance is there to help ease the burden of costly illness. From a financial point of view, insurance eases the need to liquidate investments (especially those involved in your factor investing approach).

TIP

To make sure you have adequate insurance coverage in your personal situation, contact your insurance professional for a thorough review.

Plan Your Estate

Estate planning is important because it addresses your assets and related issues (debt, expenses, and heirs for example) in the event of your death. Including what happens to the investments you built during your life.

TIP

Contact an estate planning specialist to discuss your situation and what you will need to make sure your estate plan is optimal so that a greater share of your assets is dispensed to your loved ones and other choices (such as charities) versus being absorbed by estate taxes.

Watch the News

There is a factor investing approach when economic times are good (such as when the economy is growing). There is a factor investing approach when economic times are bad (such as during a recession or inflation).

The economy of 2019 was very different from the economy of 2022. The stock market performed very differently in both years.

The point here is that an informed investor will be a step ahead of the uninformed or passive investor. Reading the news — especially the financial news — is critical for being proactive and getting your portfolio and approach in order before the economy and financial markets make their major moves.

Monitor the Companies

Stocks are only as good as the underlying companies so regularly monitor the financial health of these companies. Good companies are consistently profitable, for example, so be wary if profits start to decline. Of course, profit is just one thing to watch for. There are also sales, debt, market share, and so on.

The point is that a stock belongs in your factor investing approach when it adheres to the factors (covered throughout this book, of course) and the moment that it veers away from critical factors, you should know it.

TIP

Many brokerage sites and other financial sites give you the ability to be alerted via email or texts when material changes occur in the status of a company and its condition. Get set up to learn as early as possible if a stock no longer meets your factor investing criteria.

Know How the Federal Reserve Works

Few single entities have as much of an effect on the economy and financial markets as America's central bank, the Federal Reserve (Fed) (www.federalreserve.gov). When the Fed opens the spigots and sends money into the economy and financial markets, stock prices trend upward. When the Fed increases interest rates, real estate prices and stocks trend downward.

The bottom line is that you should be familiar with the Fed's activities because it can have a major material effect on your current and future portfolio moves.

Maintain Your Career

Career is about your main cash flow. This is the money that pays your expenses and debts. When your career is at risk, your factor investing approach can be at risk which, in turn, means that you won't be able to optimize it as a wealth-building approach.

Given that, make sure that

>> Your job is doing well.

>> Your place of employment is secure.

>> Your skills are up to date.

>> Your industry is trending positively.

Keep on top of what is going on in your career specialty with the wealth of job-related blogs and websites.

Practice Diversification

Lastly, because you're focused on factor investing, the question for you is what is happening with the rest of your money? How about your other assets? Here are some issues for you to address (perhaps with your advisor):

>> Are you diversified beyond stocks in your brokerage account? How about exchange-traded funds and mutual funds?

» How diversified is your 401(k) plan and/or other retirement plans?

» Are there any bonds involved? Are they investment quality (rated A, AA, or AAA)? See Chapter 17 for more details.

» Do you have any hard assets, such as precious metals, real estate, collectibles, or other assets of value?

» Is your mix of assets and investments appropriate for your profile and for the safety and benefit of your loved ones?

Chapter **24**

Ten Financial Problems You Can Navigate with Factor Investing

L
ife on Planet Earth is still much more random, less predictable, and a lot less linear than we like to admit. Natural and manmade events often develop or superimpose themselves to create financial and economic crisis that can negatively affect the investment markets and your portfolios.

As this is being written, the world is still dealing with the COVID-19 pandemic and the effects of governments' response to it. In early 2020, entire countries were put into lockdown in an attempt to arrest the spread of the novel virus. As a result, hundreds of thousands of small businesses closed their doors, many permanently, and tens of millions of people lost their income. In 2022, many regions are still (or even back) in lockdown, and the unprecedented monetary stimulus with which governments around the world responded to the stalled economy, combined with broken and interrupted product supply lines, has now created the highest inflation rate in 50 years. This relentless 9 percent (and climbing) inflation is slamming stocks 20–50 percent or more, and bonds, a traditional place to take refuge in a stock market downturn, aren't faring well either, because the Fed is raising interest rates at a record rate to try to contain inflation.

Governments have a long history of taking actions that end up having unintended consequences and the idea that civilization is on a constant upslope to a sunnier future is periodically and rudely interrupted by events that remind us why many cultures feel human civilization is cyclical, and that history is doomed to, if not repeat, at least rhyme.

It's safe to say that periodic financial crisis will remain a part of modern life, and that you need to find a way to cope with it.

Fortunately, factors are an excellent coping mechanism, and history shows that using them helps you not only survive but potentially thrive in a wide variety of financial crises.

Here are ten examples of financial problems that factors can help you navigate.

Recessions

A *recession* is a period of temporary economic decline (defined by at least two quarters of declining Gross Domestic Product) in which industrial and trade activity are reduced. There have been 12 recessions since 1948, which averages out to about one every six years.

During a recession, most companies have to hunker down, cut costs, and announce layoffs to stay operational. When less cash is coming in, companies with more debt have to focus on making their interest and principal payments to stay solvent.

Meanwhile, a select group of companies is able to not only weather the storm but also take the lunch money (or at least acquire new assets at bottom-dollar prices) from distressed companies holding fire-sales to raise cash to stay solvent. Like Spartan warriors of old, these companies are already lean and mean, and carry all the supplies they need to get through rough times. They have the pick of other companies laid-off employees, can acquire distressed companies' debt at fire-sale prices, and have the room to act opportunistically instead of merely reactively. In tough economic times, the best companies not only survive, but take advantage of economic dislocations, positioning themselves to gain market share and thrive even more once the recession inevitably ends.

We're talking, of course, about the quality factor (see Chapter 1). High-quality stocks with more stable earnings, higher margins, and stronger balance sheets tend to outperform low-quality stocks, over time.

Subprime Lending Crisis

Whenever Wall Street finds a new toy, they tend to play with it until it breaks. The Subprime Mortgage crisis was a key component of the 2008 great recession and financial crisis. It was the result of years of expanded mortgage lending, as profits and political pressure pushed lenders to extend credit to lower income and asset individuals. The United States wound up with the so-called NINJA (No Income No Job No Assets) loans, where lenders gave out mortgages with little or no effort to find out the borrowers' ability to pay. The reason they didn't care, incidentally, was that they weren't planning to actually hold on to those mortgages for long. Wall Street had found a nifty way to segment the risk into CMOs (collateralized mortgage obligations) where millions of mortgages were sliced, diced, bundled, and resold as bonds. Failure (default) to pay was going to be someone else's problem.

What factors would have steered savvy investors away from this gathering storm that brought down 100-year-old institutions run by the so-called smart money crowd? Companies that have the quality, value, (and sooner or later) momentum factors (see Chapter 1).

High Inflation

Inflation is a measure of the increase in the cost of living or rise in the overall level of prices. Gnawing inflation means individuals find it harder and harder to make ends meet, pay bills, or have money left for discretionary things such as vacations or travel.

Inflation can hurt stock prices in several ways. Because the Federal Reserve moves to raise interest rates to combat inflation, heavily indebted companies find their borrowing costs increasing and their profit margins shrinking.

In addition, as consumers realize their dollar is not stretching as far, they begin tightening their belts and reduce discretionary spending, which reduces the sales and revenue of most companies not selling or producing essentials items of daily use such as energy, staple foods, and other basics.

Often the hardest hit are growth stocks, which have often borrowed heavily for expansion, and are trading at high price-earnings (P/E) multiples, reflecting high investor expectations for future growth. When inflation uncertainties muddy the water, these stocks can fall hard.

Cheap stocks, or the value factor, is the port in the storm here. Though stocks that fit these factors can be expected to correct along with the general market, they tend to fall less and behave in a less volatile manner because they're priced much lower in terms of stock price per unit of earnings. We introduce the value factor in Chapter 1 and cover it in detail in Chapter 6.

Market Crashes

Since 1950, the S&P 500 index has declined by 20 percent or more on 12 different occasions. The average stock market price decline is -33.38 percent and the average length of a bear market is 342 days.

Within a bear market, much of the damage can occur on just a few pivotal down days, often loosely referred to as a *stock market crash,* which is a sudden and dramatic drop in the value of stocks listed on an exchange. Crashes are almost impossible to predict dependably and can be caused by many factors including rumors, geopolitical events such as war or a country defaulting on its debt, or just compounding herd behavior.

Investors often confuse stock market crashes with market corrections, but there are specific thresholds for each. A stock market crash is a drop of 20 percent or more from a recent market high, but a correction is widely defined as a drop of 10 percent or more.

Many investors move to cut their losses after a vicious down day, but this is usually a mistake. Almost diabolically, Mr. Market likes to serve up record up days within weeks or even days of historical down days, and research shows that if you missed just a few dozen such days over the past decades, you missed most of the benefits of investing in the market.

TIP

In general, the best thing you can do during a market crash is to remain calm. This comes down to having rock-solid confidence in your investment strategy.

Using factors and a portfolio built on factor principles puts the most powerful forces in market history on your side. Though it may take patience to ride the recovery, factors are what determined the surest and most dependable stocks that continued to prosper after crash events such as the bombing of Pearl Harbor, the Cuban Missile Crisis, and the Black Monday crash of October 19th, 1987 when the Dow Jones Industrial Average plummeted 22 percent, marking the largest one-day decline in U.S. stock market history. (See Figure 24-1.)

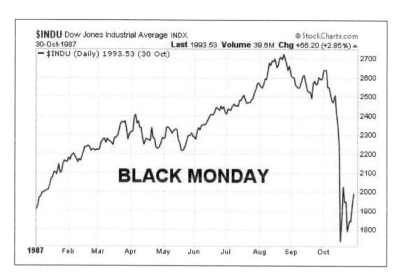

FIGURE 24-1:
Black Monday,
1987 crash chart.

Pandemics

The most recent pandemic/global health crisis occurred in 2020 as COVID-19 spread worldwide. Because it's been over 100 years since the Great Influenza and Spanish Flu pandemics that swept the world between 1918 and 1920, this risk had fallen off most investors' radars.

During the week of February 24, the Dow Jones Industrial Average tumbled 11 percent, marking the biggest weekly decline to occur since the financial crisis of 2008. The Dow went on to decline by 9.99 percent on March 12 — its largest single-day drop since 1987's Black Monday — following up with an even deeper plunge of 12.9 percent on March 1.

Yet unlike prior crashes where recovery took a year or two, the stock market made a V-shaped turn, rebounding back to its pre-COVID 19 peak by May of 2020, fueled by an unprecedented amount of stimulus money and trillions in direct aid packages.

What group of stocks rebounded the most dependably? You guessed it. Stocks with these factors: quality, momentum, value, and low volatility. (See Chapter 1 for an explanation of these factors.)

Government Overreach

It's been said that the most dangerous sentence in life is "we're from the government and we're here to help."

For all the good they can do in helping society run in an orderly fashion, governments have a long history of inadvertently making bad economic situations worse through the pressure from citizens and re-election committees to do something, thereby interfering with normal self-corrective and cleansing market forces that economist Adam Smith famously called the invisible hand.

Rising inflation? Make higher prices illegal! (Price fixing never works as President Nixon soon learned when capping prices at the gas pump.)

Overspent budgets running out? Raise taxes! (The Laffer curve illustrates that lowering taxes actually results in higher tax revenue intake.) Many leaders, including John F. Kennedy who called for 30 percent tax cuts and Ronald Reagan, believed in the power of lower tax rates. Note what happened to the IRS coffers when President Trump took a lesson from history and slashed taxes during his administration! According to a June 2022 study, this propelled higher income growth and higher income and payroll taxes. The government expects to bring in more tax revenue in the decade following the 2017 Trump tax cuts than it had projected prior to the passage of tax reform. However, many of the Trump tax cut provisions are now set to expire over the next few years. You can read the study at `https://www.heritage.org/taxes/commentary/the-numbers-are-trumps-tax-cuts-paid`.

Banking crisis? Call them too big to fail and bail them out with trillions in taxpayer money to keep them solvent at all costs. (Bankruptcy of poorly run companies is a painful yet vital process that re-allocates assets to better run more productive enterprises that can provide more jobs and real growth such as the companies' factors identify.)

When the government comes knocking with a grand solution, there are often unintended consequences that actually make a bad situation worse, prolong the economic pain, or result in an entirely new set of problems. More than one cynic has observed that when it comes to government intervention no good deed goes unpunished. That's life.

The good news is that factors help you identify the investments most likely to be positioned to survive, thrive, and even take strategic advantage of government inefficiencies and boondoggles.

Hyperinflation

When monetary policy (government money printing) and lack of confidence and faith in a country's currency combine in the perfect, nasty way, you have a recipe for hyperinflation. This is not just the annoying rise in the price of goods and services, but a situation where prices skyrocket and currency loses its purchasing power (two sides of the same coin) at alarming and life-altering rates. We're talking about food prices doubling in just weeks, or — an extreme example from Zimbabwe in 2008 — the price of a cup of coffee doubling between the time a customer walks into a restaurant and the time they pay their bill! Hyperinflation became so extreme in Zimbabwe that the government wound up printing 100 trillion dollar notes so that people wouldn't have to cart wheelbarrows of money just to go shopping. As the government continued to print notes, inflating the money supply, the currency lost so much value that the system eventually collapsed. (Barter and the U.S. dollar are what drive commerce in Zimbabwe today.) Figure 24-2 shows the highest denomination note ever printed in history. 100 trillion would have bought you little more than breakfast at the peak of Zimbabwe hyperinflation. (Curiously, 2009 uncirculated Zim notes are now worth $300 apiece on the collector's market. Talk about being worth more dead than alive!)

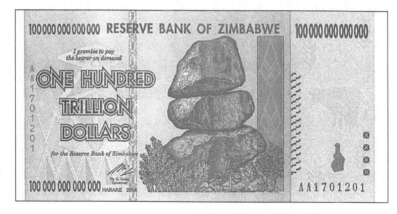

FIGURE 24-2:
The Zimbabwe 100 trillion dollar note.

Hyperinflation, while relatively rare, has happened in dozens of countries over the last century, with some notable examples of the dilution of buying power of their currency as follows:

Weimar Republic of Germany 1920–23: 1/466 billionth of starting value

Zimbabwe 2003–2008: 8 quadrillionth of starting value

Former Soviet Union 1993–2002: 1/14 of starting value

Argentina 1975–1983: 1/1000th of starting value

Bolivia 1984–86: 1/1000th of starting value

Bosnia-Herzegovina 1992-93: 1/100,000 of starting value

Stocks actually tend to fare better than most assets under hyperinflation. In Weimar Germany, stocks soared thousands of percentage points in the local currency as stock prices revalued to account for a dropping and rapidly diluting currency purchasing power. Under hyperinflation a stock rising 1000 percent is simply retaining purchasing power versus a currency that loses 90 percent of its purchasing power, which isn't necessarily growth but rather keeping what you have, in many cases.

Although stocks have often soared in terms of the currency that is experiencing hyperinflation, no one has done an academically rigorous analysis of which factors lead to stock outperformance under these bizarre conditions. (Hint to any enterprising graduate student still searching for a thesis topic!)

Stocks that exhibit factors tend to outperform lesser companies.

Tight Labor Market/Talent Shortage

This situation is usually the result of a booming economy, but recent events have shown that for technology and other fields, the shortages can also come about through travel and visa restrictions enacted by governments in response to a global event such as the COVID-19 pandemic.

Here again, factor companies win. The best companies win because they have the resources and cash flow to pay higher wages, throw in more job perks, and strategize to attract scarce talent. In addition, the track record of these companies' stocks tends to be superior, making perks such as corporate stock options (which value depends on future performance) more attractive. Winners tend to keep on winning, even in a talent war.

Black Swan Events

Asteroid impact, EMP pulse frying electronics over huge areas, North Korean nuclear attack. These sorts of unexpected events of large magnitude and consequence have been made famous in recent years by risk analyst Nassim Talib.

These events are named after black swans because they are considered impossible. (The first black swan event happened in 1697 when Dutch explorers in Western Australia first saw black swans.)

The 2017 study "Black Swans, Major Events and Factor Returns" (https://caia.org/blog/2019/03/24/black-swans-major-events-factor-returns) analyzed 9/11 and a dozen other black swan type events, and concluded that factors outperformed in many situations but the pattern of which factors outperformed wasn't clear.

They concluded that a diversified mix of factors would give investors the best portfolio to recover from a black swan event.

Market Shutdowns

Markets, especially U.S. markets, normally run so efficiently and dependably that the risk of authorities hitting the off switch doesn't even occur to many investors.

However, there have been several market shutdowns around the world in recent decades, usually as a result of civil unrest or terrorism.

In the United States, trading was frozen for four days following the Sept. 11, 2001 attacks that destroyed the World Trade Center.

When World War I broke out, the New York Stock Exchange was halted for four months starting July 31, 1914. Many European governments had large holdings of U.S. stocks that market makers knew would be sold off to raise war funding, so the closure almost certainly prevented a gigantic run on the U.S. stock market.

Analysis of Warren Buffett's winning stock selection methods has continuously uncovered his focus on the factors of value and quality. This is what gives him the confidence not to worry about a market shutdown — even a ten-year shutdown! He knows that, when it comes to selecting investments that can survive and thrive despite a lengthy market shutdown, the quality and value factor companies are ones to bet on.

6 Appendixes

Appendix A

Resources for Factor Investors

To stay on top of your investing strategies (factor-based or not), getting and staying informed are critical for success. We have compiled in this appendix a list of the most relevant information sources.

Factor Investing Books

This book gives you the low-down on factor investing, but we know that we are not the be-all and end-all of factor investing. Here are some star-studded factor investing books for your perusal.

Asset Management: A Systematic Approach to Factor Investing

by Andrew Ang (2014)

Published by Oxford University Press

Dual Momentum Investing

by Gary Antonacci (2014)

Published by McGraw Hill

Equity Smart Beta and Factor Investing for Practitioners (1st Edition)

by Khalid Ghayur, Ronan G. Heaney, Stephen C. Platt (2019)

Published by John Wiley & Sons

The Fundamental Index: A Better Way to Invest

by Robert D. Arnott, Jason Hsu, John West (2008)

Published by John Wiley & Sons

Index Fund Management: A Practical Guide to Smart Beta, Factor Investing, and Risk Premia 1st ed.

by Fadi Zaher (Author) (2019)

Published by Palgrave Macmillan

Investing Amid Low Expected Returns: Making the Most When Markets Offer the Least 1st Edition

by Antti Ilmanen (2022)

Published by Wiley

Machine Learning for Factor Investing: R Version (Chapman and Hall/CRC Financial Mathematics Series)

by Guillaume Coqueret and Tony Guida (2020)

Published by Chapman and Hall/CRC

Quantitative Momentum

by Wesley Gray and Jack Vogel (2016)

Published by John Wiley & Sons

Quantitative Portfolio Management: The Art and Science of Statistical Arbitrage 1st Edition

by Michael Isichenko (2021)

Published by Wiley

Quantitative Value

by Wesley Gray and Tobias Carlisle (2008)

Published by John Wiley & Sons

Risk-Based and Factor Investing 1st Edition, Kindle Edition

by Emmanuel Jurczenko (2015)

Published by ISTE Press – Elsevier

Shareholder Yield: A Better Approach to Dividend Investing

by Mebane Faber (2013)

Published by The Idea Farm

Your Complete Guide to Factor-Based Investing: The Way Smart Money Invests Today

By Andrew Berkin and Larry Swedroe (2016)

Published by Buckingham

Other Valuable Books for Factor Investors

These books cover areas this books doesn't cover to give you a more well-rounded approach to factor investing. These books help drill down on the concepts and ideas that underpin factor investing.

Fundamental Analysis For Dummies

By Matt Krantz

Published by John Wiley & Sons, Inc.

High-Level Investing For Dummies

By Paul Mladjenovic

Published by John Wiley & Sons, Inc.

The Intelligent Investor: The Classic Text on Value Investing

By Benjamin Graham

Published by HarperCollins

Security Analysis: The Classic 1951 Edition

by Benjamin Graham and David L. Dodd

Published by McGraw-Hill

Stock Investing For Dummies, **6th Edition**

By Paul Mladjenovic

Published by John Wiley & Sons, Inc.

The Wall Street Journal Guide to Understanding Money & Investing

By Kenneth M. Morris and Virginia B. Morris

Published by Lightbulb Press, Inc.

Periodicals and Magazines

Factor-based investing is an ongoing process. The periodicals and magazines listed here (along with their websites) have offered many years of guidance and information for investors, and they're still top-notch.

Barron's

online.barrons.com

Forbes **magazine**

www.forbes.com

Investing.com

www.investing.com

Investor's Business Daily

www.investors.com

Money **magazine**

www.money.com

Value Line Investment Survey

www.valueline.com

The Wall Street Journal

www.wsj.com

Resources on the Big Picture for Factor Investors

When the economy and financial markets are uniquely hazardous, you should be aware of the risks.

The Coming Bond Market Collapse: How to Survive the Demise of the U.S. Debt Market

By Michael G. Pento

Published by John Wiley & Sons, Inc.

Crash Proof 2.0: How to Profit from the Economic Collapse

By Peter D. Schiff with John Downes

Published by John Wiley & Sons, Inc.

Dollar Collapse

By John Rubino

www.dollarcollapse.com

The Economic Collapse Blog

By Michael Snyder

www.theeconomiccollapseblog.com

Mish's Global Economic Trends Analysis

By Michael Shedlock

www.mishtalk.com

Trends Research Institute

By Gerald Celente

www.theeconomiccollapseblog.com

Investing Websites

The following sites are among the best information sources online.

General investing websites

Bloomberg

www.bloomberg.com

CNN Money

www.money.cnn.com

Financial Sense

www.financialsense.com

Forbes

www.forbes.com

Invest Wisely: Advice From Your Securities Industry Regulators

www.sec.gov/investor/pubs/inws.htm

Investing.com

www.investing.com

MarketWatch

www.marketwatch.com

MSN Money

www.money.msn.com

Micro-factor resources

These blogs offer a wealth of opinions and insights from experts on investing. Peruse them to round out your research.

Best of the Web Blog Directory

https://blogs.botw.org/Business/Investing/

Minyanville

www.minyanville.com

Seeking Alpha

www.seekingalpha.com

StockTwits

www.stocktwits.com

StreetAuthority

www.streetauthority.com

Other blogs that are useful for stock investors

Greg Hunter's USAWatchdog.com

www.usawatchdog.com

HoweStreet

www.howestreet.com

King World News

www.kingworldnews.com

Market Sanity

www.marketsanity.com

SafeHaven

www.safehaven.com

Zero Hedge

www.zerohedge.com

Fee-Based Investment Sources

The following are fee-based subscription services. Many of them also offer excellent (and free) email newsletters tracking the stock market and related news.

The Bull & Bear

www.thebullandbear.com

The Daily Reckoning (Agora Publishing)

www.dailyreckoning.com

Elliott Wave International

www.elliottwave.com

Hulbert Financial Digest

http://hulbertratings.com/

Investing Daily

www.investingdaily.com

Investor Junkie

www.investorjunkie.com

InvestorPlace

www.investorplace.com

Mark Skousen

www.mskousen.com

The Motley Fool

www.fool.com

The Value Line Investment Survey

www.valueline.com

Weiss Research's Money and Markets

www.moneyandmarkets.com

Exchange-Traded Funds

ETF Database

www.etfdb.com

ETF Site

www.etf.com

ETF Trends

www.etftrends.com

ETFguide

http://etfguide.com/

Sources for Analysis

The following sources give you the chance to look a little deeper at some critical aspects regarding stock analysis. Whether it's earnings estimates and insider selling or a more insightful look at a particular industry, these sources will be useful to you.

Earnings and earnings estimates

Earnings Whispers

www.earningswhispers.com

Thomson Reuters

www.thomsonreuters.com

Yahoo's Stock Research Center

finance.yahoo.com

Zacks Investment Research

www.zacks.com

Sector and industry analysis

Hoover's

www.hoovers.com

MarketWatch

www.marketwatch.com

Standard & Poor's

www.standardandpoors.com

Macro-factor resources

It's important to pay attention to how events drive macro factors (which in turn, drive financial markets). The sources cited here can help you see what is coming.

American Institute for Economic Research (AIER)

www.aier.org

Center for Freedom and Prosperity

www.freedomandprosperity.org

Federal Reserve Board

www.federalreserve.gov

Financial Sense

www.financialsense.com

Foundation for Economic Education

www.fee.org

Ludwig von Mises Institute

www.mises.org

Moody's Analytics

www.economy.com

RealClear Politics

www.realclearpolitics.com

USA Debt Clock

http://www.usadebtclock.org

Government Information

These sites provide the data that all the rest of the financial media cite in their news and commentaries. Get familiar here because this is where the data for macro factors originates.

Bureau of Economic Analysis

www.bea.gov

Bureau of Labor Statistics

www.bls.gov

Securities and Exchange Commission (SEC)

Phone 800-732-0330

www.sec.gov and www.investor.gov

St. Louis Federal Reserve

www.stlouisfed.gov

Appendix **B**

Factor-Based ETFs

Appendix B helps you choose the ETF(s) that fit your needs.

Scroll down to your favorite category or sub-category to zero in on a factor-based fund. Then go to your favorite financial site and do a search for that fund using the symbol provided.

TABLE B-1   **Alternatives: Absolute Returns**

ETF	Symbol	Investment firm
AltShares Merger Arbitrage ETF	ARB	Water Island Capital Partners LP
ASYMshares ASYMmetric S&P 500 ETF	ASPY	SYMmetric ETFs
Global X Alternative Income ETF	ALTY	Mirae Asset Global Investments Co., Ltd.
IQ Hedge Event-Driven Tracker ETF	QED	New York Life
IQ Hedge Multi-Strategy Tracker ETF	QAI	New York Life
IQ Merger Arbitrage ETF	MNA	New York Life
IQ Hedge Long/Short Tracker ETF	QLS	New York Life
IQ Hedge Macro Tracker ETF	MCRO	New York Life

(continued)

TABLE B-1 *(continued)*

ETF	Symbol	Investment firm
IQ Hedge Market Neutral Tracker ETF	QMN	New York Life
ProShares Hedge Replication ETF	HDG	ProShares
ProShares Merger ETF	MRGR	ProShares

TABLE B-2   ## Asset Allocation: Global Target Outcome

ETF	Symbol	Investment firm
Amplify High Income ETF	YYY	Amplify Investments
Akros Monthly Payout ETF	MPAY	Exchange Traded Concepts
Invesco CEF Income Composite ETF	PCEF	Invesco
Invesco Zacks Multi-Asset Income ETF	CVY	Invesco
iShares Morningstar Multi-Asset Income ETF	IYLD	BlackRock
Multi-Asset Diversified Income Index Fund	MDIV	First Trust

TABLE B-3   ## Asset Allocation: U.S. Target Outcome

ETF	Symbol	Investment firm
ETRACS Monthly Pay 1.5X Leveraged Closed-End Fund Index ETN	CEFD	UBS
Multi-Asset Diversified Income Index Fund	MDIV	First Trust
Virtus Private Credit Strategy ETF	VPC	Virtus Investment Partners
WisdomTree Alternative Income Fund	HYIN	WisdomTree

TABLE B-4   ## Commodities

ETF	Symbol	Investment firm	Sector
Abrdn Bloomberg All Commodity Longer Dated Strategy K-1 Free ETF	BCD	Abrdn Plc	Commodities – Broad Market
Abrdn Bloomberg All Commodity Strategy K-1 Free ETF	BCI	Abrdn Plc	Commodities – Broad Market
Abrdn Bloomberg Industrial Metals Strategy K-1 Free ETF	BCIM	Abrdn Plc	Commodities – Industrial Metals

ETF	Symbol	Investment firm	Sector
ETRACS Bloomberg Commodity Index Total Return ETN Series B	DJCB	UBS	Commodities – Broad Market
ETRACS CMCI Total Return ETN Series B	UCIB	UBS	Commodities – Broad Market
Harbor All-Weather Inflation Focus ETF	HGER	ORIX Corp.	Commodities – Broad Market
iPath Bloomberg Commodity Index Total Return ETN	DJP	Barclays Capital Inc.	Commodities –Broad Market
iPath Series B Bloomberg Agriculture Subindex Total Return ETN	JJA	Barclays Capital Inc.	Agriculture
iPath Series B Bloomberg Energy Subindex Total Return ETN	JJE	Barclays Capital Inc.	Commodities – Energy
iPath Series B Bloomberg Grains Subindex Total Return ETN	JJG	Barclays Capital Inc.	Agriculture Grains
iPath Series B Bloomberg Industrial Metals Subindex Total Return ETN	JJM	Barclays Capital Inc.	Commodities – Industrial Metals
iPath Series B Bloomberg Livestock Subindex Total Return ETN	COW	Barclays Capital Inc.	Agriculture Livestock
iPath Series B Bloomberg Precious Metals Subindex Total Return ETN	JJP	Barclays Capital Inc.	Commodities – Precious Metals
iPath Series B Bloomberg Softs Subindex Total Return ETN	JJS	Barclays Capital Inc.	Agriculture Softs

TABLE B-5   ## Currency ETFs

ETF	Symbol	Investment firm	Sector
Invesco DB U.S. Dollar Index Bearish Fund	UDN	Invesco	Currency – Long G10 Basket, Short USD
Invesco DB U.S. Dollar Index Bullish Fund	UUP	Invesco	Currency – Long USD, Short G10 Basket
WisdomTree Bloomberg U.S. Dollar Bullish Fund	USDU	WisdomTree	Currency – Long USD, Short Global Basket

International ETFs

ETF	Symbol	Investment firm	Region*
Affinity World Leaders Equity ETF	WLDR	Regents Park Funds	Developed Markets – Total Market
Fidelity Dividend ETF for Rising Rates	FDRR	Fidelity	Developed Markets – Total Market
First Trust Asia Pacific ex-Japan AlphaDEX Fund	FPA	First Trust	Developed Asia-Pacific Ex-Japan – Total Market
First Trust Brazil AlphaDEX Fund	FBZ	First Trust	Brazil – Total Market
First Trust China AlphaDEX Fund	FCA	First Trust	China – Total Market
First Trust Developed Markets ex-US AlphaDEX Fund	FDT	First Trust	Developed Markets Ex-U.S. – Total Market
First Trust Developed Markets ex-US Small Cap AlphaDEX Fund	FDTS	First Trust	Developed Markets Ex-U.S. – Total Market
First Trust Europe AlphaDEX Fund	FEP	First Trust	Developed Europe – Total Market
First Trust Eurozone AlphaDEX ETF	FEUZ	First Trust	Developed Europe – Total Market
Global X MSCI SuperDividend EAFE ETF	EFAS	Mirae Asset Global Investments Co., Ltd.	Developed Markets Ex-North America - High Dividend Yield Index
Goldman Sachs ActiveBeta Europe Equity ETF	GSEU	Goldman Sachs	Developed Europe – Total Market
Goldman Sachs ActiveBeta International Equity ETF	GSIE	Goldman Sachs	Developed Markets Ex-U.S. – Total Market
Goldman Sachs ActiveBeta World Low Vol Plus Equity ETF	GLOV	Goldman Sachs	Developed Markets – Total Market
Hartford Multifactor Developed Markets (ex-US) ETF	RODM	The Hartford	Developed Markets Ex-U.S. – Total Market
iShares International Equity Factor ETF	INTF	BlackRock	Developed Markets Ex-U.S. – Total Market
iShares MSCI Intl Small-Cap Multifactor ETF	ISCF	BlackRock	Developed Markets Ex-U.S. – Small Cap

ETF	Symbol	Investment firm	Region*
John Hancock Multifactor Developed International ETF	JHMD	John Hancock	Developed Markets Ex-North America – Total Market
JPMorgan Diversified Return International Equity ETF	JPIN	JPMorgan Chase	Developed Markets Ex-North America – Total Market
Nuveen ESG International Developed Markets Equity ETF	NUDM	Nuveen Securities	Developed Markets Ex-North America – Total Market
O'Shares Europe Quality Dividend ETF	OEUR	O'Shares Investments	Developed Europe – Large Cap
Pacer Global Cash Cows Dividend ETF	GCOW	Pacer Advisors	Developed Markets – Large Cap
Pacer Cash Cows Fund of Funds ETF	HERD	Pacer Advisors	Developed Markets – Total Market
SPDR MSCI EAFE Strategic Factors ETF	QEFA	State Street Global Advisors	Developed Markets Ex-North America – Total Market
SPDR MSCI World StrategicFactors ETF	QWLD	State Street Global Advisors	Developed Markets – Total Market
VanEck Africa Index ETF	AFK	VanEck	Africa – Total Market
VictoryShares Developed Enhanced Volatility Wtd ETF	CIZ	Victory Capital	Developed Markets Ex-U.S. – Large Cap
VictoryShares International High Div Volatility Wtd Index ETF	CID	Victory Capital	Developed Markets Ex-U.S. – Large Cap
VictoryShares International Volatility Wtd ETF	CIL	Victory Capital	Developed Markets Ex-U.S. – Large Cap
VictoryShares USAA MSCI International Value Momentum ETF	UIVM	Victory Capital	Developed Markets Ex-U.S. – Total Market
WisdomTree Europe Quality Dividend Growth Fund	EUDG	WisdomTree	Developed Europe – Total Market
WisdomTree International Quality Dividend Growth Fund	IQDG	WisdomTree	Developed Markets Ex-North America –Total Market
Xtrackers MSCI EAFE High Dividend Yield Equity ETF	HDEF	DWS	Developed Markets Ex-North America – High Dividend Yield Index

*If the ETF excludes a given region or country, it's typically in the fund's name. If it's Pacific Rim but excludes Japan, it shows "ex-Japan".

TABLE B-7   ## Developed Markets Ex-US

ETF	Symbol	Investment firm
Fidelity International Multifactor ETF	FDEV	Fidelity
First Trust Emerging Markets AlphaDEX Fund	FEM	First Trust
First Trust Emerging Markets Small Cap AlphaDEX Fund	FEMS	First Trust
First Trust International Developed Capital Strength ETF	FICS	First Trust
FlexShares Developed Markets ex-US Quality Low Volatility Index Fund	QLVD	Northern Trust
Global X MSCI SuperDividend Emerging Markets ETF	SDEM	Mirae Asset Global Investments Co., Ltd.
Goldman Sachs ActiveBeta International Equity ETF	GSIE	Goldman Sachs
Goldman Sachs ActiveBeta Emerging Markets Equity ETF	GEM	Goldman Sachs
Hartford Multifactor Developed Markets (ex-US) ETF	RODM	The Hartford
Invesco FTSE International Low Beta Equal Weight ETF	IDLB	Invesco
Invesco International Developed Dynamic Multifactor ETF	IMFL	Invesco
Invesco S&P International Developed High Dividend Low Volatility ETF	IDHD	Invesco
iShares MSCI Emerging Markets Multifactor ETF	EMGF	BlackRock
John Hancock Multifactor Emerging Markets ETF	JHEM	John Hancock
Pacer Developed Markets International Cash Cows 100 ETF	ICOW	Pacer Advisors
PIMCO RAFI Dynamic Multi-Factor International Equity ETF	MFDX	PIMCO
Xtrackers FTSE Developed ex U.S. Multifactor ETF	DEEF	DWS
VictoryShares Emerging Market High Div Volatility Wtd ETF	CEY	Victory Capital

TABLE B-8   ## Emerging Markets

ETF	Symbol	Investment firm
Fidelity Emerging Markets Multifactor ETF	FDEM	Fidelity
First Trust Emerging Markets AlphaDEX Fund	FEM	First Trust
FlexShares Emerging Markets Quality Low Volatility Index Fund	QLVE	Northern Trust
Franklin LibertyQ Emerging Markets ETF	FLQE	Franklin Templeton
Goldman Sachs ActiveBeta Emerging Markets Equity ETF	GEM	Goldman Sachs

ETF	Symbol	Investment firm
Hartford Multifactor Emerging Markets ETF	ROAM	The Hartford
iShares MSCI Emerging Markets Multifactor ETF	EMGF	BlackRock
John Hancock Multifactor Emerging Markets ETF	JHEM	John Hancock
JPMorgan Diversified Return Emerging Markets Equity ETF	JPEM	JPMorgan Chase
Nuveen ESG Emerging Markets Equity ETF	NUEM	Nuveen Securities
Pacer Emerging Markets Cash Cows 100 ETF	ECOW	Pacer Advisors
PIMCO RAFI Dynamic Multi-Factor Emerging Markets Equity ETF	MFEM	PIMCO
SPDR MSCI Emerging Markets StrategicFactors ETF	QEMM	State Street Global Advisors
VictoryShares USAA MSCI Emerging Markets Value Momentum ETF	UEVM	Victory Capital

TABLE B-9   ## Specialized Global Markets

ETF	Symbol	Investment firm	Sector
ALPS Disruptive Technologies ETF	DTEC	SS&C	Global Broad Technology
ALPS Global Travel Beneficiaries ETF	JRNY	SS&C	Global Hotels, Resorts & Cruise Lines
Fidelity Small-Mid Multifactor ETF	FSMD	Fidelity	U.S. – Extended Market
First Trust Dorsey Wright Focus 5 ETF	FV	First Trust	
First Trust Dorsey Wright International Focus 5 ETF	IFV	First Trust	
First Trust Germany AlphaDEX Fund	FGM	First Trust	Germany – Total Market
First Trust Japan AlphaDEX Fund	FJP	First Trust	Japan – Total Market
First Trust Latin America AlphaDEX Fund	FLN	First Trust	Latin America - Total Market
First Trust Switzerland AlphaDEX Fund	FSZ	First Trust	Switzerland - Total Market
First Trust United Kingdom AlphaDEX Fund	FKU	First Trust	U.K. - Total Market

(continued)

TABLE B-9 *(continued)*

ETF	Symbol	Investment firm	Sector
FlexShares Global Quality Real Estate Index Fund	GQRE	Northern Trust	Global Real Estate
FlexShares International Quality Dividend Defensive Index Fund	IQDE	Northern Trust	
FlexShares International Quality Dividend Dynamic Index Fund	IQDY	Northern Trust	
FlexShares International Quality Dividend Index Fund	IQDF	Northern Trust	
FlexShares Morningstar Global Upstream Natural Resources Index Fund	GUNR	Northern Trust	Global Natural Resources
Franklin LibertyQ Global Equity ETF	FLQG	Franklin Templeton	
Global X SuperDividend REIT ETF	SRET	Mirae Asset Global Investments Co., Ltd.	Global REITs
Global X SuperDividend U.S. ETF	DIV	Mirae Asset Global Investments Co., Ltd.	U.S. – High Dividend Yield
Goldman Sachs ActiveBeta Japan Equity ETF	GSJY	Goldman Sachs	Japan – Total Market
Grayscale Future of Finance ETF	GFOF	Digital Currency Group, Inc.	Global Digital Economy
Hartford Multifactor Diversified International ETF	RODE	The Hartford	
iShares Exponential Technologies ETF	XT	BlackRock	Global Information Technology
iShares MSCI Global Multifactor ETF	ACWF	BlackRock	
KraneShares Electric Vehicles and Future Mobility Index ETF	KARS	CICC	Global Mobility
Roundhill IO Digital Infrastructure ETF	BYTE	Roundhill Investments	Global Internet Services & Infrastructure
Schwab International Dividend Equity ETF	SCHY	Charles Schwab	Global Ex-U.S. - High Dividend Yield
Sprott Junior Gold Miners ETF	SGDJ	Sprott, Inc.	Global Gold Miners
Xtrackers MSCI All World ex U.S. High Dividend Yield Equity ETF	HDAW	DWS	Global Ex-U.S. – Total Market
WisdomTree Global ex-U.S. Quality Dividend Growth Fund	DNL	WisdomTree	

ETF	Symbol	Investment firm	Sector
Vident International Equity Fund	VIDI	Vident	
VanEck Morningstar International Moat ETF	MOTI	VanEck	
WisdomTree Battery Value Chain and Innovation Fund	WBAT	WisdomTree	Global Mobility

TABLE B-10   ## U.S. Large-Cap Stocks

EFT	Symbol	Investment Firm	Sector
AVDR US LargeCap Leading ETF	AVDR	New Age Alpha Advisors LLC	
Columbia Research Enhanced Core ETF	RECS	Columbia Management Investment Advisers, LLC	
Fidelity Momentum Factor ETF	FDMO	Fidelity	
Fidelity US Multifactor ETF	FLRG	Fidelity	
First Trust Large Cap Core AlphaDEX Fund	FEX	First Trust	
First Trust Mid Cap Core AlphaDEX Fund	FNX	First Trust	
FlexShares US Quality Large Cap Index Fund	QLC	Northern Trust	
Franklin LibertyQ U.S. Equity ETF	FLQL	Franklin Templeton	
Franklin LibertyQ U.S. Mid Cap Equity ETF	FLQM	Franklin Templeton	
Global Beta Low Beta ETF	GBLO	Global Beta Advisors	
Goldman Sachs ActiveBeta U.S. Large Cap Equity ETF	GSLC	Goldman Sachs	U.S. – Large Cap
Hartford Multifactor US Equity ETF	ROUS	The Hartford	
Invesco Defensive Equity ETF	DEF	Invesco	
Invesco Russell 1000 Enhanced Equal Weight ETF	USEQ	Invesco	
Invesco Russell 1000 Dynamic Multifactor ETF	OMFL	Invesco	
Invesco Russell 1000 Low Beta Equal Weight ETF	USLB	Invesco	

(continued)

TABLE B-10 *(continued)*

EFT	Symbol	Investment Firm	Sector
Invesco S&P 500 High Dividend Low Volatility ETF	SPHD	Invesco	
Invesco S&P 500 Minimum Variance ETF	SPMV	Invesco	
Invesco S&P 500 QVM Multi-Factor ETF	QVML	Invesco	
Invesco S&P Midcap 400 QVM Multi-Factor ETF	QVMM	Invesco	
Invesco S&P Midcap Quality ETF	XMHQ	Invesco	
Invesco Zacks Mid-Cap ETF	CZA	Invesco	
iPath Shiller CAPE ETN	CAPD	Barclays Capital Inc	
iShares Factors US Blend Style ETF	STLC	BlackRock	
iShares Factors US Mid Blend Style ETF	STMB	BlackRock	
iShares MSCI USA Mid-Cap Multifactor ETF	MIDF	BlackRock	
IQ Chaikin U.S. Large Cap ETF	CLRG	New York Life	
John Hancock Multifactor Large Cap ETF	JHML	John Hancock	
John Hancock Multifactor Mid Cap ETF	JHMM	John Hancock	U.S. – Mid Cap
JPMorgan Diversified Return U.S. Equity ETF	JPUS	JPMorgan Chase	
JPMorgan Diversified Return U.S. Mid Cap Equity ETF	JPME	JPMorgan Chase	
KFA Value Line Dynamic Core Equity Index ETF	KVLE	CICC	
Nuveen ESG Dividend ETF	NUDV	Nuveen Securities	
Nuveen ESG Large-Cap ETF	NULC	Nuveen Securities	
O'Shares U.S. Quality Dividend ETF	OUSA	O'Shares Investments	
Pacer U.S. Cash Cows 100 ETF	COWZ	Pacer Advisors	
Siren DIVCON Dividend Defender ETF	DFND	SRN Advisors	
Siren DIVCON Leaders Dividend ETF	LEAD	SRN Advisors	
SPDR Russell 1000 Low Volatility Focus ETF	ONEV	State Street Global Advisors	

EFT	Symbol	Investment Firm	Sector
SPDR Russell 1000 Momentum Focus ETF	ONEO	State Street Global Advisors	
Timothy Plan High Dividend Stock ETF	TPHD	Timothy Plan	
Timothy Plan High Dividend Stock Enhanced ETF	TPHE	Timothy Plan	
Timothy Plan US Large/Mid Cap Core Enhanced ETF	TPLE	Timothy Plan	
Timothy Plan US Large/Mid Cap Core ETF	TPLC	Timothy Plan	
VictoryShares Dividend Accelerator ETF	VSDA	Victory Capital	
VictoryShares US 500 Enhanced Volatility Wtd Index ETF	CFO	Victory Capital	
VictoryShares US 500 Volatility Wtd ETF	CFA	Victory Capital	
VictoryShares US EQ Income Enhanced Volatility Wtd ETF	CDC	Victory Capital	
VictoryShares US Large Cap High Div Volatility Wtd ETF	CDL	Victory Capital	
Virtus Terranova U.S. Quality Momentum ETF	JOET	Virtus Investment Partners	
Xtrackers Russell U.S. Multifactor ETF	DEUS	DWS	

TABLE B-11   ## U.S. Small-Cap Stocks

ETF	Symbol	Investment firm	Sector
First Trust Small Cap Core AlphaDEX Fund	FYX	First Trust	
Franklin LibertyQ U.S. Small Cap Equity ETF	FLQS	Franklin Templeton	
Goldman Sachs ActiveBeta U.S. Small Cap Equity ETF	GSSC	Goldman Sachs	
Hartford Multifactor Small Cap ETF	ROSC	The Hartford	
IQ Chaikin U.S. Small Cap ETF	CSML	New York Life	
Invesco Russell 2000 Dynamic Multifactor ETF	OMFS	Invesco	
Invesco S&P SmallCap 600 QVM Multi-Factor ETF	QVMS	Invesco	
Invesco S&P SmallCap High Dividend Low Volatility ETF	XSHD	Invesco	U.S. – Small Cap

(continued)

TABLE B-11 *(continued)*

ETF	Symbol	Investment firm	Sector
iShares Factors US Small Blend Style ETF	STSB	BlackRock	
iShares MSCI USA Small-Cap Multifactor ETF	SMLF	BlackRock	U.S. – Small Cap
IQ Chaikin U.S. Small Cap ETF	CSML	New York Life	
John Hancock Multifactor Small Cap ETF	JHSC	John Hancock	
JPMorgan Diversified Return U.S. Small Cap Equity ETF	JPSE	JPMorgan Chase	
Nuveen ESG Small-Cap ETF	NUSC	Nuveen Securities	
O'Shares U.S. Small-Cap Quality Dividend ETF	OUSM	O'Shares Investments	
Pacer U.S. Small Cap Cash Cows 100 ETF	CALF	Pacer Advisors	
Principal U.S. Small-Cap Multi-Factor ETF	PSC	Principal	
VictoryShares US Discovery Enhanced Volatility Wtd ETF	CSF	Victory Capital	
VictoryShares US Small Cap High Div Volatility Wtd ETF	CSB	Victory Capital	
VictoryShares US Small Cap Volatility Wtd ETF	CSA	Victory Capital	
VictoryShares USAA MSCI USA Small Cap Value Momentum ETF	USVM	Victory Capital	
WisdomTree U.S. Smallcap Quality Dividend Growth Fund	DGRS	WisdomTree	

TABLE B-12 ## U.S. Stocks – Total Market

EFT	Symbol	Investment firm
American Century STOXX U.S. Quality Value ETF	VALQ	American Century Investments
Direxion Fallen Knives ETF	NIFE	Direxion
Fidelity Stocks for Inflation ETF	FCPI	Fidelity
First Trust Dorsey Wright Momentum & Dividend ETF	DDIV	First Trust
First Trust Dorsey Wright Momentum & Value ETF	DVLU	First Trust

EFT	Symbol	Investment firm
FlexShares Morningstar US Market Factor Tilt Index Fund	TILT	Northern Trust
FlexShares Quality Dividend Defensive Index Fund	QDEF	Northern Trust
FlexShares Quality Dividend Dynamic Index Fund	QDYN	Northern Trust
FlexShares Quality Dividend Index Fund	QDF	Northern Trust
FlexShares US Quality Low Volatility Index Fund	QLV	Northern Trust
Global X Adaptive U.S. Factor ETF	AUSF	Mirae Asset Global Investments Co., Ltd.
Innovator IBD 50 ETF	FFTY	Innovator
Invesco Dynamic Market ETF	PWC	Invesco
iShares ESG MSCI USA Min Vol Factor ETF	ESMV	BlackRock
iShares US Equity Factor ETF	LRGF	BlackRock
Legg Mason Low Volatility High Dividend ETF	LVHD	Franklin Templeton
Lyrical U.S. Value ETF	USVT	Lyrical Partners
PIMCO RAFI Dynamic Multi-Factor U.S. Equity ETF	MFUS	PIMCO
Principal Quality ETF	PSET	Principal
SPDR MSCI USA Strategic Factors ETF	QUS	State Street Global Advisors
VanEck Morningstar ESG Moat ETF	MOTE	VanEck
VictoryShares U.S. Multi-Factor Minimum Volatility ETF	VSMV	Victory Capital
VictoryShares USAA MSCI USA Value Momentum ETF	ULVM	Victory Capital
Vident Core U.S. Equity Fund	VUSE	Vident
WisdomTree US Quality Dividend Growth Fund	DGRW	WisdomTree
WisdomTree U.S. Growth & Momentum Fund	WGRO	WisdomTree
WisdomTree U.S. Multifactor Fund	USMF	WisdomTree

Factor-based Sector ETFs

ETF	Sybmol	Investment firm	Sector
First Trust Consumer Discretionary AlphaDEX Fund	FXD	First Trust	U.S. Consumer Discretionary
First Trust Consumer Staples AlphaDEX Fund	FXG	First Trust	U.S. Consumer Staples
First Trust Energy AlphaDEX Fund	FXN	First Trust	U.S. Energy
First Trust Financials AlphaDEX Fund	FXO	First Trust	U.S. Financials
First Trust Health Care AlphaDEX Fund	FXH	First Trust	U.S. Health Care
First Trust Industrials/Producer Durables AlphaDEX Fund	FXR	First Trust	U.S. Industrials
First Trust Materials AlphaDEX Fund	FXZ	First Trust	U.S. Materials
First Trust Nasdaq Bank ETF	FTXO	First Trust	U.S. Banks
First Trust Nasdaq Food & Beverage ETF	FTXG	First Trust	U.S. Food, Beverage & Tobacco
First Trust Nasdaq Oil & Gas ETF	FTXN	First Trust	U.S. Energy
First Trust Nasdaq Pharmaceuticals ETF	FTXH	First Trust	U.S. Pharmaceuticals
First Trust Nasdaq Semiconductor ETF	FTXL	First Trust	U.S. Semiconductors
First Trust Nasdaq Transportation ETF	FTXR	First Trust	U.S. Transportation
First Trust Natural Gas ETF	FCG	First Trust	U.S. Oil, Gas & Consumable Fuels
First Trust RBA American Industrial Renaissance ETF	AIRR	First Trust	U.S. Industrials
First Trust Technology AlphaDEX Fund	FXL	First Trust	U.S. Information Technology
First Trust Utilities AlphaDEX Fund	FXU	First Trust	U.S. Utilities
Global Beta Rising Stars ETF	GBGR	Global Beta Advisors	U.S. Information Technology
Invesco Dynamic Biotechnology & Genome ETF	PBE	Invesco	U.S. Biotechnology
Invesco Dynamic Building & Construction ETF	PKB	Invesco	U.S. Construction & Engineering
Invesco KBW Bank ETF	KBWB	Invesco	U.S. Banks

ETF	Sybmol	Investment firm	Sector
Invesco Dynamic Energy Exploration & Production ETF	PXE	Invesco	U.S. Oil, Gas & Consumable Fuels
Invesco Dynamic Food & Beverage ETF	PBJ	Invesco	U.S. Consumer Staples
Invesco Dynamic Leisure and Entertainment ETF	PEJ	Invesco	U.S. Hotels, Restaurants & Leisure
Invesco Dynamic Oil & Gas Services ETF	PXJ	Invesco	U.S. Energy Equipment & Services
Invesco Dynamic Media ETF	PBS	Invesco	U.S. Media & Entertainment
Invesco Dynamic Networking ETF	PXQ	Invesco	U.S. Information Technology
Invesco Dynamic Pharmaceuticals ETF	PJP	Invesco	U.S. Pharmaceuticals
Invesco Dynamic Semiconductors ETF	PSI	Invesco	U.S. Semiconductors
Invesco Dynamic Software ETF	PSJ	Invesco	U.S. Software
Invesco KBW Property & Casualty Insurance ETF	KBWP	Invesco	U.S. Property & Casualty Insurance
John Hancock Multifactor Consumer Discretionary ETF	JHMC	John Hancock	U.S. Consumer Discretionary
John Hancock Multifactor Consumer Staples ETF	JHMS	John Hancock	U.S. Consumer Staples
John Hancock Multifactor Energy ETF	JHME	John Hancock	U.S. Energy
John Hancock Multifactor Financials ETF	JHMF	John Hancock	U.S. Financials
John Hancock Multifactor Healthcare ETF	JHMH	John Hancock	U.S. Health Care
John Hancock Multifactor Industrials ETF	JHMI	John Hancock	U.S. Industrials
John Hancock Multifactor Materials ETF	JHMA	John Hancock	U.S. Materials
John Hancock Multifactor Media and Communications ETF	JHCS	John Hancock	U.S. Communication Services
John Hancock Multifactor Technology ETF	JHMT	John Hancock	U.S. Information Technology
John Hancock Multifactor Utilities ETF	JHMU	John Hancock	U.S. Utilities
VictoryShares Protect America ETF	SHLD	Victory Capital	U.S. Aerospace & Defense

TABLE B-14   Bonds

ETF	Symbol	Investment firm	Sector
AAM Low Duration Preferred and Income Securities ETF	PFLD	Advisors Asset Management	Fixed Income: U.S. – Corporate, Preferred Short Term
FlexShares Credit-Scored US Corporate Bond Index Fund	SKOR	Northern Trust	Fixed Income: U.S. – Corporate, Broad-based Investment Grade Short Term
FlexShares Credit-Scored US Long Corporate Bond Index Fund	LKOR	Northern Trust	Fixed Income: U.S. – Corporate, Broad-based Investment Grade Short Term
iShares Edge High Yield Defensive Bond ETF	HYDB	BlackRock	Fixed Income: U.S. - Corporate, Broad-based High Yield
iShares Edge Investment Grade Enhanced Bond ETF	IGEB	BlackRock	Fixed Income: U.S. – Corporate, Broad-based Investment Grade
iShares Edge U.S. Fixed Income Balanced Risk ETF	FIBR	BlackRock	Fixed Income: U.S. – Broad Market, Broad-based
iShares J.P. Morgan EM Corporate Bond ETF	CEMB	BlackRock	Fixed Income: Emerging Markets – Corporate, Broad-based
iShares USD Bond Factor ETF	USBF	BlackRock	Fixed Income: U.S. – Broad Market, Broad-based
iShares Yield Optimized Bond ETF	BYLD	BlackRock	Fixed Income: U.S. – Broad Market, Broad-based
VanEck CEF Muni Income ETF	XMPT	VanEck	Fixed Income: U.S. – Government, Local Authority/Municipal Intermediate
Vident Core U.S. Bond Strategy ETF	VBND	Vident	Fixed Income: U.S. – Broad Market, Broad-based Intermediate
WisdomTree Yield Enhanced U.S. Aggregate Bond Fund	AGGY	WisdomTree	Fixed Income: U.S. – Broad Market, Broad-based Investment Grade
WisdomTree Yield Enhanced U.S. Short-Term Aggregate Bond ETF	SHAG	WisdomTree	Fixed Income: U.S. – Broad Market, Broad-based Investment Grade

TABLE B-15   Leveraged ETFs

ETF	Symbol	Investment firm	Sector
Direxion Daily Pharmaceutical & Medical Bull 3X Shares	PILL	Direxion	U.S. Pharmaceuticals
ETRACS Monthly Pay 2xLeveraged U.S. High Dividend Low Volatility ETF	HDLB	UBS	U.S. – Large Cap

Index

First Bank of the United States, 17

5-day moving average, 135

Forbes magazine, 244, 246

Form 1040-ES, 200

Form 4952, 198

Form 8949, 198

Foundation for Economic Education (website), 251

401(k) plans, 204

fraud, 48

Frazzini. Andrea, 75

French, Kenneth, 23–24, 45, 71, 74, 114

FTSE Russell Smart Beta, 116

fundamental analysis

about, 53–54

intrinsic (book) value, 55

market value, 55

price-earnings ratio, 56

price-to-book ratio, 57

price to sales ratio, 57

Fundamental Analysis For Dummies (Krantz), 54, 243

The Fundamental Index (Arnott et al.), 242

fundamentals, 8–9

G

General Motors, 49

Ghayur, Khalid, 242

Giglio, Stefano, 30

Global Financial Data, 35

global investing

about, 121

best performing markets, 124–125

diversification and, 124–125

environmental, social, and governance (ESG), 125–128

forecast composition of global equity market, 122

good ideas overseas and, 123–124

new asset classes and, 123

reasons for, 122–125

shifting global economies and, 122–123

good-til-canceled orders, 96–97

Google, 50

Gore, Al, 222

government overreach, 234

government spending, 185–186

government-sponsored enterprises (GSE), 166

Graham, Benjamin, 9, 16, 45, 244

Gray, Wesley, 242, 243

Great Depression, 18, 186–187

greed, 60, 218

Gross Domestic Product (GDP)

about, 102

chart for the US, 102–103

as coincident economic indicator, 103

defined, 11–12

global economies, 122

global investing, 184

tracking, 103

growth factor

about, 10, 43

history, 45

low-turnover strategy, 50

non-quality growth stocks, 46–48

profitability, 44–46

return on equity, 44–45

stable earnings and, 46–48

vs. value, 46–48

growth stocks

non-quality, 48–49

screening, 143, 144–146

Guida, Tony, 242

H

Hamilton, Alexander, 17

Hammerstone Markets (website), 147

head and shoulders patterns, 133–134

healthcare sector, 157–158

health insurance, 225

Heaney, Ronan, 242

high inflation, 231–232

High-Level Investing For Dummies (Mladjenovic), 181, 244

high technology stocks, 11

high-volatility stocks, 10–11

holding period, 194

holistic approach, 117–118

Holmes, Elizabeth, 48

Hoover's (website), 251, 252

HoweStreet (blog), 248

Hsu, Jason, 242

Hulbert Financial Digest (website), 249

human need, 212

Hunter, Greg, 248

hype, 218–219
hyperinflation, 235–236

I

I bonds, 170
icons, in this book, 2
illiquid companies, 30
Ilmanen, Antti, 242
income
  dividend, 85–86
  interest, 193
  investment, 192–193
  personal, 112
  taxes on, 192–193
indexes
  about, 34–36
  Dow Jones Industrial Average, 35
  historical performance of, 35
  history of, 34–35
  S&P 500 Stock Composite Index, 35–36
Index Fund Management (Zaher), 242
India, 123
individual retirement accounts (IRA), 192, 202–203
industrial goods sector, 158
industrial production, 112
industry top 20%, 213–214
inflation
  about, 12, 104
  asset bubbles and, 107–108
  asset *vs.* consumer price, 106
  Consumer Price Index and, 106
  Dividends and, 80
  defined, 104
  dividends and, 80
  high, 231–232
  interest rates and, 108
  monetary, 12, 105
  price inflation, 12, 104–105
  Purchasing Managers Index and, 107
  vs. supply, demand, and flow, 105–106
  tracking, 106
  volatile periods and, 188
initial job claims, 111
Institute for Supply Management (ISM), 107

insurance, 225
intangible assets, 55
The Intelligent Investor (Graham), 9, 244
interest income, 193
interest rates
  about, 12–13
  vs. bond pricing, 168–169
  inflation and, 108
  low, 108
  rising, 108
  tracking, 109
Internal Revenue Service (IRS), 21, 191
international ETFs, 256–257
Internet stock bubble, 187
Internet stocks, 11, 46, 108
intrinsic (book) value, 55
inverse ETFs, 67
Invesco World Bond Factor Fund, 158
investability, 30
investable factors, finding, 29–30
Investing Amid Low Expected Returns (Ilmanen), 242
Investing.com (website), 137, 141, 211, 245, 247
Investing Daily (website), 249
Investing in Commodities For Dummies (Bouchentouf), 189
investment interest, 200
investment time period, 15
Investopedia (website), 206
Investor Junkie (website), 249
InvestorPlace (website), 249
Investor's Business Daily, 245
Invest Wisely: Advice From Your Securities Industry Regulators (website), 247
iShares (IVV), 68
Isichenko, Michael, 243
Israel, Ronen, 75

J

Jegadeesh, Narasimhan, 64
job openings rate, 111
Journal of Finance, 64, 74
Journal of Financial Economics, 75
junk bonds, 163
Jurczenko, Emmanuel, 243

K

K-1 form, 198
Kennedy, John F.
Kennedy, Joseph P.
King World News (blog), 248
Kiplinger's (website), 205
Kodak, 49
Krantz, Matt, 54, 243
Kulkarni, Padmakar, 126

L

labor force, 236
Laffer curve, 234
lagging economic indicators, 111
large-cap assets, 9
large-cap stocks, 13, 71, 261–263
leading economic indicators, 110–111
leverage, 219–220
leveraged ETFs, 268
life insurance, 225
limited order, 92–93
listed (marginable) stock, 99
Litner, John, 22
Livermore, Jesse, 16
long form, 198
long-term capital gains, 193
look-back period, 61
low-turnover strategy, 50
Ludwig von Mises Institute, 251
Lynch, Peter, 39

M

Macedonia, 124
Machine Learning for Factor Investing (Coqueret and Guida), 242
macroeconomic factors. *See also* style factors
about, 11, 101, 183
defined, 8
economic growth, 11–12
Gross Domestic Product, 101–103
inflation, 12, 104–108
interest rates, 12–13, 108–109
sector ETFs and, 156–158

sources, 251–252
watching, 112
magazines, 244–245
major market moves
about, 183
Federal Reserve and, 186–187
government spending factor in, 185–186
regulation factor in, 185
tax factor in, 184–185
volatile period, 187–188
management efficiency, screening stocks with, 143
manufacturing and trade sales, 112
margin interest, 200
margin trading
about, 97
factor investing and, 100
maintaining balance requirements, 98–99
mistakes to avoid, 219–220
requirements for different types of securities, 99
tips, 99–100
when stock price goes down, 98
when stock price goes up, 97
when stock price trades sideways, 98
market, 33
market beta, 22
market beta premium, 23
market capitalization, 9, 55, 73, 141
market crashes, 232–233
market order, 93
Market Sanity (blog), 189, 248
market shutdowns, 237
market strategy, 36–37
market timing
beating the market and, 33, 37
defined, 33
vs. factor investing, 40
hurdles in, 33
missing the best days, 40
Pearl Harbor attack and, 37
market value, 55
MarketWatch (website), 109, 141, 189, 205, 211, 247, 251
maximum daily price return, 30
Melas, Dimitris, 126
microeconomic factors. *See* style factors
mid-cap stocks, 13, 71

stocks. *See also* bonds
  vs. bonds, 162
  diversification with, 162
  with downward momentum, 65
  vs. ETFs, 153
  in factor-based portfolio, 13
  with macro factors, 1
  short-selling, 64–67
  during volatile periods, 188
  when to sell, 95
Stocks & Commodities magazine, 137
StockTwits (blog), 247
stop-loss order, 93–95
StreetAuthority (blog), 247
style factors. *See also* macroeconomic factors
  about, 1, 183
  defined, 8
  dividends, 10
  growth, 10
  momentum, 11
  quality, 9
  resources, 247
  size, 9
  value, 8–9
  volatility, 10–11
subprime lending crisis, 231
supercomputer factors, avoiding, 28–29
supply, 12, 105–106
support, 133
survivorship bias, 28
Swedroe, Larry, 243
systematic approach, 18
  about, 15
  disciplined strategy, 18–20
  persistent strategy, 16–18
  saving, 16–17
  saving time, 16–17
  using modern advances, 17

T

Taiwan, 124
tangible assets, 55
taxes
  about, 21, 191–192
  capital gains taxes, 192–196

capital losses and, 196–197
on charitable contributions, 201–202
deductions, 199–202
on dividends, 192–193
dividends and, 80
ETFs *vs.* mutual funds, 153
financial sites with tax info, 205–206
foreign taxes on investments, 201
gains and loss scenarios, 197
on interest income, 193
investment interest and, 200
IRS publications, 204–205
on long-term capital gains, 193
low-turnover strategy and, 50
major market moves and, 184–185
miscellaneous expenses and, 201
momentum investing and, 69
non-deductible items, 202
on ordinary income, 192
planning for, 225
resources, 204–206
on short-term capital gains, 193
wash-sale rule, 199
websites, 205
tax forms, 198
Tax Foundation, 184
Tax Foundation (websites), 205
Tax Mama (websites), 205
tax-sheltered accounts, 21, 30, 192
TC2000 (website), 147
technical analysis
  about, 129
  advanced, 137
  charts, 132–134
  head and shoulders pattern, 133–134
  moving averages, 134–136
  relative strength index (RSI), 129–131
  resistance, 133
  resources, 137–138
  reverse head and shoulder pattern, 134–135
  screening stocks with, 143
  support, 133
  timing and, 129
  trend lines, 133
Technical Analysis For Dummies
    (Rockefeller), 137

About the Authors

A native of Hastings, England, **James Maendel** lives with his wife Nicole, and four children in the lakes district of S.E. Michigan. Together, they founded Maendel Wealth, a thriving boutique investment advisory firm in Bloomfield Hills, Michigan in 1999 (www.maendelwealth.com). James is a credentialed Behavioral Financial Advisor (BFA) and also holds the Accredited Asset Management Specialist (AAMS) professional designation. In addition, as one of the first investment advisors to earn the DACFP/RIADAC Certificate in Blockchain and Digital Assets from the New York Institute of Finance, James has been honored to be accepted as a member of the Digital Assets Council in conjunction with the NY Institute of Finance.

James holds the Uniform Securities Agent State Law (Series 63) license, and the Uniform Investment Adviser Law (Series 65) license, along with Life, Health, and Variable Contracts Insurance licenses. He was awarded the Accredited Investment Fiduciary (AIF) Designation from the Center for Fiduciary Studies, the standards-setting body for Fi360 and the U.S. first full-time training and research facility for fiduciaries. A multi-year winner of the Five Star Wealth Manager award, James and his firm, Maendel Wealth, have been featured in *Hour Detroit* and *DBusiness Magazine (per website)*, as well as receiving the 2018 Best of Bloomfield Hills Award in the Financial Planner category. By drawing on his experience living in the United States, Europe, and the Middle East, James employs an inquisitive, globally informed approach to wealth management and investing, relentlessly seeking to optimize stability and outperformance. At Maendel Wealth, James and his team have constantly refined their investment process, guiding clients through the dot-com bubble, the 2008 great recession, and the global pandemic. Navigating these black swan events kindled his passion for enhancing predictability of investment performance through studying historically persistent metrics (the essence of factor investing) and market cycles. James also enjoys helping young people to get excited about the positive impact investing and financial intelligence can have in their lives through Invest It Forward (https://investitforward.sifma.org) and by participating as a volunteer judge in the annual SIFMA Stock Market Challenge and Essay Contest (https://www.stockmarketgame.org).

Paul Mladjenovic was a certified financial planner (CFP) from 1985-2021. He is a national seminar leader, author, and consultant. Since 1981, he has specialized in investing, economics, financial planning, and home business issues. Since 1983, he has done 2,500+ national seminars and workshops including "The $50 Wealth-Builder," "Home Business Goldmine," and over a dozen other courses. Besides co-authoring this book, Paul also wrote the bestselling *Stock Investing For Dummies*, *High-Level Investing For Dummies*, *Micro-Entrepreneurship For Dummies*, *Zero-Cost Marketing*, *Precious Metals Investing For Dummies*, and co-authored *Affiliate Marketing For Dummies*. His national (and online) seminars include "The $50 Wealth-Builder," "Ultra-Investing with Options," and the "Home Business

Goldmine," among others. The full details on his (downloadable) financial and business startup audio seminars can be found at www.RavingCapitalist.com. A page at this site (www.RavingCapitalist.com/factor) provides resources and views to help factor-based investors navigate today's uncertain markets and gives them a venue for questions. Paul's online courses can also be found at educational venues such as Udemy.com, Freeu.com, and MtAiryLearningTree.org. Since 2000, Paul has built a reputation as an accurate economics and market forecaster. His long record includes accurate forecasts of the housing bubble, the energy crisis, 2008's great recession, record stagflation during 2022, and much more. He has been interviewed or referenced by numerous media sources, such as Comcast, CNN, MarketWatch, Bloomberg, OANN, Fox Business, *Futures* magazine, Kitco.com, GoldSeek.com, Safehaven.com, FinancialSense.com, PreciousMetalsInvesting.com, and other popular media venues.

You can view Paul's profile at www.linkedin.com/in/paulmladjenovic/ and follow him at www.gab.com/paulmlad and you can also check out the author's page at www.amazon.com/author/paulmladjenovic. Readers can email questions or inquiries directly to paul@mladjenovic.com or at the bio page at www.RavingCapitalist.com.

Authors' Acknowledgments

First and foremost, we offer our appreciation and gratitude to the wonderful folks at Wiley. It has been a pleasure to work with such a top-notch organization that works so hard to create products that offer readers tremendous value and information. We wish all of you continued success! Wiley has some notables whom we want to single out.

We thank Rebecca Senninger, our project manager, for her dedication and professionalism. Thank you so much!

The technical editor, Christopher Mollan, was invaluable and helped us immensely keeping our content accurate.

With deep and joyful gratitude, we thank Tracy Boggier, our superb acquisitions editor. Thank you so much for being our champion at Wiley and shepherding yet another *For Dummies* guide. *For Dummies* books are great, and they appear on your bookshelf only through the planning and professional efforts of publishing pros like Tracy.

Personal from Paul Mladjenovic: Fran, Lipa Zyenska, thank you and my boys Adam and Joshua with all my heart for your support and being my number one fans throughout the writing of this book. I am grateful to have you by my side always! I thank God for you, and I love you beyond words!

Personal from James: Thank you to my wife Nicole for being the best friend, mother, and business partner I could ever have hoped for, and for banishing my writer's block with her killer keto coffee. Our sons Gavin, Merrick, Kai, and Nicholas are the best "factors" we have ever invested in. I love you guys!

Lastly, we want to acknowledge you, the reader. Over the years, you've made the *For Dummies* series the popular and indispensable books they are today. Thank you, and we wish you continued success!

Publisher's Acknowledgments

Acquisitions Editor: Tracy Boggier

Project Editor: Rebecca Senninger

Technical Editor: Christopher Mollan

Production Editor: Mohammed Zafar Ali

Cover Image: © mstanley/Shutterstock

Take dummies with you everywhere you go!

Whether you are excited about e-books, want more from the web, must have your mobile apps, or are swept up in social media, dummies makes everything easier.

Find us online!

dummies.com

dummies
A Wiley Brand

PERSONAL ENRICHMENT

9781119187790
USA $26.00
CAN $31.99
UK £19.99

9781119179030
USA $21.99
CAN $25.99
UK £16.99

9781119293354
USA $24.99
CAN $29.99
UK £17.99

9781119293347
USA $22.99
CAN $27.99
UK £16.99

9781119310068
USA $22.99
CAN $27.99
UK £16.99

9781119235606
USA $24.99
CAN $29.99
UK £17.99

9781119251163
USA $24.99
CAN $29.99
UK £17.99

9781119235491
USA $26.99
CAN $31.99
UK £19.99

9781119279952
USA $24.99
CAN $29.99
UK £17.99

9781119283133
USA $24.99
CAN $29.99
UK £17.99

9781119287117
USA $24.99
CAN $29.99
UK £16.99

9781119130246
USA $22.99
CAN $27.99
UK £16.99

PROFESSIONAL DEVELOPMENT

9781119311041
USA $24.99
CAN $29.99
UK £17.99

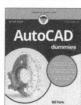

9781119255796
USA $39.99
CAN $47.99
UK £27.99

9781119293439
USA $26.99
CAN $31.99
UK £19.99

9781119281467
USA $26.99
CAN $31.99
UK £19.99

9781119280651
USA $29.99
CAN $35.99
UK £21.99

9781119251132
USA $24.99
CAN $29.99
UK £17.99

9781119310563
USA $34.00
CAN $41.99
UK £24.99

9781119181705
USA $29.99
CAN $35.99
UK £21.99

9781119263593
USA $26.99
CAN $31.99
UK £19.99

9781119257769
USA $29.99
CAN $35.99
UK £21.99

9781119293477
USA $26.99
CAN $31.99
UK £19.99

9781119265313
USA $24.99
CAN $29.99
UK £17.99

9781119239314
USA $29.99
CAN $35.99
UK £21.99

9781119293323
USA $29.99
CAN $35.99
UK £21.99